Praise for Griffith Review

'*Griffith Review* is the sound of Australian , ᵍ ⁻ ⁻⁻ loud.'
Geordie Williamson, *The Australian*

'Where the news cycle tends to feed cynicism, *Griffith Review* is the necessary counterpoint: a place of ideas and possibility. It's a relief to find the quality writing, reflection and observation nurtured in its pages.'
Billy Griffiths, historian and writer

'[*Griffith Review*] traverses genre and form, culture and continent...in what is a vibrant and impressive cross-section of modern Australian writing.'
Good Reading

'A literary degustation... The richness of these stories is amplified by the resonance between them. It's hard to think of so much fascinating story being contained within 270-odd pages.'
Ed Wright, *The Saturday Australian*

'...informative, thought-provoking and well-crafted.'
The Saturday Paper

'[An] outstanding collection of essays, reportage, memoir, poetry and fiction.'
Mark McKenna, *Honest History*

'The *Review* doesn't shirk from the nuanced and doesn't seek refuge in simplistic notions or slogans. It remains Australia's primary literary review.'
Professor Ken Smith, Dean and CEO ANZSOG

'This is commentary of a high order. The prose is unfailingly polished; the knowledge and expertise of the writers impressive.'
Roy Williams, *Sydney Morning Herald*

'For intelligent, well-written quarterly commentary...*Griffith Review* remains the gold standard.'
Honest History

'*Griffith Review* is Australia's most prestigious literary journal.'
stuff.co.nz

'*Griffith Review* is a must-read for anyone with even a passing interest in current affairs, politics, literature and journalism. The timely, engaging writing lavishly justifies the Brisbane-based publication's reputation as Australia's best example of its genre.'
The West Australian

'This quarterly magazine is a reminder of the breadth and talent of Australian writers. Verdict: literary treat.'
Herald Sun

SIR SAMUEL GRIFFITH was one of Australia's notable early achievers. He occupied positions of authority during some of the most momentous events in the history of Queensland; the frontier wars, the 'blackbirding' trade of people from Melanesia, the shearers' strike and Federation. At times he challenged power, at others he used it – he was a complex yet pragmatic man of words, a man of his times. Not all his decisions have stood the test of time. Sir Samuel was twice the premier of Queensland, its chief justice and author of its criminal code, remembered most for his pivotal role in drafting the Constitution adopted at Federation, and as the new nation's first chief justice.

Griffith died in 1920 and is now most likely to be remembered by his namesakes: an electorate, a society, a suburb and a university. In 1971, ninety-six years after he first proposed establishing a university in Brisbane, Griffith University, the city's second, was created. Griffith's commitment to public debate and ideas, his delight in words and art, and his attachment to active citizenship are recognised by this publication that bears his name.

Like Sir Samuel Griffith, *Griffith Review* is iconoclastic and non-partisan, with a sceptical eye and a pragmatically reforming heart. Always ready to debate ideas. Personal, political and unpredictable, it informs and provokes Australia's best conversations.

During Griffith's lifetime, and while he was in positions of power, the First Nations of Queensland resisted invasion. Sir Samuel made it possible for some Aboriginal people to testify in court when charges were brought against settlers. The First Australians survived, but at a terrible cost. In the twenty-first century, the need for a thorough and lasting settlement is urgent, one that respects and honours the rights, history and culture of the descendants of those who were dispossessed.

Griffith Review staff acknowledge and pay particular respect to the traditional custodians of the lands on which their office is located, the Jagera and Turrbal people in South-East Queensland.

Griffith
UNIVERSITY
Queensland, Australia

GriffithReview79
Counterfeit Culture

Edited by Carody Culver

GriffithReview79

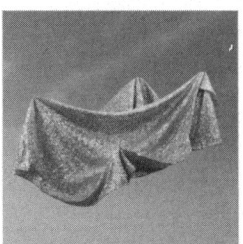

Gerwyn Davies, *Poof* 2021
Archival inkjet print, 80 x 120 cm
Edition of five, plus one artist proof
Image courtesy of the artist

Griffith Review gratefully acknowledges the support
and generosity of our founding patron, the late
Margaret Mittelheuser AM and the ongoing support
of Dr Cathryn Mittelheuser AM.

GriffithReview79 2023
Griffith Review is published four times a year by Griffith University.

Publisher	Scott Harrison
Editor	Carody Culver
General Manager	Katie Woods
Managing Editor	John Tague
Assistant Editor	James Jiang
Marketing & Events Co-ordinator	Emma Reason
Business Co-ordinator	Cieon Hilton
	Esha Buch
Proofreader	Sonia Ulliana
Publicist	Cinnamon Watson
Typesetting	Midland Typesetters
Printing	Ligare Book Printers
Distribution	NewSouth Books/ADS

ISBNs
Book: 978-1-922212-80-1
PDF: 978-1-922212-81-8
Epub: 978-1-922212-82-5

ISSN   1448-2924

Contributions by academics can, on request, be refereed by our Editorial Board.
Details: griffithreview.com

GRIFFITH REVIEW
South Bank Campus, Griffith University
PO Box 3370, South Brisbane QLD 4101 Australia
Ph +617 3735 3071 Fax +617 3735 3272
griffithreview@griffith.edu.au griffithreview.com

SUBSCRIPTIONS: See griffithreview.com/product-category/subscriptions
Institutional and bulk rates available on application

FEEDBACK AND COMMENT griffithreview@griffith.edu.au

Genuine article

The paradox of authenticity

Carody Culver

THINK BACK TO when you were a kid and of all the things you believed in that turned out not to be true: Santa Claus. Unicorns. Your parents' infallibility. The concept of fairness. Bill Murray. These unmaskings may, in some cases, have been sudden and shocking; in others, the dawning of truth may have been more gradual, your naïveté slowly disappearing beneath the ineluctable horizon of maturity and cynicism.

As we grow older and the make-believe fables and protections of childhood fall away, we're often expected to understand the difference between what's real and what's not – it's simply part of how we must navigate the world as adults. But quite aside from the vexed circumstances of being alive in the twenty-first century – a time of relentless counterfeit both online and off, from filters and fillers to influencers and identity fraud – our very existence as humans who must coexist with other humans necessitates a constant and complicated process of distinguishing the authentic from the artificial. It's never easy – even when you've known for decades that Santa isn't real.

In her book *Authenticity*, writer Alice Sherwood observes that the very word 'authenticity' now has dual meanings that are 'almost completely opposite'. There's the original meaning – the objective notion of whether something is a fact, a verifiable claim. And there's a more recent meaning that's altogether more nebulous – what Sherwood calls 'personal authenticity', or 'being true...to your own, internal sense of self', 'looking to feelings rather than facts'.

These competing, sometimes contradictory, concepts can create a circle that's difficult to square. So perhaps the question we should be asking isn't about whether something is real but about how we're defining – and redefining – the terms of that reality and the values we ascribe to it.

COUNTERFEIT CULTURE NAVIGATES this maze of modern deception with a compelling and wide-ranging collection of nonfiction, fiction, poetry and visual essay. The pieces in this edition mine the social, cultural and emotional ramifications of our shifting relationship with reality: the power of deepfakes, the possibilities of AI-generated art, the changing face of cosmetic surgery, the performance of pornographic pleasure, the dangers of corporate greenwashing, the allure of conspiracy, the bureaucratisation of art, the psychic release of fake news, the limits of national identity, the stigma of selling out, the complexities of gender transitioning and much more. This edition's short fiction offerings include an unsettling trip to a strange town, a macabre memorialisation of a beloved family pet and the outlandish escapades of a psychic shaman oracle medium visionary prophet saint. *Counterfeit Culture* won't deceive you (at least not intentionally), but it's sure to entertain you – and perhaps you'll think about it the next time you find yourself unsure whether what you're reading, seeing or hearing is, in fact, fake.

I'd like to thank the Copyright Agency Cultural Fund for their generous support of our Emerging Voices competition – one of our five winning entries from 2022, Alex Philp's 'Taxidermy', appears in this collection. You can enjoy the final two winning pieces from last year's competition in our next edition, *Griffith Review 80: Creation Stories*.

I hope you enjoy reading this collection as much as the *Griffith Review* team enjoyed working on it. Just like Coca-Cola, it's the real thing.

28 November 2022

The future is hackable

Apocalypse and euphoria in a deepfake world

Anna Broinowski

*How we move forward in the age of information
is gonna be the difference between whether we survive
or whether we become some kind of fucked-up dystopia.*
Obama deepfake, 2018

WHICH OF THESE is true? An onscreen Salvador Dalí posed for selfies in a Florida museum; Volodymyr Zelensky urged Ukrainians to surrender three weeks into the Russian invasion; the judges of *America's Got Talent*, none of whom sing opera, performed Puccini's 'Nessun Dorma'; David Beckham broadcast an anti-malaria appeal in fluent Arabic and Mandarin; Snoop Dog read tarot cards on a psychic TV hotline; Obama publicly labelled Trump a 'complete dipshit'; Mark Zuckerberg boasted 'whoever controls the data controls the future'; and Kim Kardashian confessed she loves 'manipulating people online for money'.

All are true in the sense that they happened. All are also fake: none of the people featured in these videos actually said, or did, these things. This post-truth era paradox is possible thanks to the astonishingly deceptive capabilities of deepfake technology, which uses Generative Adversarial Networks (GANs) to create credible 'real-world' audiovisual content that is, in fact, AI-generated illusion.

Initially the toxic plaything of incel misogynists incubated in the dark underbelly of the web, deepfakes emerged on Reddit in 2017 when an anonymous user pasted the faces of Gal Gadot, Taylor Swift and Scarlett Johansson onto the bodies of female actors in pre-existing porn videos. Since this insalubrious debut, deepfake technology has evolved at lightning speed: it is now possible to create convincing deepfake videos from a single photograph, and for deepfake simulations to converse with real people on Zoom. Deepfake apps are widely available and easy to use, and the wealth of data on our social-media feeds means that ordinary people – former partners, business rivals, local politicians, your next-door neighbour – are as likely to be targeted by deepfakes as celebrities.

For many AI-developers, deepfakes are just one tool in the increasingly sophisticated synthetic media arsenal revolutionising education, science, entertainment and commerce: part of a 'golden decade' of accelerating deep learning in which computers – if Blake Lemoine, the AI engineer who was sacked for claiming Google's LaMDA chatbot had feelings, is to be believed – have already developed sentience. Elon Musk has warned humanity is 'summoning the demon' by working with AI and may 'do something very foolish' without regulation. Futurist Ray Kurzweil prophesies we're headed for an ominous 'Singularity' in which machines 'will surpass human intelligence', rupturing 'the fabric of human history'. Stephen Hawking predicted AI would either 'infinitely help' or 'destroy' us. Deepfakes occupy a central place in this dystopian imaginary: by removing the gold standard of evidentiary truth, the non-fiction video, and in fulfilling the 'realism heuristic', which predisposes us to trust visual representations over written ones, deepfakes have turbo-charged fake news. They disrupt established assumptions about screen 'truth' so successfully that even filmmakers (myself included) have difficulty detecting them.

I FIRST ENCOUNTERED deepfakes in 2018, when filmmaker Jordan Peele puppeteered Obama in a piece-to-camera on YouTube, warning viewers we are 'entering an era in which our enemies can make it look like anyone is saying anything'. Having used digital effects to explore the tenuous fact/fiction boundary in multiple documentaries, from the animated manipulations of Japanese *otaku* in *Hell Bento!!*, to hoax-author Norma Khouri's labyrinthine deceptions in *Forbidden Lie$* and the celluloid propaganda of North Korean filmmakers in *Aim High in Creation!*, my curiosity was piqued. It became an obsession in 2021, when extraordinarily convincing Tom Cruise deepfakes began appearing on TikTok. A collaboration between Cruise-impersonator Miles Fisher and Belgian VFX engineer Chris Ume, the TikTok Cruises went viral, reaching eleven million views within a week. To create them, Ume pasted AI-generated data of Cruise's face onto Fisher's body, enabling Fisher to 'drive' Cruise with his physical and oral performance.

Touted by the media as 'the most alarmingly lifelike examples so far of the high-tech hoax', the Ume-Fisher deepfakes were a dazzling testimony to the speed at which AI had evolved. Unlike earlier deepfakes such as Peele's, which featured talking-heads in locked-off frames to eliminate illusion-shattering camera movements AI had yet to learn to control, the Cruise TikToks were shot handheld in interior and exterior locations, shifted between close-ups and wides without edits and used foreground props. Their single-take amateurism heightened their authenticity: Cruise licked a lollipop, fell over a podium, cleaned a kitchen, danced to George Michael's 'Freedom!' and, most spectacularly, vanished a coin, pronouncing 'magic is the real thing'. I was stunned by the verisimilitude of the deception, and my inability to spot it.

Deepfakes point to a future that is simultaneously euphoric and apocalyptic: philosophers have positioned them as 'an epistemic threat to democracy', journalists have called them 'the place where truth goes to die', futurists have portrayed them as the digital harbinger of a mass 'reality apathy' in which even video will be a lie. But for artists like Ume, and the growing network of VFX enthusiasts who create and share deepfakes in a dynamic interplay of performance and spectatorship, the technology is just a cool new toy to be harnessed for illusionary one-upmanship and fun.

These radical oppositions suggest equally contradictory possibilities. Are deepfakes really the end of truth as we know it? Or simply an innovative special effect, which, like the panoply of audiovisual trickery through-out film's evolution – from the analogue illusions of nineteenth-century cine-magician Georges Méliès to the docu-fakery of Orson Welles and the digital avatars of James Cameron – can be used for good or evil, depending who's pressing the buttons? Who are the scientists, artists, propagandists and criminals making deepfakes, and who is consuming them? Can deepfakes be accurately detected? Does awareness we are watching a deepfake affect its ability to persuade us? When are deepfake viewers unwitting dupes and when are they knowing spectators? What are the ethical implications of using real people to create fake videos? Are deepfakes *inherently* malicious, or does moral responsibility rest with their designers and viewers? To repurpose an insidious pro-gun mantra – do deepfakes deceive people, or do *people* deceive people? Is it possible to still ask these questions as synthetic media systems rapidly approach a state of 'full' AI, in which computers will be able to think for themselves?

To unpack this conundrum it is worth noting the uncertainty deepfakes generate is not new: history is riddled with alarmist prophesies about emerging technologies that did not live up to the hype. The mass-produced eighteenth-century novel generated anxieties about addicted readers; the patenting of light bulbs inspired fears of blindness; cinema prompted gatekeepers to denounce it as 'commercialised voyeurism' and the death knell of theatre; the radio insti-gated worries about weakened 'social morality'; and television was pilloried for encouraging violence. Coupled with a pervasive belief that technology is an unstoppable, autonomous force, the emergence of the internet, and its subsequent enhancements (search engines, social media, interactive gaming), generated similarly grim (but perhaps more accurate) predictions of technol-ogy-addicted users, with games causing 'aggression', smartphones causing 'depression' and social media causing a rise in narcissism and psychopathy. In 2007, ten years before deepfakes appeared on Reddit, the ease with which digital technology could manipulate reality was already creating concern that analogue markers of truth would, as film theorist Mary Ann Doane put it, lose their 'credibility as a trace of the real', and legacy media faced a 'crisis of legitimation' in which its 'referential grounding' would collapse.

The credibility of video now seems quaintly old-fashioned, the nostal-gic artefact of a more innocent time. As I write this, my smartphone dings with fresh alerts about the digital mischief perpetrated by deepfakery and its proliferating AI cousins: DALL-E, which creates artworks from text prompts; GPT-3, which writes screenplays to order; CogVideo, which delivers synthetic films from one-sentence synopses; Deepnude.to, which gives users X-ray vision, enabling them to 'nudify' pictures of women they know. An AI-generated artwork has won first prize in a Colorado fair; a TikTok influencer has deepfaked himself to convince followers his entire online persona is fake; and FN Meka, a Black cyborg created by two non-Black musicians, has been dumped by Capitol Records for a racially offensive deepfake showing him being beaten by White cops. Right now, a man is deepfaking a friend, a relative, a stranger he filmed on the bus, into a public sex video of his choice – without her knowledge.

Everywhere I look, deepfakes are being weaponised. The conflict between the beneficial potential of synthetic media and the corrosion of evidentiary, ethical and civil standards caused by AI's expanding capabilities is intensifying. The following deep dive into dystopian and utopian predictions about deepfakes, and the extent to which they have come true (assuming 'truth' is still a legitimate term), is cloaked in the cognitive life-jacket of Amara's Law: we 'overestimate the effect of a technology in the short run and underestimate the effect in the long run'. I hope, as we wade through the pixelated currents and dissolving truths of the synthetic media sea, an answer to the crucial question underlying deepfakery – will the power of screen deception ultimately belong to humans or machines? – can be glimpsed.

One caveat: this might have been written by AI. It's impossible to know.

DEEPFAKES OCCUPY THE epicentre of an escalating tension between fact and belief in the digital media economy. Their rise coincides with the emergence of video as the preferred information format for the majority of consumers. The text-driven churn of Twitter now vies with the visual distractions of TikTok: recent studies indicate that users retain 95 per cent of audiovisual messaging and only 10 per cent of messaging read as text. In a post-truth arena already besieged by the comparative virality of fake stories over real ones, with public faith in 'facts' and 'expertise' eroding across the legal, political, academic and media spheres, deepfakes, in their five-year life span, have inspired dystopian prophesies that swerve from dread to moral panic. In 2019, US Congressman Adam Schiff warned deepfakes could 'turn a world leader into a ventriloquist's dummy'. Political researchers Cristian Vaccari and Andrew Chadwick concurred, asserting the 'stakes are too high' for deepfakes to be treated as 'mere technological curiosities'. In the lead-up to the 2020 US election, computational scholars modelled seven credible deepfake scenarios that could undermine democracy. Mainstream media took up the charge, branding deepfakes as 'weaponised disinformation' on a 'catastrophic scale', the fiendish heralds of a looming 'infopocalypse' that, left unchecked, would generate a 'perfect storm of misinformation', wherein our inability to distinguish truth from trickery would damage civic society, leading to the collapse of reality.

The deepfake nightmare is one in which our fate is 'hackable' as malicious actors scrape the web for data, flooding social media with video hoaxes designed to manipulate elections, swing markets, embezzle corporations, implant false memories, sabotage court testimony, wage espionage, promote conspiracies, disseminate propaganda and blackmail ordinary people. It is a world in which video could become 'the biggest lie of all', generating an existential crisis in which citizens ignore the news altogether or exercise the liar's dividend, Trump-style, by dismissing genuine recordings (lest we forget the grab-them-by-the-pussy tape) as 'fake news'.

Deepfakes also trigger a cascading collapse of journalistic truth-markers: corroborating a story, technology researcher Mika Westerlund cautions, may not be possible because deepfakes cruel the assumption that 'whatever is said in public, a real person has said it, even though the statement may be false'. Videos may no longer be fact-checkable because deepfakes can be generated from real footage. Media literacy, which advocates identifying a video's provenance to gauge its veracity, could also be unravelled by deepfakes, which are often undetectable to the human eye and constantly repurposed and shared, obscuring their original source. The greatest danger of deepfakes, Westerlund concludes, is not their ability to deceive us but that 'people will come to regard everything as deception'.

This techno-paranoia is fuelled by the fact that deepfake detection programs can be harnessed to produce more convincing deepfakes in an AI-reboot of Frankenstein's monster. The accelerating deep-learning arms race has seen digital forensics researchers repeatedly outgunned, with the most accurate detection models, like those generated for Facebook's 2020 Deepfake Detection Challenge, only able to identify deepfakes 65.18 per cent of the time. The simulative power of synthetic media is considered so malignant by some US and EU legislators that they've enacted laws to control it: not since legal actions against Google Glass and the VCR has a screen technology inspired such a punitive juridical response. The apocalyptic endgame of deepfakery is envisaged as nuclear war, catalysed by a convincing forgery of a world leader threatening to drop the bomb – or doing so.

THESE PREDICTIONS ARE chilling, but how many, to date, have come to pass? It is, in fairness, too early to confirm claims deepfakes will destroy 'truth' as we know it: despite the speed at which AI is evolving, such a cataclysm would take time to unfold and, if it did occur, reductio ad absurdum, there would be no mechanisms left to confirm it. Deepfakes are also yet to kill off American democracy: apart from Ume's 2020 satirical deepfake *Run Tom Run* showing Cruise running – literally – for president, the fake news disrupting US elections since 2016 predominantly uses conventional image and video manipulations, not AI.

Outside the US, however, deepfakes are being used to subvert political discourse, disseminate propaganda and wage espionage. In 2018, Belgium's Socialist Party released a deepfake of Trump declaring, 'I had the balls to withdraw from the Paris climate agreement…so should you', alarming party members who thought it was real. In 2019, a broadcast by Gabon President Ali Bongo Ondimba instigated civic upheaval when his static gaze convinced opponents he'd released a deepfake to hide his ill health, leading to an (unsuccessful) military coup. In 2020, video 'sock puppets' (synthetic humans generated from deepfake photos) appeared on a Zionist Facebook page, claiming to be left-wingers compelled to support Israel's conservative Prime Minister Benjamin Netanyahu. Delighted users circulated the deepfakes on far-right sites, unconcerned by their provenance. In 2021, Leonid Volkov, Russian opposition leader Alexei Navalny's chief of staff, supposedly conducted video calls with several EU officials who later realised they had been discussing sensitive diplomatic issues with an AI, prompting speculation the deepfake Volkov was a digital spy. In 2022, pro-Russian agents struck twice: in March, with Zelensky's deepfake surrender, and again in September when a deepfake of Kyiv Mayor Vitali Klitschko met EU mayors online, claiming Ukrainian refugees were cheating the German welfare system and demanding their deportation back to Ukraine.

Deepfake researcher Hany Farid sees such deceptions as the 'the tip of the iceberg' in a burgeoning information war deploying deepfakery to achieve lucrative political and commercial goals. Deepfake crime is flourishing: in 2019 fraudsters deepfaked phone-audio of a German CEO to extract US$243,000 from his UK subsidiary; in 2021 grifters combined deepfakes with fake emails to convince a UAE company employee to transfer US$35 million to their account. The 2022 Black Hat cybersecurity conference report shows 66 per cent of cyberattacks now involve deepfakes. Deepfake human-rights abuses are also mushrooming globally, fulfilling predictions the technology will be used to attack and disempower citizens online: in 2018, Indian hackers deepfaked *Washington Post* journalist Rana Ayyub into a widely circulated porn video after she demanded justice for an eight-year-old Kashmiri girl who had been raped and murdered. Ayyub joins a line of high-profile professional women stripped and degraded by deepfake porn:

UK poet and broadcaster Helen Mort; US politicians Lauren Book and Alexandria Ocasio-Cortez; Australian lawyer Noelle Martin. Thousands of ordinary women and girls are being similarly abused: data collated by Sensity AI indicates malicious deepfakes double every six months, and of the 85,047 deepfakes circulating by 2020, 90 to 95 per cent were non-consensual porn, 90 per cent of which targeted women. At the time of writing, these figures remain largely unchanged. Tellingly, while considerable attention and resources have been devoted to the technological and legislative prevention of political deepfakes (with dubious success), the fact that the overwhelming majority of deepfake victims are female remains insufficiently acknowledged and regulated. Microsoft, despite pledging to remove its DeepNude app in 2019, still hosts the original AI source code. From the shadows of the web, toxic men continue to attack women with impunity.

AS A NASCENT technology, deepfakes are in what media theorist Simone Natale labels the 'interpretive flexibility' phase where different stakeholders compete 'to impose a specific meaning on the novelty'. Utopian deepfake predictions separate the technology from the intentions of its users, depicting a positive and transformative future that incorporates two 'emotional forces' bioethical researcher Emilio Mordini identifies as integral to the harmonious integration of all new technology: curiosity and wonder. Freed from reductive, dystopian portrayals of deepfakery as the digital bastard of malicious hackers and fake news, the technology can be viewed neutrally – as a novel special effect in film's ongoing quest for verisimilitude. Locating deepfakes in the illusionist traditions of cinema and magic, which trick the gaze but not the mind, widens the focus from machines that produce and control deepfakes to the humans who construct and circulate them. Deepfake creators – just as early technology-adopters have always done – are now repurposing this powerful tool to enrich and improve our lives. Their work illuminates an expanding site of cultural and social innovation, suggesting deepfakes might not, after all, be 'the place where truth goes to die'.

Psychologists envisage using deepfakes to de-age the relatives of Alzheimer's sufferers to strengthen memory bonds and to help gender-reassignment and body-dysmorphia patients imagine their future selves. Grieving families are already finding solace in deepfakes of the deceased – most notably in 2020 when Kim Kardashian viewed a talking hologram of her dead father. Communications researchers are developing deepfake personal 'assistants' (the video equivalent of Siri); deepfake 'skins' that enable multilingual exchanges online; deepfake 'mannequins', which can be used to try on virtual outfits; and deepfake 'influencers', such as Lil Maquela, a progressive Augmented Reality robot with 3.6 million followers. In entertainment, deepfakes participate in live TV debates, awards nights and comedy shows; fans deepfake themselves into movies and games; and musicians are being 'youthified' in concerts – such as Abba's 2022 'Voyage' extravaganza, in which the Swedish band performed as their '70s digital 'ABBAtars'. In education, deepfakes are being used to speak truth to power: *Joaquin Oliver Comes Back to Life* (2020) resurrects a shooting victim in a posthumous video, urging American voters to stop gun violence.

In cinemas, galleries and the YouTube showground, artists are using deepfake technology to provoke, subvert and astonish, fulfilling a perceptual contract as old as magic itself – in which our wonder springs from knowing we'll be deceived, but still being surprised when we are. These artists treat deepfakes as a new VFX in a screen lineage rewinding back through the digital (green screen, motion-capture) and the analogue (rear-projection, superimposition) to cinema's magical origins in the trick films of the 'Godfather of CGI', Méliès.

But deepfake artistry also responds to a more ancient dream, the human automata, whose ancestors are glimpsed in the mechanical puppets of ancient Greece, the tea-pouring robot of twelfth-century engineer Ismail al-Jazari, Wolfgang von Kempelen's eighteenth-century chess-playing android and Peter Jackson's twenty-first-century cyborg Gollum in *The Lord of the Rings*. In 2020 the synthetic human was given new form by deepfake artist Shamook, who created a full-bodied, de-aged Mark Hamill in *Luke Skywalker Deepfake*, which was so superior to the 'dead-eyed' CGI Luke of Disney's *The Mandalorian* that Lucasfilm offered Shamook a job. Shamook belongs to an expanding community of practitioners and fans who circulate deepfakes with a playful cinephilia that rewards excellence (*Princess Leia Fixed using Deepfakes*), humour (*Elon Musk Star Trek Deepfake*) and believability (*Keanu Reeves stops A ROBERRY!*). Deepfake automata, such as the Skolkovo Institute's talking portrait of the Mona Lisa and the Florida Dalí Museum's *Dali Lives,* exhibit a similar fascination with spectacular AI simulacra. The technologically literate and knowing viewers these works attract undermine dystopian predictions of stupefied audiences rendered powerless by deepfake deception.

Some political artists are harnessing this deception to reveal deeper truths: Stephanie Lepp's *Deep Reckonings* (2020) reimagines polarising figures, such as US Supreme Court Justice Brett Kavanaugh, as their 'morally courageous selves'; *In Event of Moon Disaster* (2019) subverts the fake moon-landing conspiracy with a deepfake of Nixon delivering a real speech, written in case Apollo's 1969 mission failed; James Coupe's *Warriors* (2020) harnesses deepfakes and facial recognition software to critique the in-built bias of AI.

For mainstream filmmakers AI deception has a more utilitarian function, with synthetic media tools poised to vastly reduce editing, grading, special effects and production costs. Deepfakes can substitute deceased or absent actors with convincing simulations, dub their voices in perfectly lip-synched foreign languages and replace jarring documentary re-enactments with seamless archival and dramatised scenes. Ethical concerns around the use of AI trickery in non-fiction film are growing: in *Roadrunner* (2021), director Morgan Neville used deepfake audio of the deceased Anthony Bourdain to make him speak words he'd never said. David France's *Welcome to Chechnya* (2020), on the other hand, used deepfakes to disguise refugees from Chechnya's anti-gay purges. In a captivating illustration of AI's expressive power, the deepfake 'skins' worn by France's subjects kept them safe, were more engaging than conventional pixelation and operated as a cinematic metaphor for the masks LGBTQI+ people must often wear in the face of violent discrimination.

It is clear from these works and the contradictory narratives proliferating around deepfakes that the synthetic media horizon is still expanding. It will soon be possible to create an entire feature film, in any genre, using nothing but keyboard prompts. The screen industry is alight with predictions AI will put filmmakers out of work, but I'm ambivalent. Art shows us what it is to be human. As long as AI's mechanical imposters are trained in the Silicon Valley bubble, their stories will be neither diverse nor original – once the novelty of watching computers 'do art' wears off. The prevention of malicious deepfakery needs to focus on its abusers and victims, not the technology: in our AI-enhanced future, ethical and legal regulation is vital. As deepfakes become more embedded in our on-screen lives, it is likely the dystopian stench around them will dissipate and a more nuanced understanding of the technology, as one of a suite of synthetic media tools that can cause harm or happiness, will emerge.

For now, and perhaps not much longer, the moral responsibility for deepfake deception rests not with AI but with us. One thing is already true: as the current zenith of screen-illusionism, the creative power of deepfakes is limitless.

Based on the author's research for 'Deepfake Nightmares, Synthetic Dreams: A Review of Dystopian and Utopian Discourses Around Deepfakes', Journal of Asia-Pacific Pop Culture, *Vol. 7, No. 1: 109–135 (Pennsylvania State University Press, 2022).*

Anna Broinowski is a Walkley Award-winning filmmaker and author who documents counter-cultural subjects. Her films include *Aim High in Creation!* (about North Korean cinema), *Forbidden Lie$* (about hoax-author Norma Khouri) and *Helen's War* (about nuclear campaigner Dr Helen Caldicott). She is the author of *The Director is the Commander* (2015) and *Please Explain: The Rise, Fall and Rise Again of Pauline Hanson* (2017).

From Russia with love

Fake news and the Bolshevik 'socialisation of women'

Jeff Sparrow

[A]LL GIRLS OF 18 and over are public property and are compelled to register in the free love department of the Bureau of Public Assistance…

That was how, on 20 July 1918, the Melbourne *Age* introduced to Australia a bizarre but wildly influential claim about the early Soviet Union: namely, that Bolshevism entailed the 'socialisation of women'.

Perhaps wary of readerly scepticism, *The Age* offered its 'shocking revelations' initially at an almost parodic remove. The information, it explained, came from *The New York Times*, which reported that the English suffragette leader Emmeline Pankhurst had read an article in the French paper *La Liberté* quoting the Bolshevik *Isvestria* (sic) about a state-run program in Saratov, south-western Russia, that made all women sexually available to all men.

On 5 November, however, *The Age* returned with more definite intelligence. It now cited a Soviet journal – more accurately rendered as *Izvestia* ('The News') – as publishing a decree from Bolsheviks in Vladimir (not Saratov) establishing 'a Bureau of Free Love', at which women were obliged to register so they could be chosen by amatory men, with any children issuing from the pairings deemed 'state property'.

Across Australia, individual newspapers headlined the same sparse details in a variety of ways. A sarcastic Adelaide *Advertiser* declared revolutionary Russia 'an abode of love'. Its rival, the Adelaide *Register*, decried 'Bolshevik Morals'. The *Newcastle Morning Herald and Miners' Advocate* attacked 'Bolshevik

Immorality', the Brisbane *Telegraph* denounced 'Bolshevik Depravity' and the Hobart *Mercury* simply reported: 'A Bureau of Free Love'.

For the next months, what the Boulder *Evening Star* called 'the Bolshevik scheme for state-organised vice' dominated the coverage of Russia, with the revolutionaries' supposed sexual dissipation receiving as much or more attention as their expropriation of the capitalists. When, for instance, a resident from the central coast of NSW wrote to his local paper inquiring as to what this 'Bolshevism' involved, he was told that it entailed the elimination of every 'pure woman or chaste wife' from the community. Bolshevism, said the editor of the *Gosford Times and Wyong District Advocate*, meant 'women and men are to be mated at the will of the "bosses", just as a studmaster mates the males and females of his flocks and herds'.

These lubricious tales about the Bolshevik program were not, of course, true (though, as we shall see, they were not entirely false either). If we were to adopt contemporary terminology, we might describe the whole trope as 'fake news'. An analysis of how and why the 'Bureau of Free Love' story spread illuminates something more general about the nature of disinformation: then, as now, new technology facilitated misrepresentations that suited the interests of the powerful and provided psychic release for genuine anxieties about gender, sexuality and social change.

THE 'SOCIALISATION OF women' narrative arose from journalistic innovations associated with the First World War. In response to an unprecedented demand for up-to-date news, the Australian press had embarked on rapid technological change. Editors installed steam- and rotary-powered printing machines, established distribution fleets of automobiles and trucks, and hooked up their newsrooms to telephone lines. They also embraced the wire services that provided near real-time reportage of European battles.

The 'Bureau of Love' tale epitomised that new journalistic internationalism. It seems to have originated with a Moscow anti-Bolshevik paper called *Svoboda Rossii*, which, in April 1918, published a 'private letter' detailing the socialisation plans of the Saratoff Anarchist Club. When the anarchists denied the allegation, another right-wing paper in Moscow explained that the 'free love' bureau (and an accompanying 'League of Men Free for Selection') had, in fact, been established in Khvalynsk – and by Bolsheviks rather than anarchists.

That was the basis of the first *New York Times* report. The later stories in the Australian press derived from a weekly political magazine called the *New Europe*, which, on 31 October 1918, described an *Izvestia* decree said to 'substitute prostitution for marriage'. On 4 November, the British *Daily Telegraph* repackaged the *New Europe*'s claims under the heading 'Latest Bolshevik Infamy'. Within twenty-four hours, outlets as distant as the *Aberdeen Journal* in north-east Scotland and the *Goulbourn Evening Penny Post* in NSW could, because of cable technology, discuss the supposed matrimonial relations prevailing in Soviet Vladimir.

The Australian obsession with Russian free love thus represented a local iteration of an international preoccupation, one cultivated by the world's most respected newspapers. In the United States, the salacious coverage in *The New York Times* (according to which 'enthusiasts for nationalisation, naturally all males, [were] raid[ing] whole villages, seiz[ing] young girls, and demand[ing] proof that they are not over 18') ensured that headlines about sexual socialisation remained a staple of the American press well into the 1920s.

In Britain, the 'free love' narrative circulated in the newspapers of record (particularly the *Times* of London) as well as the penny press, so much so that *The Guardian*'s special correspondent, Professor WT Goode, deemed the 'stories of the nationalisation of women' as most responsible for fanning 'wildly excited feeling against Bolshevism'.

But if war internationalised journalism, it also fostered an intimate relationship between the news and the nation state, in ways that fundamentally shaped the reporting on Russia.

In 1914, Roderick Jones, the general manager of the Reuters wire service, had approached the imperial authorities to place his company 'at the disposal of the government for the fullest dissemination all over the world of British and Allied intelligence'. The British government accepted his patriotic offer, thereafter using Reuters' cables as a conduit for articles selected, and in some cases entirely fabricated, by the Department of Information. That meant, for instance, that the infamous (and totally bogus) account of a German 'corpse factory' rendering cadavers into soap made its way down the wires to the *Ballarat Courier* ('Boiling down the dead, Huns crowning infamy'), the *Sydney Sun* ('Fat from the dead: Horrible German method') and the Melbourne *Herald* ('The German Beast: A nation dehumanised').

The local press was not, however, entirely innocent of manipulation by the imperium. In Australia, as elsewhere, the Great War brought tremendous political polarisation, a genuine social crisis now obscured by the twenty-first-century perception of Gallipoli as a locus of national unity. Less than a week after the declaration of hostilities, the syndicalists of the Industrial Workers of the World (IWW) headlined their paper *Direct Action* with a trenchant evaluation of what the fighting meant. 'WAR! WHAT FOR?' the front page asked. 'FOR THE WORKERS AND THEIR DEPENDENTS: DEATH, STARVATION, POVERTY AND UNTOLD MISERY. FOR THE CAPITALIST CLASS: GOLD STAINED WITH THE BLOOD OF MILLIONS, RIOTOUS LUXURY, BANQUETS OF JUBILATION OVER THE GRAVES OF THEIR DUPES AND SLAVES. WAR IS HELL! SEND THE CAPITALISTS TO HELL AND WARS ARE IMPOSSIBLE.'

With Labor leader Andrew Fisher committing Australia 'to the last man and the last shilling', the IWW's assessment initially constituted a distinctly minority position. Yet a sharp decline in living standards meant that, as early as 1915, working-class women were protesting food prices in Melbourne streets.

The suppression of Dublin's Easter Uprising in 1916 intensified disquiet, with local Catholics suggesting Britain's treatment of Ireland exceeded in its brutality the widely condemned German outrages against 'poor little Belgium'. The newspapers celebrated Anzac heroism but recruitment rates slowed, particularly after the Australian Imperial Force retreated from the Dardanelles and the horror of the Western Front became evident in the swelling casualty lists.

Desperate to maintain what the British MP Sir Edward Carson called 'the necessary supply of heroes', Prime Minister Billy Hughes vowed to draft recalcitrants, a proposal backed by the entirety of what we'd now call the political class. Yet the people of Australia thought otherwise. A mass campaign by trade unions, Irish Catholics and socialists narrowly defeated the first conscription plebiscite; the resulting tensions within the Labor Party saw Hughes expelled from the NSW party and then lead his followers out of the federal caucus. The schism further radicalised the labour movement: when Hughes united with conservatives to win the 1917 election for the new Nationalist Party, the treachery of a 'Labor rat' turned more unionists against the war. The second conscription referendum held in December that year was defeated by an even greater margin than the first. Meanwhile rising industrial militancy culminated in the near-insurrectionary NSW general strike – and then the convulsions of the immediate postwar era led, in 1919, to the greatest number of days lost to disputation in Australian history.

Domestic conflict shaped the journalism of the era. The War Precautions Act of 1914 allowed the Australian Government to suppress statements that 'might cause disaffection or alarm during the war, or prejudice the recruiting, training, discipline or administration of the forces'. The next year, legislative amendments forbade editors from even revealing they'd been censored.

The few journalists reporting from the frontline had their copy redacted – first in the field and then again when it reached Australia. But the censorship regime bore down hardest on the publications of the anti-war and anti-conscription movement. In 1914, soldiers with fixed bayonets raided Vida Goldstein's pacifist paper, *Woman Voter*. With the Unlawful Associations Act, the government outlawed *Direct Action* and criminalised the IWW, an organisation Hughes described as 'hold[ing] a dagger to the heart of society'. Later, the War Precautions Act even prohibited displays of red flags, leading to mass arrests of socialists and the nation's first ever hunger strike (by the activist Jennie Baines after a six-month jail sentence for flag flying).

The major newspapers – all solidly pro-war – supported the censors, despite occasional grumbles about delays to their despatches. An April 1918 meeting between twenty-six editors and Minister of Defence George Pearce culminated in 'Rules for Censorship' that lauded 'the evident devotion of the Press of Australia to the public interest, and an unswerving loyalty to the cause of the Allies unexcelled in any other part of the world'.

Avowed partisanship meant a press more committed to ideology than accuracy. 'It is striking how poorly the conflict was reported,' write Fay Anderson and Richard Trembath in *Witnesses to War* (2011), their history of Australian frontline journalism. 'Battles were censored to the point of inaccuracy and were consistently portrayed in a positive light; news was delayed for months; and the lexicon of war remained upbeat and victorious: failure, carnage and defeat did not enter the vocabulary.'

THE EARLY COVERAGE of the Russian Revolution in 1917 – and the subsequent civil war – followed the same pattern. The big papers simply ignored the repeated challenges (in the labour press and elsewhere) to their 'free love' stories. Even more importantly, they also paid no attention to reports in the Brisbane *Worker* and Ezra Norton's muckraking *Truth* exposing the role of a tiny Australian contingent in the multinational anti-Bolshevik intervention organised by Winston Churchill.

Parliament casually fobbed off the few questions asked about the local contribution to the Russian Civil War. Yet the presence of Australian troops fighting on Soviet soil indicated how much the early response to the Bolsheviks represented a continuation of the Great War. Western governments condemned Lenin (whose famous 'sealed train' had travelled to Russia through German territory) as an overt agent of the Kaiser; the press presented the revolution as a conspiracy, in the words of the Brisbane *Daily Mail*, 'arranged by the German general staff and financed by the German Imperial Bank'.

The 'free love' narrative thus built upon the Great War coverage of German depravities. Allied propaganda consistently depicted 'the Hun' as racially different to the genial Brit, producing, as a kind of ideological collateral damage, widespread xenophobia. 'Anyone with a German sounding name is treated as a German,' complained the Swiss consul. 'The Australian people are too lazy to study the difference between the Nations.'

Russophobia manifested itself as early as 1914 when jingoistic stevedores in Melbourne bashed their Slavic co-workers for being suspiciously exotic. By 1916, the press was already condemning the activists among the Russian population in Brisbane (which numbered perhaps several thousand in total) as 'defenders of German "kultur"', denouncing these left-wing exiles' insufficient enthusiasm for the Tsarist dictatorship they'd fled.

After the revolution the sentiment intensified. When members of the Brisbane Russian community met with Finnish, Polish, Greek, Belgian, German and local radicals to celebrate May Day in 1918, the Brisbane *Courier* mocked the assembly as a 'polyglot gathering' in which 'disloyal sentiments' had been voiced in 'a babel of tongues, brogues and accents'.

The next year, the *Daily Mail* ran a sustained campaign against a Bolshevism it labelled 'a propaganda of indecency'. Sketching a dire vision of a Brisbane under Soviet rule, it warned of the police station in George Street becoming a bomb store, a tribute to Lenin replacing the Queen Victoria statue and the public library giving way to a Free Love Bureau.

When Russians marched against the War Precautions Act and its ban on the red socialist ensign, some seven thousand ex-soldiers retaliated with a violent attack on Brisbane's immigrant ghetto. The so-called 'Red Flag riots' – which one émigré described as a 'formal pogrom, exactly like the pogroms of Jews organised during the reign of the Czar' – culminated in diggers gathered outside the Russian Association Hall, singing the recruiting song, 'Australia will be there', and chanting, 'burn them out!…hang them!'

The violence revealed the ideological consequences of prolonged xenophobia. But it also showed how the stories of Russian 'free love' played upon long-running domestic anxieties.

IN THE DECADES prior to the war, a profound unease about sexuality and gender had developed in Australia as it transitioned from slow-paced rurality to a bustling, impersonal economy centred on huge cities. The historian David Walker describes the extraordinary late nineteenth-century proliferation of patent medicines treating what one advertiser called 'Failing Manhood, Nervous Twitchings and Nervous Debility'. The wide array of evils attributed to *spermatorrhoea* – semen lost through masturbation or nocturnal emissions – reflected a broader uncertainty about masculinity once traditional male roles associated with the colonial frontier had given way to soulless and emasculating industrial wage labour.

Not coincidentally, the masculine insecurity about seminal continence coincided with suffragette campaigns for women's participation in the public sphere. The proportion of women remaining single rose sharply between 1891 and 1901 while the rate of fertility declined, leading Melbourne's pre-eminent gynaecologist, a man with the splendidly Victorian name of Walter Balls-Headley, to warn in *The Evolution of the Diseases of Women* (1894) that trade unions and 'state socialism' were contributing to 'deficiency in marriage'.

The good doctor was not alone in his diagnosis. In a colonial settler state obsessed about the teeming masses of Asia, barren wives undermined national security even more than their enfeebled husbands. NSW established a royal commission in 1904 to investigate the birth rate crisis and its ensuing report stressed that the 'future of the Commonwealth, and especially the maintenance of a "White Australia" depend[ed] on the question of whether we shall be able to people the vast areas of the continent'.

The next year, the leaders of the conservative Women's National League identified a religious duty 'to fight with all our strength against [the] repulsive doctrines with which socialism is intimately associated'. In rhetoric that would later be recycled almost wholesale about the Bolsheviks, they warned that a 'socialistic' ALP intended that 'all men should hold in common the means of production, manufacture and exchange, as also their lands and houses, and even their wives and children'.

The patriotic ecstasy of 1914 reflected, in part, a conservative conviction that war provided an alternative to such a fate; that the hostilities meant social and sexual redemption; and that combat would restore the virility of men, put women in their place and buttress a tottering social order. 'War prevents us from slipping into the abyss of degeneracy and becoming flabby,' exulted Prime Minister Hughes. 'War like the glorious beams of the sun has dried up mists of suspicion [with] which class regarded class. War has purged us, war has saved us from physical and moral degeneracy and decay.'

The Anzac mythos also crystallised at the intersection between battle, nation and revived masculinity. In his famous despatches from Gallipoli, CW Bean described the diggers as sustained by 'an idea of Australian manhood'; on the first anniversary of the landing, the Returned Soldiers' Association explained how the campaign meant that 'Australia became fully one with the Empire…as a true man goes to his bride.'

Such fantasies utterly disoriented soldiers returning to a nation far more divided than the one they'd left. In 1918, for instance, an ex-serviceman called Eric Bannister faced an assault charge after punching a stranger embracing a woman in George Street, Sydney. 'What right do you have to kiss a girl,' he had allegedly shouted, 'when you haven't been to war?' Men like Bannister had understood the trenches as reviving a traditional sexual hierarchy (exemplified by the extraordinary image of the diggers marrying the empire) – and then found their treasured hyper-masculinity imperilled by shirkers smooching in the street.

Depictions of the Bolsheviks as bearded, women-ravaging *muzhiks* provided the angry veterans with an ideal target. At a 1918 meeting of the Queensland Loyalty League condemning socialistic free love, one member declared: 'The Union Jack had saved our woman folk from that sort of thing.' Alas, it clearly hadn't, a failure that the league vowed to set right.

The coverage about Russia revived a tired fantasy of the right, a cliché that rendered the Bolsheviks instantly familiar as well as dangerously exotic. The Brisbane *Worker* aptly described the 'free love' trope as 'a hardy annual

[that] grows well in the manure-like imaginations of anti-socialists and capitalist journalists'.

At the same time, conservative fears about the socialist threat to sexual morality during the war and immediately after also bore an undeniable kernel of truth.

BY THE TURN of the century, the so-called 'Woman Question' preoccupied the left as a whole. The German socialist August Bebel developed Friedrich Engels' critique of bourgeois marriage into his own 1879 tract, *Woman and Socialism*, a book that ran into an astonishing fifty editions by 1909 and helped German social democracy grow into a mass movement. In 1910, Clara Zetkin, another Social Democratic leader, proposed at the International Socialist Women's conference an annual celebration of 'International Women's Day'. By the next year more than a million people celebrated the date (the forerunner of today's IWD).

So when the local paper from the tiny Western Australian town of Meekatharra warned that Bolshevism had adopted 'the old German socialists' idea of free love', it did not wholly fabricate its reports, despite its tendentious conflation of women's emancipation with Bolshevik licentiousness and of 'free love' with 'free lust' (as the paper put it). The revolutionaries in Russia certainly drew heavily on the German tradition (Bebel and Zetkin, but also pioneering sexologists such as Magnus Hirschfeld) as they implemented ideas previously only expounded as abstractions.

Under the leadership of Alexandra Kollontai, the first Commissar of Social Welfare, the Bolsheviks developed a program of gender equality that granted women property rights, entry to education and the professions, and legislated for equal pay – all of which they had been denied under the Tsarist state and by the Orthodox Church. The family code of 1918 removed the religious system in which wives pledged obedience to husbands and instead transformed marriage into a secular agreement between two equals, terminable at any time by either party. Illegitimate and legitimate children received the same rights. Abortion became entirely legal in 1920; the Tsarist laws criminalising homosexuality were repealed, opening a window of relative freedom that even included some same-sex weddings. The state funded childcare alongside communal laundries, kitchens and facilities. The historian Wendy Z Goldman rightly describes the Bolsheviks as responsible for 'nothing less than the most progressive family legislation the world had ever seen'.

Such was the real foundation on which the fake news about female social-isation was constructed. The effects on politics in Australia were palpable.

In January 1919, when the Melbourne *Argus* reported on the syndicalist plan to found One Big Union covering all workers, it did so through a visceral deployment of the rhetoric used by the Women's National League back in 1905. 'OBUism means IWWism,' the paper snarled. 'IWWism means Bolshevikism and Bolshevkism means the tearing of young girls from their homes and mating them like animals to men selected for them by a government bureau.' The OBU idea was indeed backed by remnants of the old IWW; many of its supporters did endorse the Bolsheviks. But the *Argus* ignored remarkably broad enthusiasm for the Soviet regime in an Australia tired of war. In Sydney, even the Christian socialists of the Free Australian Association declared their wish that 'what happened in Russia be not so far off in the world'. In Melbourne, Alf Wallis from the Victorian Trades Hall council explained that 'when the time came for the revolution in Australia, the Trades Hall would expect to see the Soviet system of Government established in Australia'.

More importantly, the *Argus* – along with almost the entirety of the Australian press – misrepresented the statistical registers by which the new secular system in Russia recorded marriages, divorces, births and deaths. The notorious 'bureaus' facilitated 'free love' only insofar as they permitted wives to separate from abusive husbands – a right that, after 1918, women reportedly exercised in huge numbers. The fake news from Russia entirely reversed the meaning of the Bolshevik bureaus, presenting facilities designed for female empowerment as institutions fostering male desire.

Despite publishing a memoir under the title *Autobiography of a Sexually Emancipated Communist Woman* the cultured and deeply intellectual Kollontai was scarcely a libertine – and many of her arguments now seem entirely unexceptional. 'The sexual act,' she wrote, 'must not be seen as something shameful and sinful but as something which is as natural as the other needs of a healthy organism such as hunger and thirst.' As Grigorii Batkis from the Moscow Institute of Social Hygiene explained in 1923, the Bolsheviks advocated for 'the absolute non-interference of the state and society into sexual matters, so long as nobody is injured and no one's interests are encroached upon'.

Yet, even had those perfectly sensible positions been presented accurately by the Australian press, Bolshevik sexual morality would have remained controversial – not because it compelled women but precisely because it didn't. The 1904 Report from the New South Wales Beale Royal Commission into the Decline of the Birth Rate had, after all, recommended an intensified campaign to suppress information about contraception so as to force women to fulfil 'their true duty to themselves, their fellow countrymen and posterity'. To put it another way, the outrage over Russia reflected Western backwardness as much as Bolshevik radicalism. When an incredulous American journalist inquired whether divorce was available on demand in the Soviet Union, Trotsky asked, with equal incredulity, whether it was truly banned elsewhere.

SO WHAT HAPPENED to the 'socialisation of women' scare?

All through the 1920s, a hostile press attacked radicals for their supposed immorality but the trope delivered ever-diminishing returns. As more information circulated about the Bolsheviks – and a steady stream of outsiders published tracts about visiting the 'Land of the Soviets' – the more outlandish accusations served only to diminish the credibility of those who made them: early hysteria about sexual mores became increasingly an object of mockery. 'In Russia still are lovers,' quipped one Labor humourist, 'lovers' lies pinched from Above / You can lead a man to Russia but you cannot make him Love.'

In the Soviet Union, the prolonged civil war and economic blockade impeded attempts to provide equality through communal facilities for childcare, cooking and other facets of social and familial life. By the late 1920s, the rise of Stalin signalled a degeneration of the revolution's liberatory ideals. In 1934, the Soviet Union reintroduced laws against sodomy, with the novelist Maxim Gorky explaining that homosexuality should be considered 'bourgeois degeneracy'. Divorce once more became difficult and Stalin proclaimed childcare 'the honourable social duty of mothers'. Kollontai, who'd joined the anti-Stalinist opposition, eventually capitulated to the dictator, surviving the terror of the 1930s only by remaining quiescent while the regime systematically demolished the policies she'd implemented.

A corresponding revision took place within the communist movement abroad. In its early years, the Communist Party of Australia provided an oasis of sexual tolerance in a socially conservative nation, so much so that one party branch in the 1920s even boasted a drag queen as a member. By the 1930s, however, the Stalinisation of international communism led the CPA to crack down on what its leader Jack Miles called 'loose practices' among members. Bolshevism, Miles decreed, 'demands a steel-like character and that has to apply on sex questions as well as on other questions'. With communists avowing their commitment to traditional sexual ideals, scare stories about 'free love' bureaus lost their potency.

Obviously, the specifics of the 'socialisation of women' narrative belong to a vanished time: the lost world of Great War radicalisation. Yet if we zoom out from the complexities of that moment, we can recognise elements familiar from the 'fake news' in our own era. Like the cables of 1914, the new information technology of the twenty-first century provides tremendous opportunities for propagandists and fabricators. Almost by definition, the most successful 'fake news' serves powerful interests. As such, it often gets boosted by supposedly reputable sources, with, for instance, *The New York Times* doing as much as any publication to foster phoney stories about weapons of mass destruction prior to the invasion of Iraq.

As with the tales of 'free love bureaus', fake news today is invariably overdetermined, circulating as an expression of multiple and contradictory social neuroses. Yet even in its most lurid manifestations it draws upon certain real events and phenomenon. A paedophilic conspiracy does not, despite the assertions of the QAnon cult, govern the Western world – but the sex trafficker Jeffrey Epstein did associate with some very powerful people. 'This is at once a bogus age and an age of bogies,' explained Brisbane's Labor paper *The Daily Standard*, somewhat wearily, in 1917. 'And the bogus men of this bogus age are ever creating fresh bogies w[h]ere with to fool their unwary fellows'.

More than a century later, the same might still be said.

Jeff Sparrow is a Walkley Award-winning writer, editor and broadcaster. He is the author of ten books, his most recent being *Crimes Against Nature: Capitalism and Global Heating*, published by Scribe in 2021.

Taxidermy

Alex Philp

1.

THE PROCESS IS difficult. An effort to get underway. I watch my father on FaceTime: frozen, moving, frozen, blurry, then, finally, clear.

'They're butchering it,' he says.

His audio is glitching. His voice is blubbery – wet, as if underwater. I realise he's crying.

'I don't think that's an appropriate way to put it,' Mum says.

All three of us – Dad, my brother and I – zero in on her face. She's leaning back into her chair at the call centre, where she's on nightshift. My brother and I nod to agree.

'Okay,' Dad says. A lick of snot hesitates under his left nostril. 'Okay. But they're not making it easy. You know what they wrote in the email? Your *beloved companion*. Not even his name. Completely impersonal.'

My eyes flick to the rectangle that is my brother. I can tell that Josh is holding his tongue. He wants to remind Dad that not only were we all sent the email, but also that Dad forwarded it to us, so we're doubly aware of the email's contents. Something beeps on Josh's end. He looks over his shoulder, iPhone jostling. A forklift is moving. He's on his break.

'Yes.' Mum nods, slowly. 'But, to be fair, they'd be doing this several times a week. This is a job for them.'

'Is that what you want?' Dad says. 'For him to be treated like everyone else?'

He bends out of frame. The screen lags. Behind him, our kitchen becomes visible: fiddle-leaf fig by the bench, a tray from tonight's pasta bake sudsy in the sink. When Dad pops up, his image takes a moment to catch up to real time.

'Cullen-speed,' I say. Josh is the only one who laughs.

Dad lifts Hercules in front of his phone. The dog wags his tail. His eyes are milky, half-blind. Dad rests his cheek against Hercules' back. He speaks and a piece of spit flies from his mouth. Instinctively, I move to wipe it from my face.

'They might as well position him like a fish, if you don't care. They can position him with his mouth open, like he's an idiot.'

Mum, Josh and I look beyond our screens, as if to a wall, somewhere in our house, where the mount will soon be placed.

After the call, I put my phone on charge. I click my ceiling fan up a level and pull my sheet tight around me.

I hear my father coming down the hall. Behind him is the slow, depressing patter of Hercules. Dad pauses at my door before walking on. I wonder if he wants to debrief. I wonder if Dad feels like Mum and Josh were dismissive of his feelings, and that I'm his only ally. I conjure the sound of his crying – heavy, laboured – and I have the image of him deep underwater, his face not lifted towards the surface, but down, towards the ocean floor.

2.

HERCULES IS SIXTEEN. He's a Shih tzu. He has an overbite. He swings his arse when he walks. It's not eating his own shit that's killing him. It's stomach cancer.

When we got him, he was the size of a Calypso mango. Josh and I would wash him in the bathroom sink. He'd whimper if he didn't feel close to you.

Dad and Josh are in the kitchen when I go to get a glass of water before uni. They're sitting on breakfast stools and reading a brochure. Josh gives me a look when Dad closes his eyes to rub at his contacts. I lean back against the fridge.

'Where's Mum?'

Dad shrugs, still rubbing. He looks like an overtired baby. He reaches for his phone.

'Oh, no. Don't worry.'

'Is it something I can answer?'

'I don't want anything. Just wondering.'

Josh stands. He picks up his keys. 'I'm off.'

He points to his Coles shirt before I can ask. When Josh leaves, I put my glass into the dishwasher, search for my tote bag. Silently, Dad lifts it.

'Thanks.' I reach for it, but he lowers it away from me.

'Look at this,' he says.

'I'm late for class.'

'Just for a second.'

I sit on the stool beside him.

'I suspect,' Dad points to a glossy photo in the brochure, 'that they must brush them with a varnish, to keep the coats shiny.'

I consider the photo. A long-haired, yellowish Chihuahua, not on a wall mount, but on a stand. You could put it on a coffee table.

'Yeah,' I say. 'Yeah, probably.'

Dad's phone rings. It's Mum. He lets it ring out and then immediately plays her voicemail. He puts it on speaker.

'She always sounds, I don't know…' He taps the phone against the bench top. 'Huffy? Like she's walking up a hill when she speaks.'

3.

IN THE LECTURE hall, I try to concentrate. It's my fourth semester and I've switched from psychology to occupational therapy. Halfway through the second hour the lecturer is explaining how to make a splint when my phone buzzes. It's a group text from Dad: *Walnut, Beech, Pine or Cherry???* He sends a link to a website. *Pine*, Josh texts back. Mum doesn't reply, but gives a thumbs-up reaction to Josh's message. *Pine*, I type.

After the lecture, my friend Abby asks if I want to get drinks. We catch up to the others, who are walking down the hill.

'Okay, but—' Steph says.

Remi turns on her. 'No *okay but*. He's a socialist!'

I laugh along with Abby and Tom, though I'm not sure if any of us know what socialism actually is. We stop to get sushi to take to the uni bar. The woman at the counter gives me a raw salmon and avocado one instead of the smoked salmon one with cream cheese. At the bar, we leave tiny pieces of rice stuck to the table and slosh our schooners as we yell. I don't know why the bar staff let us stay. If I were them I would ask us to leave.

'Lib? Do you think?'

I look at Abby. 'Yeah,' I say.

Abby blinks back. 'Yeah, what?'

'What?'

They look at me. Tom hoots, grabs my shoulders, gives me a little shake. 'Wake up, Jeff.'

4.

MUM MAKES MORNAY for dinner.

Josh asks Dad to pass the pepper. Dad is further away from the pepper than Mum is. He makes a gesture to suggest this. I grab the pepper, give it to Josh.

'It's not a *big* deal,' Mum says.

'It is a big deal,' Dad says. 'Logistically.'

At noon, Dad had a phone call from Conroy and Sons. They have to delay the job a couple of days – the head taxidermist has sprained his wrist, needs to RICE it – which means that there will be a two-day gap between when we take Hercules to the vet and when we take him to a warehouse-like building in Oxley that Conroy and Sons have informed us is their workshop. The mount we ordered has arrived. It sits on the kitchen bench. I feel the wet of a small mouth at my ankles. Hercules is asking to see the mount. I nudge his head away.

The mount company made a mistake. The mount they sent is cherry, not pine. Before dinner, Dad spent the evening holding up the mount to different walls in the living room. Then, he made me hold it up, my arms straining, as he told me to reach higher, until the hem of my shirt was at the top of my ribs, so that he could see how it would look if he were a person just entering the room. Mum half-watched from the couch, the varicose veins in her calves the colour of the merlot in her glass. 'It's not art, Paddy,' she said. When I was maybe eleven, once I'd figured out what Mum's days were really like, she and I would play a game. When I wanted to talk, even if she were right beside me, I'd pick up the phone and call her. She'd answer, eyes glittering. 'Welcome to Optus. This is Joanne speaking. How may I redirect your call?'

Mum looks at Dad. 'Whenever we talk about it, Hercules looks upset.'

'That makes sense. He's dying.'

'When we talk about the mount he gets this—' Mum waves a hand in front of her face. 'Look in his eyes.'

'You think he'd prefer something else?'

'We need to think about what's best for Hercules.'

'This has to be a joint venture,' Dad says. 'This is a hard time.'

Josh blinks at the mornay. He wipes the inside of his wrist against his mouth and then picks up his plate. I follow him to the kitchen, grab his arm.

'You're *stoned*,' I whisper.

'You're stoned.' He tries to mock my voice, but his is off-centre, spaced out. 'When they get a divorce, who's your money on to get Hercules?'

AFTER DINNER, I lie on my bed, watching Netflix.

There's a profile for me, Mum, Dad and Josh, and then one for Mitch – the boy that I went on three Bumble dates with a year and a half ago, and that I gave my password to because I felt bad he couldn't watch *Stranger Things*. He still uses the account. Sometimes I go on his profile, just to see what he's up to. Mitch likes movies more than TV shows. The exception is *Good Witch*. He's seen every season.

Hercules lies low against my abdomen. I curl and press my nose, then my lips, to the soft fleshy fat where the vet said the tumour is. I want to text Abby. The pieces of sushi rice on the table at the bar reminded me of maggots, I want to tell her. They made me think of how rice is put into salt shakers to suck out moisture. They made me think of preserving something long dead.

My door cracks open. I close my eyes.

He assumes that I've fallen asleep watching something. From the weight of the movements, I can tell that it's Dad. He shuts the laptop, removes my earphones. He says something to Hercules, rubs his ear. Rubs his belly. The words are indistinguishable, even though he's close to me.

It's a while after I hear the door shut that I retrieve my earphones.

I end up on Google.

I start with one word. Taxidermy. Then, Dogs + Taxidermy. Then, Taxidermy + Mammals + Process. Then, thinking back to my first-year unit on effective academic writing and research, Taxidermy + Mammals + Process (OR) Instructions. I go to a few websites, then to a national association page.

There was a convention last year in Ontario. My fingers sweep the keyboard. Reddit, I click. One post notes that mammals are difficult to taxidermise because it's hard to find a dead mammal to practise on without hunting one yourself. *It's not like u can buy a dead animal with the skin still on at the butcher*, BigKen62 posted. *Try marine*, TommyFishesAmerica replied. I hover the mouse over the word. Then, click it.

I'm sitting up now. My laptop is whirring and too hot on my thighs. I click into images. They load and I scroll, shoulders hunched. There is an absence of bears. No foxes, no owls. No eagles. I scan for rabbits. For scraggly terriers. All I see are scales. Scales and dead eyes. The images move into a feeling at the base of my throat.

Hercules shifts. A snore erupts from him. I look up at the window, towards the sunlight and to the dust that it illuminates beneath my ceiling fan.

5.

MARINE TAXIDERMY DIFFERS from mammal taxidermy. In marine taxidermy, fibreglass is arguably more durable. Real skin, however, is more authentic. BigKen62 said that it demonstrates commitment to a craft ethos if a marine taxidermist uses real skin. I'm certain that this is true. The Google images of fish with real skin look undeniably better. An iridescent snapper, backed on a mahogany frame. A sailfish – sharp contours, lines – has the potential to look so alive that you'd be forgiven for believing that the dorsal fin on its back might sway with a current at any moment. Bream is a popular fish to mount, though I don't know why. It doesn't look impressive.

6.

I HAVE A practical class at uni. The tutor asks us to take off our shoes and walk in a circle to warm up. Tom pretends not to laugh. We're learning how to de-escalate situations where a patient might get violent. We get in pairs and take turns lunging at each other with wild eyes while the other person holds up their hands in a defensive manner, softly bends their knees and scuttles from side to side, crab-like. No matter how raised a patient's voice gets, the de-escalator must speak calmly but firmly. They must also remember their personal buzzer, which they can press in dire situations, to alert hospital security.

'Get back,' I said, 'get back!'

The tutor doesn't believe our voices are firm enough.

On my way home, I take the bus to a shop that I've never felt the need to go to before. Strip doors slap behind me as I step inside. The air is cold.

My phone buzzes. It's a call from Mum, then a text. *Are you home for dinner?* Almost instantly, there's a call from Dad. I lock my phone.

The fishmonger looks at me. 'Ready?'

'A bream, please. Two breams.'

'Whole ones? Want me to debone them?'

'No. Thanks.'

My phone rings again as I leave the shop. I manoeuvre the parcels of butcher paper under one arm to answer it.

'Hey,' I say.

'How was class?'

'I thought you were going to ask if I'm home for dinner.'

'No.'

'Mum just called. To ask that.'

'So you picked up when she called.'

'What?'

'I just tried to call you.'

The breams are sliding. I tighten the muscles under my armpit. 'I am home for dinner.'

'I wasn't going to ask that. What else did she say?'

'Who? Mum? Hey, Dad, I have to go. I'm working on a group assignment at Abby's.'

When I get back, the house is empty. I call, but Hercules doesn't come.

I take the breams into my room. I sweep uni books off my desk and position the breams on it, side by side.

Marine taxidermy has ten steps.

Skin the fish with a scalpel or sharp fillet knife. Preserve any meat and skin unable to be removed by injecting formaldehyde and rubbing salt. Afterwards, remove the eye. Spread Borax over the wet inside of the skin to prevent shrinkage. Stretch skin over a mould and shape. Keep fins wet, spread and pinned, until skin is sewn shut and then attach them. Carefully.

1, 2, 3, 4, 5, 6...

7. *Let the fish dry. This can take several weeks.*
IN THE BATHROOM cabinet, I find a metal fingernail cleaner that can act as a scalpel. I'm making do with what I have while I wait for my Amazon order to arrive. Instead of a preserving container, I use an empty ice-cream tub. Instead of formaldehyde, I use white vinegar. Sprint shears (garden shears), varnish (nail polish).

As suggested by BigKen62, a YouTube channel is my teacher. It's created by a guy in Idaho. The Idahoan is working on a kingfish while I'm working on a bream, but I still get the gist. The Idahoan's kingfish is to be mounted on a jagged tree stump-like backing. It looks like a tree that has been struck by lightning. The kingfish will look like it was very hard to catch when mounted like this. I look down at my bream. I want to mount it on a mosaic of large pebbles.

The Idahoan's voice turns unexpectedly tender.

'Once you've finished, you need to keep it out of direct sunlight,' he says. 'When it gathers dust, you can wipe it down only, *only*, with a wet cloth.'

I chew the skin on the side of my pointer finger to taste the fish there.

8. *Using a pin, place a glass eye into the socket.*
I'M ALMOST LATE for an exam. I don't have time to take the bus. I ask Josh to drive me. The exam is where the tutor pretends to be a patient and I perform a cognitive assessment. I arrive at the exam room on the far side of campus five minutes before my time slot. Abby and Remi are in the slot just before me; Tom had his exam in the morning.

As Abby and I pass each other – she's leaving the room, I'm entering – she lifts a hand to her lips, mimes drinking. I grin, shake my head. Make my palms meet flat together, raise them to pillow my left temple. I give a faint snore, though by the time I do, she's already halfway across the lawn and there's no way she'd hear it.

WHEN I FINISH the exam, I walk towards the bus before I realise that the lone Nissan in the carpark is Josh's. I jog over, open the passenger door.

'You didn't have to wait.'

Josh shrugs. I buy him a thickshake from McDonald's on the drive home.

We eat dinner alone, apart from Hercules. He sits between us on the couch, breathing heavily. Mum and Dad are in Oxley; they're viewing the workshop, which means that more than ever Hercules is on borrowed time. Conroy and Sons said that it makes people more comfortable if they can inspect where the work is done beforehand. If Josh finds something funny on TV, he opens the entire black hole of his mouth to laugh.

Afterwards, we stand before a wall in the living room. I take a step closer to the wall, then a step away. We go into the yard. We peer through the windows and examine – from a distance now – the living room wall.

Hercules has followed us. He moves lazily through the dandelions before he starts to chomp at something ancient in the grass. It's sediment, like crumbled sandstone.

'Oi,' Josh says. 'Hey.'

I try to grab Hercules by his round hips but he lunges away. He trots to the fence and then circles back. When he lowers his head to the grass, I nudge him with my foot. Josh has resumed looking at the wall.

'It's good,' he says. 'Because when we're having afternoon drinks and nibbles out here, we'll still be able to see him.'

I look at the wall, too. I try to think of what I could say.

I've been knocking Hercules away this entire time. When I relent, Hercules doesn't believe me. He hovers his overbite over the grass and watches me as he picks up his dried shit. When I don't move, he hurries away. Gleeful. Radiant. The most active and beautiful that I've seen him in months.

'Did you really just say *nibbles*?' I laugh at, not with, Josh.

I WAKE WITH a jolt. I've been asleep an hour. My laptop is open on my bed, the Idahoan concealed in the black screen. I hear the TV on in the living room. The theme music is of Mum's show.

Mum is sitting on the couch. I sit beside her. She puts her wine onto the floor so that she can wrap both arms around me.

We watch the judges share secret looks after minuscule bites of food. Coles stocks the pantry on *MasterChef*. Josh works in the Coles warehouse. Mum watches *MasterChef*. The everyday ties between my family please me.

'Where's Hercules?'

'In our bedroom,' Mum says. 'Dad wanted to spend tonight with him.'

I let that sink in. Then, I allow my mind to wander to the bream. Unlike the Idahoan, I didn't do a good job of removing the skin; the first bream I completely ruined and the second bream isn't much better. Earlier, straight after the exam, I tried and failed to use the straw from Josh's thickshake to insert a glass eye into the bream. The supplies from Amazon arrived yesterday, the eye among them. I tried to insert the eye into the bream's eye socket with tweezers. The eye was too small; it slipped into the cavity, as if nesting in a moon crater. The eye is clear, but not shiny. Not shiny like I thought it would be.

After a while, I hear Dad open his door and start to come down the hall. I sit up and kiss Mum goodnight.

I leave through the kitchen to avoid the hall. I can hear Dad walking down the throat of it. I picture us moving on opposite sides of the living room. For a moment, I fear that I've gone the wrong way: that the direction I'm heading in is directly towards him, and that we're going to collide. That he's going to collide with me. I blink but my vision has gone strange, and I run my hand along the wall to guide me and I make it into my room and I shut the door. I go to my desk. I snap on the desk lamp and the bream is revealed.

I can hear Dad speaking to Mum even through the walls. Hercules, no doubt, sits pudgy at their feet.

'Look, I'm just telling you that, from the outside, it seems like this is just a regular night for you.'

'I've had my time with him.'

I crack open my door.

In my parents' room, I move into their ensuite. Dad's contact lenses sit in the cupboard and shimmer in their solution. I pick them up and hold them to my own eye. If placed carefully over the bream's eye, a lens would make the glass gleam.

9. *Paint and varnish.*

THE NEXT DAY I get called into work at the newsagent, for once. I have no money, so I take the shift. Dad, Mum and Josh pass me in the car as I'm walking there; Mum waves through the open passenger window and Josh gives me the finger. Hercules sits on his lap.

After my shift, the streetlights are just turning on. I walk home along Old Cleveland Road. I wrap my cardigan around me, my tote bag keeping rhythm against my thigh, and I listen to the cicadas and look up at the faint stars, like they've been half-drawn or half-erased.

I open our front door. Dad looks up from stirring the slow cooker.

'Where is he?'

Mum looks at Dad. Dad looks at Josh. Josh looks at the beer fridge freezer.

THE BREAM IS still drying. During the day, I leave it on my desk. At night, I put it on a piece of cardboard under my bed. I've just slid it under there, and am looking up a Twitter thread that Tom mentioned in the group chat, when there's a knock on my door.

I look up. After a while I say, 'Come in.'

Dad closes the door behind him. I think about making a joke about cutting onions. Dad stands by the door and his gaze wanders around my room. I make a show of locking my phone and putting it onto my desk, to indicate that he's interrupting me. Dad picks up my newsagent shirt from the floor. Then he picks up a pair of jeans. My undies. He holds their loose elastic, the thin cotton, in his fingers.

'What?' I say.

'It smells weird in here. Have these been washed?'

'It's grief.'

'What?'

'Sorry.' I sit down at my desk.

Dad sits on the edge of my bed. He still holds my undies.

'Just girl smells, probably.' He laughs. 'Did you like dinner?'

'It was nice.'

'I liked the thyme.'

'I thought that was oregano.'

'Ratatouille is French. You'd only use oregano in Italian.'

'Oh,' I say.

'Are you sad about Hercules?'

A current moves in me. *No*, I imagine saying. *In fact, I'm glad. I'm happy he's dead.*

'Yes,' I say.

'Come here.' Dad makes room on the bed. He's wearing board shorts. The material edges up as he moves, reveals the thick hair of his thighs. 'I'm sad, too.'

I say nothing. I put my fingers on the spot of my desk where I usually place the bream. I imagine how beautiful the bream's eye will look not with the contact lens, but with a real eye. On his YouTube channel, the Idahoan taught me that the art of taxidermy allows for creativity. *The body is yours to control*, he assured me. How would the bream look if I reached across and took my father's eye? How would the bream look if I dug my fingernails into his eye socket and snapped the nerves there and severed his lamina cribrosa, and watched him fall backwards, if I then collapsed the bream's face with my fist and positioned my father's green eye in the ruins?

'Come here.' Dad looks down at his thighs. We look down at them together. I think of my undies, crumpled in the pocket of the board shorts. 'Come and sit here,' he says. 'Come and sit beside me, Libby.'

10. *Mount, ready for display.*

WE HAVE DECIDED to cremate Hercules. Mum drove this decision. Conroy and Sons kept putting our order off, and she decided that she couldn't wait another day. My aunt is coming for lunch next weekend and Mum needs room in the beer fridge for spinach and feta quiche.

We're at the Wynnum waterfront. We're walking down the board-walk, ready to throw Hercules into the wind. The boardwalk is busy with people fishing, with people sipping coffee and looking out across the marina. Suddenly, Mum worries that what we're doing is illegal.

'I really don't think that you can just throw ashes wherever,' she whispers. 'No, seriously.' She tugs at my father's shirt. 'Paddy. Do we need a permit?'

In reply, Dad swerves off track. Mum, Josh and I follow. We climb down from the boardwalk, onto large black rocks pimpled with crabs, and come to a flat rock that we can all stand on, shielded from onlookers by the shadow of the yacht club shed.

Mum steps forward. She raises her hands. Though her fingers are still, I have a fear of her fumbling the urn. I'm afraid she's going to drop it. I'm afraid I'll be asked to step off the rock and into the yeasty water to retrieve it. I'm the only one wearing shorts, which are quicker to dry than jeans, so they'll make me do it. I know they will. Mum prises the lid off Hercules.

I'm still standing away. I'm closer to the shed than to the water.

Dad looks back at me. He's been rubbing at his eye. It's red, inflamed. Though I know it's impossible, I think the contact in his left eye has moved. I think half of it has slipped behind the eye, and seen up close, his iris might look like it's split, like he's looking at me twice.

This piece is one of five winners of the 2022 Griffith Review Emerging Voices competition, supported by the Copyright Agency Cultural Fund.

Alex Philp is a writer of both screenplays and prose. Working with her frequent collaborator, Luisa Martiri, she wrote the short films *Milk* (2018) and *Pools* (2020). *Pools* premiered at Flickerfest (2021) and was also an official selection for Show Me Shorts Film Festival New Zealand and CinefestOZ. Her short fiction has been published in *Overland, Westerly, Voiceworks* and in the *Review of Australian Fiction*. She won the Rachel Funari Prize for Fiction in 2017.

Melinda Bufton

Self-portrait in Joy Hester pocket mirror

All hail my inner bones, things have been troped
yet now heat up. Being Bowie gone to Berlin,
genuinely out of ideas and summoning Brian Eno
wearing just plain black things (with tiny gold crucifix at neck!).
Yes I have been in my gaudy California
and then a long stretchy phase at Intertia, which is the capital of *blergh*.
Finally at the NGV a new sign and clustering of YBAs but feel frowny re the
    Sarah Lucas
adjectival androgyny. We all dressed that way?! It was a down-low downtown
    downtime look
because casual had nothing to do with leisure, you goofs.
And then I remember oh
I did go to Germany – once – but these timelines so punked
and no longer sure if my memory files can be opened…not pixel-y enough or
    something.★
Try the 'Gwen Harwood', making up names for myself to continue the
    lifelong gambits and ardour,
but non des plumes. Artifice so hot without make-up and I'm hoping to get
    away with same.
Iteratively I summon a muscle or teardrop and, well,
affect cavalcade –
You are my molten core.
Brushing dirt from my face and streaming my own lies
to my own startled newsfeed, it turns out
I was there all along and nothing really happened without the
cut-ups *which are not cheating!* Doxing my own creative practice again
to find I can dress down for the media, eventually, and that glamour shots
mean something different to everyone. Except you and me.
I think we'll find its line, I think we'll find its buttercup I think we'll find
form.

★ *after Gig Ryan*

Melinda Bufton is the author of *Moxie* (2020), winner of the Helen Anne Bell Poetry
Bequest Award 2019.

Rogues' gallery

Art and the bureaucratisation of novelty

Kasumi Borczyk

OBSERVE ANY CULTURAL institution for long enough and it will eventually mismanage a crisis of legitimacy so large that you can witness it incline first towards decadence and then towards disorder. With this in mind, I found myself at The Lume Melbourne's digital Vincent van Gogh exhibition early in 2022. Marketed as the Southern Hemisphere's first permanent digital art gallery and housed inside the Melbourne Convention and Exhibition Centre, The Lume is brought to you by Grande Experiences – its name may evoke some sinister shopfront for a sex-tourism operator, but it produces immersive installations of artistic cash cows like van Gogh, Monet, da Vinci and Dalí. A quip once made by Andy Warhol feels especially prescient here: 'Someday all department stores will become museums and all museums will become department stores.' My visit coincided with the annual Melbourne Gift Fair, which meant the entrance hall to the exhibition was full of suppliers spending their day peddling knick-knacks wholesale.

The exhibition itself comprised 3,000 square metres of multi-sensorial discovery. One installation recreates *The Bedroom* (1888) such that you can step inside and photograph yourself sitting on a simulation of the painting of van Gogh's bed; another room contains mirrors and plastic yellow sunflowers in a tenuous homage to *Sunflowers* (1887); and yet another features a Lexus (the exhibition's presenting partner) with *The Starry Night* (1889) printed onto its exterior. In the corner of the main gallery, there is a van

Gogh-inspired café where you can order food and drinks, but the main event is a ninety-minute lightshow, replete with spicy and woody aromas, in which van Gogh's paintings, sketches and quotes are projected onto the walls and floor amid a swerving medley of classical music. The experience does not so much approximate the feeling of inhabiting a van Gogh painting, as Grande Experiences would have us believe, as it does the feeling of living inside a van Gogh-inspired screensaver.

Bruce Peterson, the founder of Grande Experiences, explains that 'there is something for everybody at The Lume. They don't need to know who Vincent van Gogh is, they just want to get, and need to get, immersed in the colour and the movement and the vibrancy.' Of The Lume's Monet exhibition, which followed the van Gogh later in 2022, he likewise adds that 'it doesn't matter that they understand who Claude Monet is, because their introduction to art and culture becomes a joyous one, an engaging one'. The aim, apparently, is just to entice the lowest common denominator – willing as they are, according to Peterson, to trade their attention for shiny beads and trinkets.

On paper, the figures speak for themselves. The revenue of Grande Experiences was forecast at $70 million for the 2022 financial year, and it's just one of many producers of digital, interactive art touring globally. This push towards the immersive and the multi-sensorial is marketed as a democratising process. Never before has the general public been persuaded to develop such a keen interest in art – exhibitions, productions and festivals are more ubiquitous and more accessible than ever, but what comes with this particularly vibrant branding of cultural life is the absorption of art into the sphere of commodified experience.

THE PRODUCER OF the digital art exhibition presents himself as a benevolent cultural figure whose love of art behooves him to share it with an otherwise uneducated public by transforming classical artworks into spectacles of light, sound and moving image (note that van Gogh and Monet's artworks are out of copyright, and therefore their digital reproductions are not subject to licensing costs and require little more than a multi-sensory Google search). This is the capitalist class's manner of operation: to repackage every product and service as a humanitarian endeavour, as ethical and non-discriminatory towards those they target as consumers.

In the case of the digital art gallery, this moral dimension is superficially noble: it presents the cultivation and preservation of art as a life-affirming project. It is a distorted echo of the sentiments espoused by nineteenth-century polymaths John Ruskin and William Morris. Morris believed that art should not be reserved for the enjoyment of ruling elites, that life should be suffused with artistic expression and that everyday access to art is tantamount to a human right. He abhorred the death of the craftsman – he who created beautiful and useful objects with pride, using both his mental and physical faculties. The rise of industrial society in the nineteenth century resulted in the division of labour between the working class and the thinking class. The former is a mere appendage to a machine, completely alienated from the kind of engineering and imagination that invests everyday life with artistic and spiritual meaning, while the latter designs the objects to be made in the factories staffed by the working class. Barbara and John Ehrenreich, consummate ethnographers of what they termed the professional-managerial class, noted that this class exists 'by virtue of the expropriation of the skills and culture once indigenous to the working class'. (Granted, most professionals in nominally creative fields these days – from graphic design to architecture and marketing – are just as unmoored from the objects of their creation, resembling ergonomic, standing-desk versions of their assembly-line counterparts.)

Decoupling art from the everyday life of the craftsman has led to the art world as we know it today: a leisure activity for the leisure class, cocooned in layers of self-indulgence and preoccupied with creating monuments to its own importance. According to Morris, the only emancipatory possibility for art is to revive the spirit of craftsmanship, to reinvest everyday life with artistic creation for all people. It is something of an unfortunate irony that Morris' critique has itself been appropriated by the leisure class in their preoccupation with DIY individualism, in their love of artisanal goods and in the cultivation of a rustic asceticism that signals their own understanding of Morris' philosophy above everybody else's. What counts as the democratisation of art today – whether it be a 'Paint & Sip class' organised by your employer as a team-bonding exercise or the digital van Gogh exhibition – is the belief that everybody deserves to experience the same bourgeois levels of artistic alienation.

The digital art exhibition attempts to suture the spirit of capitalism to the spirit of Morris' radical critique, creating a grotesque Frankenstein's monster

of artistic techno-populism. The immersive, multi-sensory experience promises to midwife art back into the everyday lives of the people. The assumption
is that interaction is tantamount to emancipation: that by interacting with the
digital reproductions of an artwork, by plotting one's own movement within
the installation, by taking one's own photographs, you somehow gain entry
into a guild of selfie-takers, transforming yourself into a digital craftsman 'in
dialogue' with the work on exhibit. What we, as participants of the digital
art gallery, are given is not just a pale imitation of craft cultivation but the
opportunity to internalise the prevailing attitudes of late-stage capitalism, to
content ourselves with the reproduction and consumption of images.

What's more, the digital art gallery acclimatises us to the neoliberalisa-
tion of public art. Angela Nagle writes in her essay 'Reprivatizing Fine Art in
the Name of Equality' that museums are trending once again towards more
relaxed rules around the 'deaccessioning' of their artworks, to wit: the sale of
works to private buyers. Citing economic strains in the aftermath of Covid,
the Brooklyn Museum was forced to sell several European pieces dating
back to the sixteenth century, bequeathed to the museum with the understanding that they would be preserved for the benefit of public enjoyment.
For Nagle, we are witnessing a reversal of 'one of modern society's great
achievements'. In another example, in 2005 the New York Public Library
sold Asher B Durand's *Kindred Spirits* (1849) to Walmart heiress Alice Walton
for $35 million. Works of art are being re-privatised for both economic
and ideological reasons, perhaps never to be appreciated in a communal
setting again, while the public is being sold the bread and circuses of their
digital simulacra.

WHILE THE LUME'S van Gogh exhibition may represent one of the
more degenerate examples of the marriage between neoliberalism and art,
it is symptomatic of the technological soap opera that is unfolding inside
the walls of our most prestigious art museums – that the meaning, function
and design of the gallery are undergoing a radical adaptation in the age of
direct-to-consumer streaming. Its animating force is no longer one of cultural
preservation but one of self-imposed innovation. Where artists once attacked
the established order through acts of aesthetic transgression, it is the art world
itself that now claims to épater la bourgeoisie by adopting the bureaucratisation of novelty as its guiding principle. The masterstroke of modern art was

in its levelling of all possible criteria for aesthetic judgement. In theory, what constitutes art is no longer subject to any benchmark of style, subject matter or technical proficiency as dictated by a coterie of artistic elites. While there may no longer be gatekeepers of artistic merit in the traditional sense, the axis of power has simply been rearranged under the guise of social justice such that the art world is now beholden to those who gatekeep the gatekeepers. As Alice Gribbin writes in her essay 'The Great Debasement', 'while the market has turned artworks into mere commodities, the vast machinery of the art world has turned artworks into artifacts, by zealously, and almost exclusively, upholding the artwork as an entity with a message to convey'. Gribbin argues that institutional powerbrokers and bureaucrats are still the auditors of good taste, but that their measure of an artwork's worth is no longer truth or beauty, but how much or how little an artwork subverts the agreed-upon status quo. Art has become a handmaiden of the information age. In this, the medium of installation art often takes centre stage, and it almost goes without saying that the Yayoi Kusama-fication of the art museum is owed in no small part to how well it photographs. Every museum attendee can recall how incidental an artwork feels when its primary importance is as the background for a selfie. Consumers expect the contemporary museum experience to involve some degree of personal, physical involvement. In some sense, we have lost the ability to grant an artwork the freedom of existing outside of our own technological compulsions. In another sense, the installation merely simulates authenticity. For an experience to be authentic, according to Byung-Chul Han, it must 'resemble a crossing during which one must expose oneself to danger'. The experience of art is to the modern museum-goer what the experience of war is to the player of a first-person shooter video game.

THE TECHNOLOGICAL SUBJECT reaches the end of a long working week and, according to Jacques Ellul,

> his joy at finishing his stint is mixed with dissatisfaction with work as fruitless as it is incomprehensible and at a far remove from really productive work… Torn between this precariousness and the absolute, unalterable determinateness of work, he has no place, belongs nowhere. Whether something happens to him, or nothing happens, he is in neither case the author of his destiny.

It is against this backdrop that he seeks out the 'artificial paradise' of diversion and amusement so as to 'permit him to live as he might have willed. For an hour or two he can cease to be himself, as his personality dissolves and fades into the anonymous mass of spectators.'

In the age of technological optimisation, we are equally as preoccupied with entertainment as we are with devoting leisure time to projects of self-actualisation. The contemporary success of art museums rests on their ability to compound the entertainment value of an amusement park with the promise of an educational experience. Unable to reconcile the simultaneity of so many different and sometimes contradictory experiences, we come away with nothing. Instead, the informational brochures do the learning on our behalf by pre-masticating the artwork's underlying message. Meanwhile, the motion-designed spectacle always exudes such an aura of diversion that whether or not we are actually being entertained is irrelevant. This leaves us free to do what we apparently really want: to self-document while bathed in pixels of light.

Han's *Saving Beauty* argues that every aspect of our 'close-up society' is suffused with a pornographic dimension, one in which images no longer 'present gaps in the field of vision' or 'contain any hide-outs'. He goes so far as to argue that information and data are pornographic by nature because 'they have no *flip sides*; they are not *ambiguous*. In this, they differ from *language* which does not permit things to come into *perfectly clear focus*.' The pornographic is smooth, clinical and hygienic so as to be consumable (even when it attempts to pass as dirty or ugly). In The Lume's exhibition, the paintings of van Gogh are digitally manipulated to imitate the movement of his brushstrokes and enlarged so as to resemble, in spirit, a centrefold, with close-ups filling the entire room. Nothing about these digital reproductions requires you to squint or to edge closer; nothing reveals itself to you as time passes or through observing the artworks from different standpoints because there are no angles with which to see them in a new light. There is only one, all-encompassing, ejaculatory money shot.

A certain stillness and time, a certain stability and rootedness are required for beauty to be appreciated, in and outside the gallery. As Elaine Scarry writes (quoting Simone Weil), beauty forces us 'to give up our imaginary position at the center': 'It is not that we cease to stand at the center of the world, for we never stood there. It is that we cease to stand even at the center of our own world. We willingly cede our ground to the thing that stands before us.' In this way, aesthetic appreciation is a radical act of reciprocal freedom. Unfortunately, no worthwhile pursuit comes freely, and the redemption of beauty will involve confronting the countervailing forces of our day. It is a pursuit antithetical to a society that attempts to induce in us the shock of the new by continually manipulating the objects of our attention.

A previous contributor to *Griffith Review*, Kasumi Borczyk has also written for *Meanjin, Damage Mag, The Independent, Rolling Stone* and *Kill Your Darlings*, among others.

Detachable penis

Gender dismembered

Sam Elkin

WHEN I FINALLY got up the courage to call Mum to tell her I was on testosterone, she took a long pause before responding.

'So, are you going to get a penis stitched on?'

Mum and I don't talk about our feelings much, much less our intimate body parts, so I didn't quite know what to say. After a beat, I managed, 'Err, no. I don't think so.'

And that was that. We've never talked about it again.

Three years pre-transition, I was walking down King Street hand-in-hand with my then girlfriend headed for the Red Rattler, a queer bar in Marrickville, when a guy leaned out of his shiny Mazda 6 with a lurid grin.

'Hey ladies, who wears the strap-on?'

I withered and died, while my girlfriend traded barbs with him.

It certainly wasn't me who wore the strap-on. Not me, not then. I felt deeply ashamed by the suggestion that I might secretly covet a penis. Why would I, a lesbian feminist, schooled in a little Dworkin at the very least, want to penetrate my partner with that ultimate symbol of terror, the enforcer of women's subjugation?

Who would want to prove Freud right?

My femme-ish partner, lipstick to my ChapStick, was not similarly oppressed. During the years we were together, she acquired a bright orange vibrating waterproof dildo, a seventeen-inch veined double dong the shade of well-chewed bubblegum and an adjustable vegan-leather harness.

It was on one of my few awkward trips to a sex shop with her that I first spied a Mr Limpy, a jiggly three-and-a-half-inch prosthetic penis that came in vanilla, caramel or chocolate skin-tones. Were they a joke, I wondered? Like a penis straw at a hens' night?

Equal parts attracted and repulsed, I covertly ordered one a week later. When my pale, wobbly contraband arrived in discreet packaging, I panicked and shoved it in a sock drawer, and quietly put it in landfill a year later.

Three years into my transition during the 2021 lockdowns, my online shopping habit became a full-blown addiction. One of the weirder things that I purchased was a petite crocheted penis and testicles, hand-stitched by a crafty 'bear' called Devon. Each package was made-to-order, so I could choose everything from the shaft length to colour and testicle size. I could've even added ball hair.

Devon emailed to thank me for my order and told me my item would take him six to eight weeks to create. That was fine, I replied, it wasn't like I was going anywhere. I waited, occasionally giggling to myself about my penis's long-pending arrival. But three months later, no longer laughing, I contacted Australia Post, asking for an update on the whereabouts of my 'bespoke textile piece'.

After further delays, I was informed that it had been delivered to another flat in error. That despite their best efforts, recovery had proved impossible. I tried to remind myself that it didn't matter; it wasn't exactly a life-or-death issue. But the fact that my hand-sewn little member was now sitting in some-body else's house, perhaps waiting to be gifted to a colleague in the annual Kris Kringle, made me feel ill. Perhaps I'd bought it as a joke, but that didn't mean just anyone had a right to laugh.

I contacted Devon to tell him what had happened. Devastated, he promised to make me a new one as soon as he'd gotten through his back orders.

A month later, Devon and I met face-to-face outside my flat for hand delivery.

'Sorry it took so long. I was really just making these to take my mind off things but this little business has really taken off,' said Devon.

He showed me some screenshots of his latest made-to-order creations: a small pink willy warmer with a rainbow thunderbolt, and a larger, tan-coloured uncircumcised member with bushy, brown testicles.

'I truly hope this gives you joy,' Devon said as he handed me mine, artfully wrapped in the *Star Observer*, Melbourne's gay street magazine.

A year later, this one hasn't had a lot of outings either. The only time I really feel the need for a packer is lifting a barbell at the gym, hyperconscious of the visibility of my bulge-less shorts to the folks on the treadmill. I try to remind myself that there are worse things you can witness at a fitness centre.

Pissing wasn't a big problem until I started passing. Then I had this new dilemma of how to use the men's room. Fortunately, men's toilets do come equipped with toilets as well as urinals, but a free stall with a functional door can be hard to come by. Even when I found one, as I sat down to wee, I was gripped by worry. What if a man entered the next stall, looked down and noticed that my feet weren't facing the wall?

So, I looked into stand-to-pee (STP) devices. There was a seemingly endless array of consumer choices, from top-end prosthetics, designed with care right down to the realistic skin folds, to the DIY folded yoghurt-pot lids that wikiHow showed me how to craft.

It hadn't been so long since the missing package debacle, so I chose to steel my nerves and buy one in person from my local camping shop. Known as the Shewee, it's a sleek purple sheath attached to a thin, shallow, pointed funnel. Marketed as 'the original female urination device since 1999', the Shewee promised me the freedom to pee simply and hygienically without removing a single item of clothing. It's even NATO-approved for use by women in the military. The woman soldiers no doubt had more practical skills to draw upon than I did, but I just couldn't make the damned thing work. Every time I tried the funnel would immediately leak piss into my pants.

I took it to a festival once, hoping to avoid a close encounter with the drop toilets.

When I got home, I forgot to wash it, and it remained in a zip-locked bag at the bottom of a duffel for six weeks. When I finally fished it out in horror, the Shewee was covered in a spider web of thin, green mould. I'd like to tell you that I threw it out, but I didn't. It's also hiding in my underwear drawer. Now washed.

My journey into gender transgression led me to seek out evidence of my own kind in history. I found one such man in a Sydney courtroom in 1920. Harry Crawford (also known as Eugene and Eugenia Falleni) was arrested for the murder of his wife Annie Birkett, whose burnt body was found in bushland near Lane Cove River in northern Sydney. The prosecution argued that Crawford killed his wife after she discovered that he was biologically female. Describing Crawford as 'practical in her deceit', the prosecution tantalised the press by indirectly alluding to the 'false phallus' confiscated during a raid on Crawford's home. The Crown never produced the unmentionable item, deemed too scandalous to be seen by the public. Crawford was convicted, his capital sentence commuted to life. But what happened to the fake penis? How did he construct it? Is it still hiding in an evidence bag somewhere, just waiting to be displayed at the Justice & Police Museum?

I'VE BEEN TAKING testosterone for four years since that phone call to my mum. It deepened my voice, widened my neck and gifted me a jungle of arse hair, but it has failed to provide me with a penis. It's done something down there, however.

The technical term for my new 'condition' is clitoromegaly, or in simple terms, an enlarged clitoris. In the definitive *Atlas of Human Sex Anatomy*, the typical clitoris is defined as being three to four millimetres in width and four to five millimetres in length. If your clitoris is double that size, then – surprise! – you've got clitoromegaly. Some women naturally develop clitoromegaly due to polycystic ovary syndrome and other disorders that increase the presence of so-called 'male' androgens in the body. In a woman's body, too much testosterone and androstenedione can result in 'virilising effects' including acne, increased facial hair and male-pattern hair growth.

I myself have gone down the unnatural route to clitoromegaly by wilfully applying a topical pharmaceutical cream. It wasn't easy to come by, of course. There were many confused, angst-filled years leading up to my putting my name on the gender clinic waitlist. Then there was the not inconsiderable wait for my first appointment. Finally, after I got the nod from a GP, a psychologist and an endocrinologist, it was determined that I had 'gender dysphoria'. This diagnosis was the ticket to my first testosterone prescription. From there, it was just a daunting trip to the chemist followed by a three-day wait to pick up my medication.

Then, all I had to do was carefully draw out two millilitres of the opaque balm with a measuring applicator and rub it into my torso. It would seep through my skin and into my bloodstream. This was the little tube that could, super-sizing my clitoral erectile tissue until it resembled the tip of my thumb.

No-one would mistake this little nub for a penis. It's more like an outie belly button attached to an inner cord that leads to God-knows-where in there. It's a wonder of modern pharmacology.

I was alarmed when I first read about this side effect of testosterone usage. Despite having met many trans men over the years, I didn't know the human body could grow a new part. Transmogrification is the stuff of nightmares.

Some call it their 'dick', their 'growth' or their 'junk'. Of those, I like 'junk' the best. Like a beat-up old jalopy, 'junk' is fun, cheap and cheerful, the kind of miscellany you might find in the discount bin of a country op shop. The trans men and non-binary folk on Reddit and Facebook are always talking about their 'junk'. Some crow about their two- to three-inch growth, while others ask what they can do to get to these great lengths. Solutions are offered, including clitoral pumps and ointments, though there's little proof that they work.

Depending on the shape of your vulva, you might have discomfort when your nub starts rubbing up against your underwear. I didn't have this problem. My little nub is safely stored away behind the folds of my labia majora.

I was surprised to find that trans men engaged in as much size talk online as other men. Because I don't think in inches, it took me a while to realize what they meant. Five to seven centimetres? Mine was nowhere near that. I realised then that, even by trans man standards, I am on the small side.

There's no official ritual that comes after growing a nub. No bar mitzvah or Rumspringa, not even an awkward trip to the supermarket with a parent to get pads. Perhaps it's time that we made one up.

There's just me and my nub. Many of my trans masculine and non-binary assigned-female-at-birth brethren consider theirs to be a penis. And I'm fine with that. I know just enough about post-structuralism to understand that there's no reality outside language and that words and categories are inescapably slippery. But despite my love of *Eva Luna* and *One Hundred Years of Solitude*, I've never been a magical thinker.

I'm always trying to get to the nub of the issue. What am I now? Am I a male with a vagina? Or am I a mannish woman with a big clitoris and an extremely hairy tummy? Or, could it be that I have crossed over into the land of the third sex like Hermaphroditus, a male and female conjoined? Have I become, through hormonal intervention, physically intersex?

I keep searching back through time to try to understand what I am.

In *'A Strange Sort of Being': The Transgender Life of Lucy Ann/Joseph Israel Lobdell, 1829-1912,* Bambi L Lobdell (second cousin four times removed) explores the life of the so-called 'female hunter of Delaware County'. Joseph Lobdell, who was assigned female at birth in Albany County, in the state of New York, lived as a male for sixty years before being arrested for vagrancy while subsisting in the forest with his wife and pet bear. Upon his admission to the Willard Asylum for the Chronic Insane in Ovid, New York, Lobdell said, 'I may be a woman in one sense, but I have peculiar organs that make me more a man than a woman.' A report from his psychiatrist goes on to say that 'she says she has the power to erect this organ in the same way a turtle protrudes its head – her own comparison.'

I felt a deep kinship with this strange wandering man, now lost to the grave. What would Lobdell have thought of this modern world?

It seems that every high-rise – from the Empire State Building to Malaysia's Petronas Twin Towers – more or less resembles a penis. One of London's tallest skyscrapers is a cylindrical glass monstrosity nicknamed the Gherkin, also known colloquially as the Crystal Phallus.

Sydney's seventy-two-foot Hyde Park Obelisk looks so much like a penis that the AIDS Council of NSW once sheathed it in a big pink condom. My home state's Eight Hour Day Monument in Carlton is just crying out for similar treatment.

Even outer space isn't safe from humanity's phallic obsession; the 2021 lift-off of Jeff Bezos' Blue Origin turned into a global roast after hundreds pointed out just what the rocket ship looked like.

FROM PENIS PUMPS, photographic touch-ups to pharmaceutical aids, there's ample evidence that penis anxiety is everywhere. Just check your spam folder.

In some cases, at least, it appears to be for good reason. In 2021 Shanna H Swan, an environmental and reproductive epidemiologist, co-wrote a bestseller disturbingly titled *Count Down: How Our Modern World Is Threatening Sperm Counts, Altering Male and Female Reproductive Development, and Imperiling the Future of the Human Race.* Swan argued that that perfluoroalkyl and polyfluoroalkyl substances (PFAS, also known as 'forever chemicals'), which are found in everything from takeaway containers to baby shampoo, are correlated with a reduction in semen quality, testicle size and penis length. The size of the average man's penis could soon be humanity's next life-or-death issue.

Instead of contributing to the propagation of my imperilled species, I've gone and made myself infertile, at least temporarily. Would it be more or less transgressive for me to now go 'the whole hog'?

Phalloplasties were not devised for the purposes of gender reassignment but in response to the tidal wave of lower-body blast wounds experienced by male soldiers during World War I. The first phalloplasty for gender reassignment was performed in 1946 by the British physician Sir Harold Gillies on a fellow doctor, Laurence Michael Dillon (born Laura Maud Dillon). It involved thirteen procedures, and remained the standard technique for forty years. I understand that they've got it down to three now. There are lots of quirks and variations, depending on the patient's body type and personal desires, so this is just a rough guide.

To create the neophallus, they've got to take the skin from somewhere, usually the forearm, leg or side. The site of the donor tissue will require a major skin graft. I wouldn't recommend looking at photos; it's gnarly.

They shape and contour this stolen flesh and attach it to the groin. At this stage, you've got something that resembles a penis, but it can't get up to too much.

The second stage, scheduled about six months later, includes lengthening the urethra to allow for urination out of the tip of the penis, creating the scrotum from genital tissue and removing the vagina. All that original plumbing has got to go.

Finally, a year later, they put in saline testicle implants and an inflatable erectile device to help the patient achieve an erection. Then, presumably, you rest.

My extensive midnight research tells me that lots can go wrong. There are moments of pain and unexpected leakage. Fistulas, frequent urinary tract infections and incontinence. Multiple follow-up appointments and unforeseen hospitalisations. Functional limitations on the arm or leg from which the tissue was removed. Unsatisfactory penis length or testicle size.

This procedure, only available to very few wealthy trans men, does not sound appealing. Don't get me wrong, I'd love a dick, but I'd also love a life of pain-free pissing.

But then one night I was accepted into a secret Facebook group called 'Jason's Phallo Journey' after my request had sat pending for a week. I leaned forward in my chair, eager to know everything about Jason's new member.

In his profile image, Jason beams in a fancy button-up shirt, arm in arm with a long-haired woman in a sensible blouse and blue, pleated skirt, smiling lovingly at him. They might be at a vineyard wedding. I scrolled down back to the start when Jason was about to go into surgery for his hysterectomy, lots of 'good luck messages' posted next to an image of him in a hospital gown. A week later, there's a photo of his hairy abdomen with fresh pinhole surgery scars. Six months later, he's back in the hospital bed for procedure number two. He sounds tired and sore afterwards; the Endone has helped with the pain but is making him constipated. Procedure three is tricky, and he's soon back in the hospital gown for a surgical revision. But when I finally get right back at the top of the timeline, I shed a tear as Jason signs off for the last time, thanking everyone for their support. He said that despite the years of pain and blow-out costs, the feeling of his dick lying against his thigh on a lazy Sunday afternoon made it all worth it.

Should I go under the surgical blade one day like Jason did? Would it make me a real man?

LORENA BOBBITT CAUSED a global news sensation when she cut off John's penis with a carving knife in the US in 1993. It was such a big news story that even I, at age ten, living on the other side of the world, heard all the grisly details in the playground. Why did this cock, temporarily removed from its undistinguished American owner, end up being so very famous? What was so very funny about a man without a penis?

The real story wasn't very funny at all. Lorena said that she'd done it after her husband John had raped her, and not for the first time in their marriage. After she cut it off, he was so drunk that he just fell asleep. Lorena drove off, threw John's penis into a field, but soon called the police to confess to what she'd done. The police collected his penis and packed it in ice, and it was successfully reattached. The urologist James Sehn, who also shot to fame as a result of the case, said in a 2019 interview that when he saw John without his penis, 'It was a kind of an out-of-body experience… It really takes your breath away to see this kind of disfigurement.'

Would my body take his breath away too?

Later that year, scientists discovered a new deep-sea worm that lies in ambush on the seafloor and attacks unsuspecting prey, often snapping them in half. They named it the 'Bobbit worm'.

In 2019, thousands of pulsating creatures resembling ten-inch disembodied pink penises washed up on a beach in California. Their Latin name is *Urechis caupo*, more commonly known as fat innkeeper worms. Twitter was alight with dick jokes. 'Ladies, if you aren't satisfied at home, remember there are plenty of fish in the sea.' I suddenly imagined myself boarding an emergency flight to LAX with all the other trans guys to rehome the fat worms into our trousers.

A more conservative surgical procedure you can get is a metoidioplasty, or 'meta'. A surgeon cuts the ligaments around the mega clitoris to release it from the pubis and give the shaft more length, typically four to six centimetres.

They say that the ancient Greeks preferred a small penis, as they believed it made a man rational, intellectual and authoritative. That's why Michelangelo's idealised David has a small one. Ancient Greek statues of satyrs, the lustful, ugly half man-half donkey attendants of Dionysus, have comically large penises, pointy equine ears and wild manes.

I wonder what the ancient Greeks would have thought of a man with a vagina. The second coming of Tiresias, foretelling the downfall of their civilisation?

Vladmir Putin recently declared that his war on Ukraine was part of a broader battle to save Russia from the imposition of the West's 'sex change operations' and its 'various supposed genders'.

Could my body bring down an empire?

A previous contributor to *Griffith Review*, Sam Elkin is a writer, arts producer and radio maker living in Naarm (Melbourne). He is a co-editor of *Nothing to Hide: Voices of Trans and Gender-Diverse Australia* and co-host of Triple R's *Queer View Mirror*. His personal essays have been published in *Growing Up in Country Australia*, *Kill Your Darlings* and *Mascara Literary Review's Resilience* anthology. In 2022 he was awarded a Scribe Varuna Fellowship to develop his first full-length book.

Rebecca Jessen

Lesbian search terms

how does a lesbian love a person
can I use a rock to tenderise meat
Amazon commercial with the lesbian couple wtf
homemade real lesbian
things that usually don't go together but end up good
how exactly do lesbians conduct sex business
boob scenes in all movies
lonely sad woman lets a lesbian comfort her
what can upset a Capricorn gay
when she keeps bringing up boys
how to give off top energy
lesbians be owning house plants
do witches wear anything else on their head besides a hat
body language between lesbians
why do gay Aries have a horrid temper
how to approach the girl at school lesbian version
why are lesbians obsessed with older women
how many types of lesbian sex do we have
what does a ripe pineapple look like
girls who like girls who like recycling
how to satisfy my lesbian part through video call
why do girls cut their middle fingernail
how to ground yourself as a baby witch
Pisces lesbian and Sagittarius bisexual soul mates
very hot lesb mommi
hand poems for the lesbians
is it a date lesbian version
should I get a job before I get a girlfriend
lesbians on TV who didn't die
how long does hummus keep in the fridge

This found poem is a selection of search terms published in Autostraddle's weekly newsletter.

Rebecca Jessen's poetry collection *Ask Me About the Future* (UQP, 2020) was shortlisted for the Victorian Premier's Literary Award for Poetry and the Kenneth Slessor Prize for Poetry and was commended in the Anne Elder Award.

The trick that tells the truth

Unmasking corporate counterfeit

David Ritter

TWO LITTLE GIRLS, maybe four or five years old, are hurtling through the knee-high grass, the blades of which appear more chartreuse than verdant under the low sun's bright light. Each child is wearing a striped singlet and long pants. There are no buildings in sight, just a lush, vacant meadow spreading in every direction, backed by dense trees casting a shadow on the near horizon. The sunbeams stream behind the speeding figures, shining through the translucent sprays of their shoulder-length hair. The lively grin of the follower and the concentration of the leader suggest that perhaps the chase is on – but there could be a thousand motives behind why they run, or none at all. The scene conjures Wordsworth: *Bliss was it in that dawn to be alive.*

Or so this piece of corporate marketing intends us to feel. A female voice is heard over the footage, intoning words of warm reassurance: 'We are moving from using high to lower emissions generation technology. Our commitment to gradually close our coal-fired power stations means we are making way for new low-carbon generation.'

The script is being read on behalf of AGL Energy, operator of three ageing coal-burning power stations and by far Australia's worst domestic climate polluter, responsible for around 8 to 10 per cent of the nation's annual emissions. At the time the video was made, AGL was planning to keep burning coal until the late 2040s, almost two decades beyond what's recommended by the International Energy Agency to meet agreed global climate goals.

As subjects of late capitalism, we've become inured to the amoral cynicism inherent in relentless corporate marketing; yet both the good faith of our human nature and the susceptibility of our lizard brains ensure that we also remain receptive. We are perhaps not quite as jaded as we think and can still be shocked when a chasm emerges between brand and reality. In 2020, the disjunction between AGL's public relations and the truth of the company's business practices was highlighted and ridiculed in the public realm, ending in a court case of profound significance on Australia's twisted road to belated action on climate change. In days of counterfeit without cease, the mask can still be torn off when a concerted effort is made to do so.

THE AUSTRALIAN GAS Light Company, as it was originally known, was founded in Sydney in 1837 and was responsible for the first public lighting of a street lamp in the city a few years later. According to a contemporary news report, '[i]n the evening a partial illumination of the town took place, and, we must notice, that gas appeared in the streets of Sydney for the first time, under the auspices and laudable exertions of the Australian Gas Company'.

For the majority of its corporate history, AGL's 'laudable exertions' no doubt seemed synonymous with progress and civility, bringing heat and power derived from coal and gas to the homes and businesses of millions of Australians. However, as the twentieth century closed, the power-generating sector faced structural disruption. Global warming – driven primarily by the burning of coal, oil and gas – was rapidly accelerating as an existential threat to humanity and nature, while renewable energy was emerging as the cleaner, superior and soon-to-be cheaper technological alternative.

As Australia's largest electricity generator, AGL was faced with a set of choices about how to respond to these new realities. In 2012, the company's leadership made a conscious decision to purchase coal power stations – effectively betting against climate action. It was not until midway through the 2010s that a newly appointed CEO, Andy Vesey, attempted to steer a new course away from burning coal and towards renewable energy. But the response from Coalition politicians, the coal lobby and the Murdoch media was protracted and savage – federal minister Josh Frydenberg personally intervened to urge that Vesey be sacked. Eventually, and under immense pressure, Vesey walked of his own accord and was replaced by AGL's Chief Financial Officer, Brett Redman.

In 2017, while still CFO, Redman made a presentation to an energy conference entitled, 'A future of storable renewable energy'. The first slide of the PowerPoint was captioned:

> Shaping a sustainable energy future for Australia.
> AGL's new brand campaign makes our position clear.

The statement of intent in the first line is undermined by the indication in the second that what is really going on here is brand positioning. Corporations engage in extensive research and marketing to very deliberately situate their brands through corporate communications and advertising strategies. The positioning of a brand must be *plausible* enough to be accepted by the target audience and not so flagrantly deceptive as to infringe consumer affairs laws and other legal restrictions. Yet the law allows a great deal of latitude for the kind of puffery, hype and myth-making that is central to the imaginary of late-capitalist marketing.

That fleeting footage of the two girls running through the paddock represented just one brief instance in a calculated pattern of words, pictures and initiatives designed to communicate AGL's preferred corporate message. Reality soon presented a stark contrast: after Vesey resigned, AGL's business strategy turned backwards. By 2020, renewables accounted for only 10 per cent of AGL's total electricity output, an increase of roughly 0.2 per cent per annum since 2015, with the vast majority still coming from coal. But the brand positioning remained consistent, with AGL continuing to claim that it was 'actively working to reduce greenhouse gas emissions' and had 'a relentless determination to make things better'.

BURNING COAL IS the single greatest source of domestic carbon pollution in Australia, responsible for around one third of annual emissions. In 2019, Climate Analytics, a leading international non-profit specialising in scientific modelling, reported that Australia needed to 'steeply decrease coal-based electricity generation in the coming years and phase it out entirely by 2030 in order to "do its bit"'. These findings were later supported by the International

Energy Agency, which released figures that specifically called for all unabated coal-fired power plants to be phased out in advanced economies by 2030.

The technological trends are clearly running against coal, but the speed of inevitable closures is inadequate in the face of the climate emergency – and could also be further decelerated via political interference. From 2019 to 2020, AGL was responsible for more than twice the amount of the next biggest emitter of greenhouse gases. If AGL's three ageing facilities continue burning coal until the end of their technical lives, the result would be around a further 750 million tonnes of carbon dioxide being belched into the atmosphere. However, if AGL could be moved to commit to closing its coal-burning power stations by 2030 then a big chunk of Australia's carbon pollution would be gone in a single decisive sweep, and the transformation of such an iconic and systemically significant actor could have profoundly positive implications.

In late 2020, a plan began to take shape across a number of collaborating climate and environment organisations, including Greenpeace, to make a renewed effort to persuade AGL to commit to early coal closures in line with the goals of the Paris Agreement. As CEO of Greenpeace Australia Pacific, I was part of the team that decided it was the right time and strategy to take on the challenge of applying pressure to Australia's worst domestic climate polluter.

However, any campaign to transform AGL from the outside would face a significant obstacle, aside from the inherent difficulty of persuading a corporate behemoth to shift business strategy. In early 2021, Greenpeace commissioned research into how AGL was perceived in the market. The findings were sobering. Relatively few people, even among Australia's most climate-alarmed, knew that AGL was the nation's number one source of onshore emissions. In fact, many believed that AGL was making reasonable progress in transitioning to renewable energy. Similarly, only a negligible fraction of media reporting on the company ever mentioned its status as Australia's worst domestic climate polluter. In short, AGL was getting away with it – and a major effort was needed to shift those public perceptions.

THE TRUTH-TELLING TRICKSTER is one of the many faces of the environmental movement. As activists and campaigners, we use verbal and visual jokes that sometimes flout the polite norms of the prevailing socio-economic order to highlight ecological crime. In particular, the subversive practice known as 'brand jamming' is the work of the ecological trickster transgressing against the protected status of intellectual property, one of late capitalism's golden calves. Unlike mere mischief, brand jamming is motivated by principle; the intention is to remedy injustice for the benefit of nature and humanity. It derives from the understanding that brand positioning is always part concealment and that, except in limited circumstances, corporations are not legally required to disclose the truth of how business strategy is impacting on the world. So it is that the reassuringly familiar brand-you-can-trust – sustained by vast marketing budgets, embedded in collective memory and personalised through social association – is rendered uncanny as its cruelty or atrocity is uncloaked: the parody video reveals an orangutan's severed finger where the chocolate bar should be; 'Coke' becomes 'Choked' on the roadside banner. Like a judo flip, this tactic uses the weight of the brand to drive the impact of the parodic reversal, subverting the usual associations attached to the widely recognised trademarks to reveal some hidden, ecological wrong-doing and create momentum for change. And it's been an effective staple of Greenpeace and other environmental and social justice organisations for decades: the trick that tells the truth.

Greenpeace revealed a new website, www.australiasgreatestliability.com, in May 2021 that used a parody of AGL's logo and its brand colours to paint the company as 'Australia's Greatest Liability' and included links to a report detailing the truth about the company's polluting activities. Hardly our finest comedic writing, but revealing enough. The launch was accompanied by widespread distribution of social media assets lampooning AGL in the same or similar terms and drawing attention to the business's dire pollution record, future plans and the impact the company's activities were having, and would continue to have, on the climate, environment and humanity. Slogans such as 'Still Australia's Biggest Climate Polluter' and 'Generating Pollution for Generations' were accompanied by a selection of shocking images from the recent summer of catastrophic fires. A little over a week later a wave of street posters followed, and the parodic rebranding began to appear on billboards and walls around Melbourne and Sydney.

A few days after the campaign commenced, Greenpeace Australia Pacific's in-house legal counsel Katrina Bullock called me at home in the early evening. We'd received a legal letter from AGL alleging that Greenpeace was infringing on the former's intellectual property rights. If we didn't remove AGL's branding from our campaign materials, we could expect legal action to be taken. But Australian intellectual property law contains some reassurance for the trickster: an explicit freedom-of-expression safeguard in the Australian Copyright Act allows use of copyrighted material where that use is fair dealing for the purpose of review, criticism, parody or satire. The intended purpose of the provision is to prevent copyright from being weaponised to inhibit the flow of information on matters of public interest.

Fossil fuel corporations have a history of unscrupulous legal threats and actions to silence charities, activists and community groups – a practice known as strategic lawsuits against public participation, or SLAPP suits. AGL is a multi-billion dollar company; Greenpeace is a community-based environmental charity. In our view, AGL was threatening a SLAPP suit. Kat and I discussed the matter briefly; there would be no cessation of campaign activities. Shortly afterwards, AGL initiated proceedings in the Federal Court of Australia and matters were put to the test.

The consequences of the case would be highly significant. If we lost, not only would the public campaign to shift AGL to 2030 coal closures suffer a severe setback, but Greenpeace could expect a costs order – and there would be broader free-speech ramifications. Previewing the case in *Crikey*, lawyer Michael Bradley concluded that '[i]f the law turns out to be on AGL's side on this question, then comedy is dead'. Alive to the consequences, a number of other charities, including the Australian Conservation Foundation, wrote an open letter to AGL, describing the company's decision to bring the case as 'an attack on civil society' amounting to 'a direct affront to free speech and the ability of organisations to hold corporations to account on climate change'.

I'D NEVER BEEN a witness in court before. Two Greenpeace staff members were called to explain our rationale and purpose in parodying AGL: myself and Glenn Walker, the latter a life-long environmentalist and highly skilled and respected campaign strategist now leading our AGL initiative in close collaboration with other organisations and community groups.

My time in the witness stand was short – what felt like an anti-climactic twenty minutes – but Glenn faced almost an hour of forensic cross-examination. The standard advice to witnesses prior to giving evidence is to take your time in answering and respond only to the precise question being asked. I watched as Glenn, nonchalant but alert, carefully took every question on its merits. The trial judge, the Honourable Justice Stephen Burley, would later highlight one particular exchange:

> Mr Hennessy SC: Why do you say it was important to use AGL's logo as opposed to – or in combination with AGL's name as opposed to AGL's name alone?
>
> Mr Walker: Because parody is imitation and it made [it] a funnier, more effective creative from our perspective to use as much of their logo and, obviously, their creative look and feel [in] the advertisements as possible while still making it very clear that [it] wasn't an advertisement from AGL because it was saying something that you wouldn't expect from AGL, and that's what grabs people's attention, the unexpected nature of a parody which is clearly labelled as by...presented by Greenpeace which we're...Greenpeace is very well known for.
>
> Mr Hennessy SC: But when it has suited Greenpeace in this campaign it has simply identified AGL by its name as distinct from the AGL – or separate from – the AGL logo, hasn't it?
>
> Mr Walker: Sometimes we identify AGL by name but there are many parts of this campaign. In this particular instance, these...the use of AGL's logo into an amended logo and into the creative materials was part...was very deliberately part of what we call 'brand jamming' or what others might refer to as parody.

After a single day's hearing, proceedings closed with Justice Burley reserving his judgement.

IN 2003, BARBRA Streisand brought a legal action for alleged privacy violation, seeking the removal of an aerial photograph of her home from a website. Prior to the case, the image in question had been downloaded six times. After the publicity generated by the trial, more than 400,000 people had digitally rubber necked the pixelated view of Streisand's mansion. The episode gave rise to a new colloquialism, 'the Streisand effect', denoting instances when an attempt to conceal instead has the ironic effect of massively increasing public awareness of the very subject that was meant to be hidden.

AGL's communications strategy had been designed to elide reality. They'd gone to court to stop Greenpeace from revealing the truth by parodying their corporate logo. Now, regardless of the result, the case drew intense and widespread media attention to the true state of things, both nationally and internationally, with features appearing everywhere from *The Washington Post* to *The New Indian Express* – a total of more than 1,500 unique news features. Much of the media duly recorded AGL's status as Australia's worst domestic climate polluter. If the aim had been to silence, then the decision to sue had severely misfired. Streisand's own lyrics came to mind:

> If we had the chance to do it all again
> Tell me, would we?
> Could we?

Ultimately, it wasn't only the media coverage that went against AGL. Justice Burley overwhelmingly rejected the company's arguments and ruled in favour of Greenpeace, finding that 'any damage caused to AGL by the campaign is caused by criticism of AGL as a corporate entity, on environmental grounds'. Following this judgement, the campaign continued on our terms. As Kat told media, the result of the case was clearly 'good news for charities, advocacy organisations, satirists and anyone else who seeks to rely on the "fair dealing" freedom of speech safeguard in the Copyright Act to criticise, review, satirise or parody powerful corporations'.

THE DEMAND FOR truth is central to the cause of climate action. The systemic deceptions of the coal, oil and gas corporations – whether through outright dishonesty or denial, willful nurturing of doubt, greenwashing or the advocacy of superficially plausible but inadequate incrementalism – have been intrinsic to stymieing effective action. When challenged, AGL didn't dispute a single fact presented by Greenpeace. In the event, one of AGL's lawyers made the company's motivation and moral economy abundantly clear in submissions to the court: 'What it is seeking to do is protect itself, protect its intellectual property rights.' Quite the motivation in a world on fire. The reality is that unless the great and powerful institutions of our societies are reorientated around the imperative of reducing emissions at emergency speed and scale, the world towards which those two little girls are hurrying is one of untold suffering and catastrophe.

Since the case was decided, the campaign has rolled on, with AGL's executive leadership challenged on the streets and screens and also, one hears reliably via various back channels, by frustrated and distressed employees within the company. Two CEOs have departed – Redman himself abruptly resigned before the campaign really kicked off. A proposed demerger collapsed. Coal closure dates have inched forward – better, but still wholly inadequate. A non-binding resolution put forward by the Australasian Centre for Corporate Responsibility – asking investors to support AGL set short, medium and long-term decarbonisation targets in line with the Paris Agreement – received 54 per cent of the vote despite the board's recommendation that shareholders vote against it. In the lead-up to the same AGM, an eighteen-year-old former school striker received enormous public attention and ultimately won around seven million shareholder votes in an attempt to be elected as a board member. Shareholder value has plummeted. Privately, business types speak of AGL as a case study in failed leadership and bungled strategy. Ultimately, though, none of this matters while the polluting goes on.

There is no joy in the humbling of a big polluter, only in securing rapid metamorphosis for the common good. Hope of a late-hour redemption still glimmers: a near future in which AGL will indeed close those coal-burning power stations and make the swift transition to becoming a pure-play renewable energy provider. Indeed, as the grim consequences of the fossil fuel order's persistent counterfeit are felt across the planet, failure is not an option if we are to build a bridge to a flourishing future. Environmental and climate activists and campaigners, a coalition of progressive investors and shareholders galvanised most prominently by the dramatic intervention of tech billionaire Mike Cannon-Brookes, and the internal staff resistance demanding change within AGL must and will collectively prevail. Such is the demand of truth in these brief years of decision, as this critical decade hurries on.

POSTSCRIPT: AFTER FURTHER highly publicised internal turmoil, AGL has now announced that it will bring forward the closure of its coal-burning power stations to 2035. Not yet 2030, but a vast improvement – and the realities of the market are such that the date could be even sooner. Writing for *The Guardian* Australia, journalist Peter Hannam reported on inside information that AGL Energy's new chair, Patricia McKenzie, had told an internal audience that even Greenpeace would be happy with the new plan. McKenzie reportedly said, 'We're in a very changed world now.'

1 November 2022

I would like to acknowledge the persistent efforts of activists, community members, researchers, journalists and campaigners who have focused on AGL for many years, particularly colleagues at the Australasian Centre for Corporate Responsibility. Thank you, too, to the legal team which so effectively represented Greenpeace in the case with AGL: Rebecca Gilsenan and Katherine McCallum from Maurice Blackburn, and barristers Frances St John and Neil Murray SC of Sydney's Tenth Floor Chambers. Thanks also to everyone who chipped in vital support to Greenpeace's legal defence fund and the AGL campaign more generally. Greenpeace never accepts any funding from government or business; our work is only possible because of generous community support.

A previous contributor to *Griffith Review*, David Ritter is the chief executive officer of Greenpeace Australia Pacific and a widely published writer.

About face

Under the skin of the cosmetic surgery industry

Phillipa McGuinness

IN THE HBO series *Hacks*, Jean Smart plays stand-up comedian Deborah Vance, a Las Vegas headliner, home-shopping network mogul and minor cultural icon – if one whose bookings are drying up. In one episode, she has routine plastic surgery; she gets work done so she can work. Viewers are to assume that the character Smart plays is around the same age she is, seventy-one. For a performer still on the job in her sixties or seventies – or, frankly, any age – *not* to have cosmetic interventions of the invasive kind is the same as retiring. Or dying.

Deborah Vance inhabits the same acid milieu as late real-life comedians Joan Rivers and Phyllis Diller, the women through whom, as a child in the 1970s, I would have first heard the word 'face lift'. Diller had her first nose job and face lift in 1971. In an 'information video cassette' about plastic surgery from 1984, a cosmetic surgery sales-pitch prototype, Diller proclaimed, 'It's more than a physical lift. It's a psychic lift and a spiritual lift. It makes you feel very much better about yourself.'

Diller and Rivers were transparent, shockingly so, about their nips and tucks, liposuctions, implants and reconstructions. Though their enhancements and modifications attracted mockery, these brassy, fearless women made themselves the butt of their jokes. They may have loathed their bodies, but they owned that self-loathing. And made a lot of money from it.

Meanwhile, the 2021 manifestation of these trailblazers, Deborah Vance, lies bandaged and bruised, begging for more painkillers after her eye 'refresh' at the fictional but hyper-real facility Seven Graces Surgical Centre and Luxury Aftercare, outside Las Vegas. When Ava (Hannah Einbinder), Deborah's employee and the zoomer to her boss's boomer, refers to the 600-thread-count sheets 'you're supposed to bleed and ooze on', the characteristically acerbic Deborah responds, 'Oh, let me guess, you don't approve of cosmetic surgery?' Ava has opinions on tap about everything else, so her response is a little surprising. But, then again, given her youth (she's in her late twenties) and her usual place of work (Hollywood), perhaps not: 'Honestly, I keep forgetting to have a take on it. It's either good or bad. I don't have an opinion.'

At the end of the episode, Ava wakes up in a hospital bed. She's recovering from surgery she almost missed out on because a male emergency room doctor dismissed her abdominal agony as dehydration. On her behalf, Deborah wielded her do-not-mess-with-me powers, which was fortunate – Ava's pain was caused by a burst ovarian cyst.

Sometimes with women's health in general – not only cosmetic procedures – it can seem like the joke is on all of us. Resigned, self-aware humour is one antidote. Another is to follow the money, which is what one investigative reporter did with Australia's cosmetic surgery industry.

WHAT DO WE mean when we talk about cosmetic surgery? The most popular procedures are liposuction, breast augmentation, blepharoplasty (eyelid surgery), rhinoplasty (nose surgery), otoplasty (ear pinning), face-lifts and abdominoplasty (tummy tucks). Investigative journalist Adele Ferguson estimates that the cosmetic surgery industry in Australia is worth $1.4 billion – but that excludes botox injections, laser resurfacing, chemical peels and dermal fillers, which generate *many* more billions of dollars in revenue. Ferguson's bio describes her as a specialist in 'markets, banking and the economy'. Indeed, she told me that when she was first contacted by a whistleblower nurse who worked in the cosmetic surgery industry, she assumed that whatever emerged would be a business story. In many ways she was right.

In a series of investigative reports, published in *The Age* and *The Sydney Morning Herald* and broadcast on *Four Corners* in October 2021 and *60 Minutes* in June and August 2022, Ferguson introduced her audience to various doctors who worked in the extraordinarily lucrative cosmetic surgery industry. Some are now suspended or must work under restrictions. Daniel Aronov was once the most popular cosmetic surgeon on TikTok, with thirteen million followers – now, according to the Royal Australian College of General Practitioners (RACGP) website, his work as a GP must be supervised and he is prohibited from working as a cosmetic surgeon. Joseph Ajaka, who founded Australia's biggest cosmetic surgery provider, Cosmos Clinics, obtained a court order ahead of the second *60 Minutes* program in 2022, later overturned on appeal in what the media outlet declared a win for press freedom. Brisbane doctor Ryan Wells, now suspended, was an associate of Dr Daniel Lanzer, perhaps the best-known face in Ferguson's gallery of disgrace. A former member of the Australasian College of Dermatologists, Lanzer is no longer registered to practise and, according to a college spokesperson, has 'not been involved in any college committees in recent years.' (Lanzer's now-redundant website stated he had been on the college's liposuction committee.) Maddens Lawyers are running a class action against Dr Lanzer and various associates on behalf of hundreds of patients who reported 'devastating experiences'. Cosmos Clinics are facing two separate class action investigations.

Ferguson's reports also introduce some of these doctors' patients, a group comprising mainly those women who chose not to be forced into silence by signing non-disclosure agreements and would not be cowed by intimidatory tactics. Many are now disfigured – stronger words such as 'maimed' or 'butchered' are used by the women themselves and various medical professionals – and live with chronic pain. Their traumatic stories are confronting.

So is the footage of surgical procedures these clinics shared on social media, often with before and after shots spliced in. Ferguson comments on air that for these doctors 'cameras were as essential as liposuction cannulas'. The clips, often showcasing Instagram influencers paid in kind, are backed by dance music, boosterish commentary and 'medical' teams performing hi-jinks. One doctor doesn't bother to watch the movement of his own hand as he frantically moves a cannula in and out of a patient's body, potentially lacerating internal organs, because he's too busy looking at the camera.

'That footage was *wrong*, on so many levels,' observes Mark Ashton, another doctor who recurs in Ferguson's reporting, but in the role of reputable surgeon. Ashton is clinical Professor of Surgery and Honorary Professor of Anatomy at the University of Melbourne and Chair of Plastic Surgery at Epworth Freemasons Hospital. In both television programs, he can be seen sitting next to Ferguson watching the cosmetic surgeons' footage. (Ashton told me when I interviewed him that what he saw was unedited; Ferguson said that the raw footage would be too rough for viewers to stomach.) His pale skin reddens and his eyes widen. Observing procedures such as mega liposuction, he expresses disbelief at the blatant carelessness, disregard for basic hygiene and lack of respect for patients. He uses the word 'barbaric', noting that post-operative care seems non-existent and that often doctors appear to be performing an operation inappropriate for what they claim they're seeking to achieve. More than anything, he's furious that patients' lives are being put at risk. Referring to the fundamental principle of informed consent, he asks 'Has anyone explained to the patients that these procedures come with risks, including the risk they might die?'

Especially disturbing to him is the increasing commercialisation of medicine, cosmetic surgery in particular: 'The patient, in effect, is a commodity [cosmetic surgeons] are utilising to derive an income or business stream. It's completely disconnected from what you're meant to be doing as a surgeon or a doctor in the first place.'

Like many plastic surgeons, Ashton does a lot of what he calls 'repair work': 'It went nuts on that Monday after the *60 Minutes* program aired. We had over 166 people ringing in just two-and-a-half hours to book in for a consultation. That's not to inquire, that's to *book in*. We're having to act like a triage service.' These were mainly women, he says, who wanted to get procedures they have had done elsewhere – usually by cosmetic surgeons – fixed. 'These people are incredibly fragile and broken. We've got to try and put them back together again. But in many cases the problem we're confronting is unfixable. One of the people we saw last week who's had aggressive liposuction, well, the best way to describe her abdomen would be one of those images you see on the news after a hailstorm where a car bonnet has all these dint marks, like pockmarks where the hailstones have hit the car. That's her abdomen. How do we fix that? We can't. It's unfixable. And so this person now has a lifelong scar, a lifelong deformity caused by someone with inadequate surgical training.'

THE QUESTION UNDERLYING all Ferguson's reporting, the inquiry it prompted, the consumer anguish and the plastic surgeons' outrage is this: Who is qualified to carry out these procedures? These now-exposed 'cosmetic cowboys' (as Ferguson titled her exposé) had been operating in plain sight for a long time – why weren't they reined in? What mechanisms exist to protect the growing number of patients wanting cosmetic surgery and happy to pay for it? One woman Ferguson interviewed who almost died of internal bleeding after liposuction went badly wrong said: 'I thought there is no way this can happen in Australia.'

In 1999, a significant report was prepared for the NSW Minister for Health. *The Cosmetic Surgery Report* was signed off by Chair of the Cosmetic Surgery Inquiry, Merrilyn Walton, who was then head of the Health Care Complaints Commission. Detailed and systematic, the report responded to the rapid growth of the industry, assessed the state of play and presented detailed proposals for better regulation. Yet nearly every concern it raised has been left unaddressed in the ensuing decades, starting with the need to regulate the standards and skills required to perform cosmetic surgery. In her executive summary, Walton wrote: 'Cosmetic surgery is mainly performed outside organised medicine where the traditional protections provide patients with a safety net.'

Sounding reflective and a little exasperated, Walton, now Professor Emerita of Medical Education at the University of Sydney, told me that 'we've known about this stuff for twenty years. There's been nothing new [that's] come out except for the failure of regulation and failure to act in the public interest.'

All the same, Ferguson said to me that when she started reporting on the cosmetic surgery industry, 'I found it hard to believe – I had to triple check – that a cosmetic surgeon can have a basic medical degree yet call themselves a cosmetic surgeon and they can do facelifts, tummy tucks, Brazilian butt lifts, you name it. And they don't have to work in a hospital, they can just flout the rules and set up their own day hospital...and it's all legal.'

For years, plastic surgeons and other medical practitioners have sought to abolish the term 'cosmetic surgeon'. Ashton confirmed the reason for Ferguson's disbelief: a medical student can indeed graduate with an under-graduate degree and put up a shingle proclaiming themself a cosmetic surgeon the very next day. But specialists who are recognised by the Royal Australasian College of Surgeons (RACS) and its various surgical subspecial-ties, including plastic surgery, have completed at least eight extra years of specialist training. Ashton says that while this is about imparting technique and experience, it's also about building an ethical framework, about knowing what to do on the spot when something goes wrong, about knowing which procedure is the right one for a particular patient and, especially, about post-operative care. Unlike all other specialists, cosmetic surgeons have a direct channel to potential clients through social media. Why wouldn't a consumer assume that a surgeon is a surgeon is a surgeon?

Not surprisingly, changing titles is part of the response that the Australian Health Practitioner Regulation Agency (AHPRA) and the Medical Board of Australia put forward in response to an independent inquiry into the cosmetic surgery industry undertaken in 2022. Led by former Queensland Health Ombudsman Andrew Brown, it was prompted by Ferguson's reports. At first glance, AHPRA's promise to better regulate the cosmetic surgery industry and penalise transgressors seemed reasonable. Many welcomed a dedicated cosmetic surgery hotline, for example. But as Walton, formerly on the AHPRA board herself, says, 'I think part of the problem with the report is that it was done by people who are in the complaints business, so they talk about underreporting and needing more resources or better trained people. That's not the problem.' Plastic surgeons responded with, well, their scalpels blazing.

Allowing only those with a surgical qualification accredited by the Australian Medical Council (a separate entity to the regulatory bodies mentioned above and one that does not recognise 'cosmetic surgery' as a medical specialty) to call themselves a surgeon would be a fundamental reform. Plastic surgeons who have long argued for this change should perhaps be grateful that Ferguson showed Federal Health Minister Mark Butler the graphic footage during her interview, because he has vowed to enshrine protection of the title 'surgeon' in law. Minister Butler has also asked the Australian Commission on Safety and Quality in Health Care (again, separate to other regulatory bodies mentioned here) to ensure that practitioners work in accredited facilities.

Dr Nicola Dean, current head of the Australian Society of Plastic Surgeons, seemed genuinely impressed by Butler's energy and commitment. But, she told me, while this could be a way of controlling cosmetic surgeons by proxy, through the facilities they work in, there are potential loopholes. Her key objection, however, arises from what AHPRA proposed as a train-ing program for cosmetic surgeons – Dean says it's one seemingly devised on the run – that would 'endorse' practitioners. Perhaps not surprisingly the Australian College of Cosmetic Surgeons, the Australasian College of Dermatologists and the RACGP support AHPRA's training proposal. Plastic surgeons, however, are vehemently opposed; for Dean, because of the training regimens already in place for surgery, the endorsement model 'for cosmetic surgery makes no sense at all'. Ideally, according to Dean, in addition to protecting the title of surgeon and insisting on better facilities regulation, basic scope-of-practice restrictions for doctors who are general, not specialist, registrants with AHPRA would need to be set up.

Based in Adelaide, Dean is unusual not only because she is the first woman to be head of the Australian Society of Plastic Surgeons, but also because she works full time in the public health system. She told me a few weeks after its response to the inquiry was released that AHPRA and the Australian Medical Board simply did not recognise 'the magnitude of transgression of these practitioners. I think there is a fundamental difference between a medical practitioner who has made an error of judgement for a particular patient, you know, they've accidentally operated on the wrong arm or given the wrong dose of a drug. That is what was envisaged when the notifications and punishments of AHPRA were set up. I think this is a fundamentally different problem. This is people setting up a commercial business that systematically neglects patients at the very fabric of its being. That is a whole different level of harm.'

In its published response to the inquiry, AHPRA included a comment about underreporting, claiming that not one of the devastating cases discussed in the media had been reported to the regulator by a medical practitioner. It includes an irrefutable line: 'Silence allows poor practice to go unchecked and this harms patients.' Dean shared with me the results of a HealthEd survey of GPs: almost one third of those surveyed had seen negative results from operations performed by underqualified cosmetic surgeons, but only 1 per cent had reported these cases to AHPRA. GPs are notoriously overworked, but how did so few of them see fit to call out a colleague for maiming a patient's body? Did the hospitals where patients arrived in ambulances direct from cosmetic surgery clinics not report negligence? What about the insurers, who presumably oversaw cosmetic surgeons' compensation payouts? Isn't reporting supposed to be mandatory?

I asked Ashton about this. 'Even when you do mandatory reporting and you ring them [AHPRA] up and you say, "well what happened?", they say, "I can't talk to you about that". Well hang on, I'm trying to help here! Blaming the doctors, blaming the GPs for underreporting, misses the point because the issue is that if you make your process of reporting so onerous and difficult that busy GPs doing a myriad of different things find it difficult to report, that reflects the process that you're operating under.' And how might someone in pain, shouted at by the doctor who operated on her, who feels ashamed and embarrassed, find the wherewithal to pursue a complaint through a complicated federated system?

Walton says that improving the complaints process or limiting doctors' scope of practice will not be enough. 'To me there's a simple fix: anyone who wants to do surgical procedures, whatever they are, must have the minimum surgical qualification.' This would happen through the Royal Australasian College of Surgeons. 'Then you introduce more credentialling on top of that. If you want to be a plastic surgeon, you do more training. If you want to be an ENT surgeon, you do more training. If you want to do cosmetic surgery, you do more training.'

WE MAY CONTAIN multitudes, but for most of us a sense of self is partly contingent on our appearance. Our image-centred world has elevated what writer Jia Tolentino calls 'Instagram face', a racially ambiguous assemblage of ethnic 'greatest hits' – wide cat-like eyes, big lips, smallish nose, high cheekbones. Few people will have a face that fits this template, nor will they exist in a body with a tiny waist, large breasts and a shapely Instagrammable Kardashian-style booty, or a six-pack, or whichever attribute next becomes fashionable. But whatever, you can pay for it.

Cosmetic procedures, whether invasive surgery or injectables, have become so normalised that Diller and Rivers might now raise their eyebrows, were they able. Our culture celebrates endless self-improvement and enhancement. It abhors, to use an icky marketing phrase, 'visible signs of ageing'.

Cosmetic surgeons aren't the only ones profiteering from this. One reason their services have become so popular is because of market forces: better trained plastic surgeons might charge more for doing the same procedures. Now we see what you get when you mix a weak safety and reporting culture with the oceans of cash that roll in for cosmetic procedures. It swept up those medical practitioners who became faux surgeons when they suppressed a basic tenet of their training: do no harm. Whether they land back on shore will be up to the regulators, the medical profession and government.

We can't keep pretending that surgery stops being surgery and becomes something trivial when you put the word 'cosmetic' in front of it. Merrilyn Walton says, 'We need to reset. Not keep seeing cosmetic surgery as fringe but treat it exactly like we do every other area of medicine.' She adds: 'Regulation is one truly democratic thing governments can do: protect the public. Put the patient's interest first. Ignore all the other stuff.'

A previous contributor to *Griffith Review*, Phillipa McGuinness is the author of *Skin Deep: The Inside Story of Our Outer Selves* (Vintage, 2022) and *The Year Everything Changed – 2001* (Vintage, 2018). A former book publisher, she is currently editor of *Openbook*, the State Library of NSW's quarterly magazine.

FICTION

Wax

Scott Limbrick

DARK CLOUDS LOOM as we draw closer to the town, like a charcoal sketch of a roiling night. It's still early morning, and the air is cool, and Em and Dougal sit quietly, for once, in their passenger seats.

The curves of the road fall away as it shifts into a long, narrow stretch, the lone street threading through a tiny community. I take us past homes with wire fences, a hardware store, a grocery, a park. A picture-book version of settlement.

I pull the car into a sharply angled spot, white lines marking the space. With the engine off, our world falls quiet: no traffic, no song of birds, no hum of daily life. The three of us climb out to stand in the deserted street, beneath the gently swirling black and grey.

'This is the place, isn't it, Mum?' Em asks, her voice puncturing the silence.

'That's the one,' I say. 'Looks interesting, doesn't it?'

Before us is a standalone wax museum, painted with neat strips of blue, maroon and gold. The entire structure seems out of time, its brilliant colours framed by the dim sky. It's exactly the kind of place I'd envisioned when I organised our trip.

I'd found the waxworks in an old guidebook, one I picked up in an op shop in another more substantial town. I couldn't find any information online – no website, images, maps or reviews. I knew this meant it was probably closed, but it was difficult to ignore the possibility of a decaying tourist trap, the vague promise of the type of experience I'd wanted to add to Em and Dougal's memories of childhood when I planned our holiday.

We were meant to be exploring forgotten pockets of the country. Places that weren't thriving, or even surviving. Places like the offbeat locations I'd seen when I was a child myself: abandoned hedge mazes; sculpture parks eroded by wind and rain; model villages with small-scale fairs and miniscule protest movements. Those strange stops that somehow remained stitched into my mind more permanently than the actual destinations of those holidays.

Patrick was going to come with us – was excited, even – but had retreated in the weeks leading up to our departure. Struggling to get out of bed, calling in sick to work. Speaking about the hopelessness of everything, the pointlessness of fighting against what we all knew was to come. Fixating on personal irritations that he saw as proof of this futility. It was the unpredictability of these periods that I found most difficult, the way his world could suddenly shift, leaving me and the kids in another world entirely. Sitting in the dark, his sharp features lit by the glow of his laptop or phone, he would trawl through articles about troop movements or failures in climate diplomacy, as if these facts justified his desire to withdraw from life.

I found myself wanting to construct pockets in time, to hold us all inside them. That way we could make the most of those periods when he wasn't folded into despair. This time, of course, it hadn't worked out that way.

The kids and I approach the museum and take stairs up to a veranda. A sign hangs from the rafters by the entrance, dangling above a box with a precise slit in the top. Crisply painted text suggests an entry fee of ten dollars, but there's no one around to enforce it.

'Do we have to talk to someone?' Dougal asks.

'I'm not sure, honey,' I say. 'It seems like a trust system.'

I go back to the car and rummage through the console, but can only scrape together a few dollars in coins. I return to the veranda to deposit them in the box, listening to the thud of coins falling straight through to hit the wooden base.

'Looks like we're getting a private tour,' I joke, mainly to myself.

'There's a guy in there,' Dougal says, pointing at a café across the road. 'Maybe he works here.' He waves, trying to catch a man's attention through the window. But the man remains in profile, sitting with both hands gripping the mug that rests on his table, oblivious to anything else.

The museum's lobby is sparse, despite some attempts at a vintage European style. Deep red rugs have been thrown down on wooden floors, mismatched chairs with flowery cushions are carefully positioned in corners. Oil paintings of landscapes, all rolling green hills and sublime storms, are set deep into ornate brass frames.

Before we enter the display areas I instruct Em and Dougal to read the labels, hoping they'll gain something from the descriptions. Em sighs, performing an exhaustion with my requests to make the most of experiences, but I know she's eager to read anything she can. Dougal complains that his phone won't turn on, and Em tells him he should have charged it in the car. He begins to argue with her, sensing that his authority as an older brother – one, he often reminds her, who is soon to enter double digits – has been undermined; but he perks up when he glimpses an elaborately costumed figure in the next room. Sensing this, Em quickly challenges him to a competition over who can read the most placards, and they rush into the first room. I follow more slowly, allowing them to go ahead, enjoying their excitement.

One gallery is filled with surf lifesavers in red and yellow caps reclining on fold-out chairs arranged on fake sand. In another, we encounter an eclectic collection of celebrities – Frank Sinatra, Rihanna, John Travolta, Nicole Kidman and others even less identifiable to children, judging by the questions Em and Dougal ask as we move past. A raised platform showcases the Beatles at various stages in their careers, their gazes catching one another across time.

As we move through the rooms, I'm stunned by the detail of the figures: the presence of stubble, the glistening lips, the fine lines stretching over hands. Their high quality adds something disturbing to the space, a melancholy that wouldn't exist if the faces were simple failures.

'How long would it take to make these, Mum?' Em asks.

'Weeks, maybe months,' I say, though I have no idea. 'It depends how many people work on them. Maybe we can look it up later?'

'Do you think they work like candles?' Dougal says, prodding Queen Elizabeth's arm.

'They'd have to have a wick to work like that, Dougs,' I say. 'The little rope bit that you light, right?'

'Yeah,' Dougal says. 'I guess that's good, so people can't just burn them down if they get scared.'

'Are you scared?' Em says, trying not to smile.

'No,' Dougal snorts. 'As if.'

I wander into a space that's been set up like a mine, crowded with prospectors digging for gold. They're trapped in moments that seem to hold some combination of hope and gloom.

I touch the wax of their pickaxes, then run my hand along the wax rock of the walls. One man squats a few metres away from the others, holding a pan. As I move towards him, I notice a label with descriptive text about Victoria's gold rush, a reminder of the foundational gruesomeness of the enterprise – the colonial history of world's fairs, or zoos, here insisting on itself in a minor carnival of the macabre.

I linger in the mine, wondering why these scenes were selected for preservation, why they had been brought into existence rather than others, until I hear Em and Dougal's raised voices carrying through from another gallery.

I find them, scowling at one another, in the middle of a debate sparked by a tableau of the moon landing that dominates the room.

'People can't live in space,' Em says, standing next to a figure I assume is either Neil Armstrong or Buzz Aldrin. 'That's so stupid.'

'No it's not,' Dougal says. 'We'll be able to stay on Mars. Or planets we don't even know yet.' He looks at me. 'Right?'

I don't tell them what I really think: that humanity will probably find a way to destroy itself before it manages anything that spectacular. It's an impulse I don't want to share, one that cuts against how I want either of them to engage with the world.

'Some people think they can make it possible to live in space,' I say. 'But maybe it's more important for us to focus on making Earth better before we worry about that.'

'Yeah,' Em says, like this is exactly what she'd meant.

'But it would be so cool,' Dougal says. 'People could live out there, exploring things forever.'

'It can't be forever,' Em says. 'Dad says that all good things must come to an end.'

'But space is different,' Dougal says. 'Space goes forever, doesn't it, Mum?'

'Good question,' I say, trying to come up with something acceptable. I'm still absorbing Em's repetition of Patrick's grim mantra, one I hadn't known she'd retained. I wanted to shield her from those thoughts, but they'd filtered through. 'Maybe there's no way to really know. Maybe if space disappeared, the whole universe, that would be the end of time as well. So that could mean it actually had lasted forever.'

'Huh,' Dougal says. Em looks horrified, and I regret my answer. I look around the gallery, searching for a way to distract them from this accidental note of dread, but all I see are more fake astronauts and a large landing module.

Dougal says, 'I'm hungry.'

WE CROSS THE road to a milk bar, next door to the café. Dougal runs ahead of Em and me, his small arms pumping through the air. When he reaches the entrance he moves to shove the door open – but as soon as he touches it, he recoils. He looks back in confusion, waiting for us to catch up.

'It feels weird,' he says, as if I should have warned him.

I wonder whether he's had a static shock, or a similar jolt. But when my hand makes contact with the metal panel, I don't feel metal. I feel something less smooth, less cool, more textured.

It's wax. I lean forward and can see that the entire door is wax. Even the window seems to be made from it, given away by a slight, almost milky, opacity. I peer through to inspect the inside of the store, where I see a lone woman standing behind a counter in the far corner, watching the till. I wait for her to glance up so that I can catch her attention and ask what's happening, but she is absolutely still.

'Are you alright, Mum?' Dougal asks.

'I'm fine, Dougs,' I say, shifting my attention away from the window. 'I just don't think this is a real store.'

'What do you mean?' Em says.

'It's like the people we just saw, all the figurines,' I say, attempting to portray an understanding of the situation I don't have. 'It's all made from wax. Even the inside, see?'

Dougal looks through the door, then emits a soft gasp. Em walks over to the café and touches the wall. 'This one is, too,' she says, her eyes wide. 'And that guy,' she says, staring at the man in the window, who I now know will always be gripping the same coffee.

'Did the book say this stuff would be here?' Dougal asks.

'No, honey,' I say. 'It didn't say anything about this.'

As we walk through the town, approaching any structure we pass by, we confirm that the only solid building is the waxworks itself, figures and structures almost seeming as if they've expanded out of it. The signs, the grass in the park, the tools in the hardware store: all wax. The town is small enough that it's possible to see from one end to the other, all the buildings along one road. Still, it's an unfathomable creation, one that, in its exposure to the elements, seems doomed.

There's no one to talk to, no one to demand answers from. Only an array of the ersatz, bathed in muted light. The sky remains filled with clouds, shrinking the boundaries of what can be perceived, but the air is warming up. My skin begins to glisten with sweat.

Em flits from object to object, building to building, eager to take in everything she can. Dougal is more withdrawn, but I can see that he's watching carefully, still making a judgement on how strange this may or may not be.

When we reach a bakery, Em gawks at the bread and pastries set out in the window, reciting the names of each one out loud in a sing-song voice before dashing into the butcher next door. Dougal says that the croissants are making him feel hungry again, a heavy-handed hint, and I pull a muesli bar out of my bag before we continue on.

'Who do you think made all this stuff?' Dougal asks, still chewing.

'A lot of people, I reckon,' I say, but even the question has made me less sure.

'Like, how many?' he asks again.

I try to give him something. 'Could be hundreds, Dougs,' I say. 'I've never seen anything like it.'

'What happens when the sun comes out?' Em asks, looking up at the clouds.

'None of this would last long,' I say. 'Not in that kind of heat.'

I consider whether I should take the kids back to the car and leave, find someone to tell, maybe even bring them back to show them; but part of me suspects that I'll never be able to find the museum, or the town, again. Instead, I rub one of Em's shoulders and ask her where she'd like us to go next.

She guides us through various buildings, structures that have somehow risen up from the dirt and may dissolve at any time. Dougal lingers in each space, gazing at the details and inspecting objects from different angles. Em rushes through rooms, in and out of doors, like she's running out of time to take it all in.

In a pub we see polished wooden booths surrounded by posters of classic rock bands and photos of Golden Age Hollywood stars. In an electronics store, sale signs blare loudly with their vivid yellows and reds. The homes are unique, each with their own layout and decor. In one, abstract paintings line the walls and modern sculptures act as centrepieces. In another, an enormous shed takes up most of the backyard, complete with a sturdy workbench covered in scraps and tools.

In every case, the detail is overwhelming. All the paraphernalia of life, its mess and chaos, captured perfectly in wax. Even up close it can be difficult to tell that nothing we see as we walk along the street is real: cats climbing trees; families sitting around dining tables, forks halfway to their mouths; patrons sipping from motionless glasses; workers reaching to restock shelves. Like the prospectors, like the celebrities, the occupants of the town live only in the moment.

I pause at the fence of a tidy home, the window providing a clear view of a family watching television. Staring at a television, at least. The children sit on the ground, the parents recline on the couch, all unmoving but apparently content.

I begin to recall old photos of nuclear test sites, with test dummies in little houses, suspended as they wait to be blown apart. Whole worlds conjured into existence purely in order to be destroyed, an apocalypse to scale.

'Where's Em?' Dougal says.

'What's that, Dougs?' I snap back to attention.

'I was going to show her this bike,' he says, gesturing to a wax bicycle propped up near the front gate.

I MARCH DOUGAL quickly along the road, both of us calling Em's name. Though the town is small, it suddenly seems expansive, capable of hiding anything. I know she must be nearby, that no one could have taken her, but still I feel the terror in my throat.

There are only a few homes we haven't been inside, at the fringes of the town, before structures give way to wide fields of grass and dirt. I'm sure Em must have entered one of these, her sense of urgency sending her hurtling ahead, desperate to see everything on offer.

I decide to begin at the end. I lead Dougal to the last building before the road unfurls alone into the horizon, smearing into a blur against the sky.

It's a neat white home with a bright red door and square windows, like one I might have drawn in notebooks as a child. The colours make the house almost unbearably cute, existing somewhere between cartoonish and lifelike.

We walk up the path, then I push the door open and lean over the threshold. The interior feels familiar, but I can't place it. It's not anywhere I've been before, but I'm overcome by how much it feels welcoming, like home.

'Em?' I call into the hallway.

Nothing. Then, from the other end: 'In here.'

When we reach her, sitting on the floor of a cosy lounge room, Em is completely unconcerned, oblivious to the flash of panic she's caused. Two figures, teenage boys, sit on chairs, their hands gripping controllers as they play a video game.

'Look,' Em says, pointing at the frame on the screen, 'it's like that game Dougs used to play.'

'Oh, yeah,' Dougal says, grinning. 'I remember that one. You could fully rip a guy's head off.'

I take a moment to slow my breathing. 'Em, you can't just run off,' I say. 'You have to stay with me.'

'Sorry, Mum,' she says. 'I wanted to see what was in here.' She stands and waves one arm in the direction of the kitchen, further into the house. 'Can I show you something?'

I don't want to reward her, but I also don't want to push back against her enthusiasm, her sense of curiosity. I want her to keep that hunger for the world.

'Okay,' I say. 'Let's see.'

She takes me by the hand and walks me through the kitchen and to the back door, Dougal trailing behind us. We spill into a small backyard, fenced in, with a table setting and barbecue beside a patch of grass. Along one side runs a tall hedge, which would, if it ever had to, block the prying eyes of those in the neighbouring home.

A figure stands near the hedge, an enormous pair of shears gripped in both hands. It's a tall man in a dark singlet with a small white skull, his eyes intently focused on the blades, eternally caught in an act of preparation.

'The guy looks like Dad,' Em says, coming to a stop beside him. 'Don't you think?'

'Yeah, he does a bit,' Dougal says, creeping closer to the figure, standing on his toes to get a better look at the carved facial features.

Now that she's said it, the man does remind me of Patrick. His cropped brown hair and angular nose, his manner a frozen mixture of concentration and concern, the way he gets when attempting a minor project, or making a decision with consequences for the remainder of his day.

'I can see it,' I say. 'But your dad's got so much more to him. And I don't think he'd wear a singlet like that, would he?'

Dougal laughs. 'No way.'

'Do you know if Dad's been feeling okay?' Em asks. We'd told them both he wasn't well, but it's sometimes difficult to tell what they take this to mean. It's a thing to be explained, when we can.

'I'm sure he's getting better, Em. We'll call him when we get back to the motel, yeah?' I say, and she smiles.

'I want to tell him about the astronauts,' she says.

'I'm going to tell him about the pub,' Dougal says. 'It was way cooler.'

I wonder what Patrick would make of this place. I wonder whether he'll believe it when he hears about it. Whether he does or not, I'm not sure I can tell him how it made me feel.

Because looking at this man, a version of Patrick with no need to move forward or backward, I understand that there's something seductive about the precipice. It's the only time those dual anxieties about things changing, and about things staying the same, can be perfectly unresolved: memory and anticipation grinding to a halt.

Dougal says that seeing the kitchen has made him hungry again, and I tell him we'll have to drive somewhere else to get food. Em mumbles that she needs the bathroom. I'm grateful for these small requests, for the pull of the world beyond, tearing me away from a sense of comfort I want to reject. We go back through the house, out onto the street, and retrace our path down the road, towards the car, towards the technicolour museum at the heart of it all.

I watch the kids as we walk, attempting to get inside their heads. More and more it has become hard to know what they're really thinking, their thoughts no longer something they readily share. Em smiles, her whole body bobbing up and down, like she's been told a joke by someone I can't see. Dougal narrows his eyes in concentration, turning something over in his mind.

As we near the car, Dougal tugs at my hand and asks if he can check out the café before we go. Glad that he's felt his own compulsion, I tell him of course he can, and he speeds ahead.

Through the window, I look on as he approaches the man he'd waved at when we arrived, taking a seat on the wax chair across the table. I wait outside and ask Em to stay with me. I can see Dougal looking directly into the man's eyes, holding his stare like he's trying to unlock something. He folds his arms on the table and leans forward slightly, his mouth falling open as he squints. After a minute or two he looks away, then climbs off the chair and walks back through the door.

'He has kind eyes,' Dougal says. 'Not all of them had kind eyes.'

Em looks back at the man, still frozen in position.

'I'm sad for him,' she says.

'Why's that, Em?' I ask.

'He seems lonely,' Em says.

'No,' Dougal says. 'I think he's happy by himself.'

I tell them that they might both be right.

EM GRIPS MY hand, wrapping my fingers tight in her sweaty palm. We stand beside our car, close to its more comprehensible surface of sleek metals and hard plastics. It will take us to the motel, then onward, to our next destination, then to others, then home to Patrick. We'll find new experiences, construct new memories. We'll probably begin to question whether today happened the way we know, right now, that it did.

I imagine what might happen if we stayed here. After a while I might feel a bead of sweat gather, then roll down my back, and recognise that the full heat of the day was making itself known. In the sky the thick clouds would move on, and the first hints of a brilliant sun would blast through. We'd see buildings all along the street begin to drip, then disappear in chunks. The people inside would meld with the walls and furniture before they fell apart.

If we stayed long enough it might become too hot, even for us, and we'd start to melt, our clothes disappearing, our skin seeping to the floor. Maybe the walls of the museum would liquefy as well and slowly sink into the ground, and then even the road around us, until we were all the same, until all three of us were sifted in completely, mixed forever with the dust and the sand.

Scott Limbrick is a writer based in Naarm (Melbourne). His fiction has appeared in *Electric Literature*, *Going Down Swinging*, *Westerly*, *Hobart*, *The Suburban Review* and *Kill Your Darlings' New Australian Fiction 2021* among others. His short-story collection *Flaring Out* was shortlisted for the Richell Prize for Emerging Writers.

Strike a pose

Seeing the world in portrait mode

Yvonne Todd and Carody Culver

An unsettled expression, an unnatural pose, an unaccountably glossy complexion: the strikingly costumed characters in New Zealand artist Yvonne Todd's photographic portraits fuse the glamorous and the ghoulish. Ever since winning the prestigious Walters Prize in 2002 for what judge Harald Szeemann declared was 'the work that irritated him the most', Todd has played with photographic precision and convention to render familiar figures and objects in a new light. And whether she's capturing an angel-faced starlet or a disembodied limb, she always has an eye for the humour that's inherent in her unexpected tableaux.

CARODY CULVER: You trained as a commercial photographer before attending art school in Auckland. What prompted your interest in portrait photography, and how has your training in commercial photography influenced your artistic practice?

YVONNE TODD: I connected with photography early. It was the medium that most intrigued me, despite my first experiences as a photographer being deeply disappointing. I had a basic point-and-shoot pocket camera as child and it took low-quality photos that never aligned with the vision I had in my mind's eye. Why didn't my photos look like the ones in books and magazines? I knew I was missing out on important specialised information and needed to find out what it was. It was illuminating to be able to learn photography at an Auckland polytech and take 'proper' photos, where I could control the look and feel of them. I needed to appease that disappointed eight-year-old whose crappy photographs of her pet budgies were an ongoing source of frustration.

The initial polytechnic photography course I did was in professional photography and there were several modules where we emulated the language of advertising photography. This meant precise studio set-ups where every-thing had to be exact. I recall a nightmarishly difficult assignment that involved constructing and photographing a floating sandwich, where each component – the bread, the cheese, the lettuce and the tomato – had to be spaced out neatly, invisibly, and not be in contact with its neighbouring ingredient. It required careful engineering and had to be done in-camera without Photoshop. The results were to be scrutinised and judged by a panel of advertising professionals. I felt a sense of desperation at the level of intricacy of this task and realised that as a photographer I couldn't be a technician for hire. I could, however, borrow the studio photography skills I was learning and turn them to my own ideas, to replicate a specific kind of photography.

I trace much of my art-making to my childhood. My parents worked long hours and I had a quiet, solitary existence where I'd spend hours arrang-ing my motley collection of dolls and ornaments into strange little tableaux. This provided me with a sense of respite from the world, especially as I found interactions with other children fraught with odd, confusing power dynamics and assumptions of 'expected' behaviour. My staged arrangements allowed me to reflect on and process my experiences – something I'm still doing as an artist. There's an ongoing compulsion to control and shape narratives after the fact.

CC: You often photograph women, and while some of these images feel remi-niscent of studio portrait photography – very exact, very staged – there's usually an element of the uncanny present, a heightened sense of artifice or an imperfection that might unsettle the viewer or make them look more closely. What's the impetus for this duality in your work?

YT: My portraits represent a bringing together of numerous strands, the repurposing of photographic conventions to make the familiar unfamiliar and vice versa. My work speaks to associations and assumptions about familiarity, particularly in regard to precise studio photography and the implied sense of intentionality that comes with it. I'm interested in the way we appraise the subject of a photo as a product to be consumed visually, and the way in which photographs connect with aspirations and the cognitive necessity of finding meaning and purpose in the visual. Artifice appeals to me as studio photography is largely an exercise in smoke and mirrors – creating a polished idea of 'perfection', a lasting document of seamless photographic subterfuge. The uncanny aspect is a by-product of this.

The meticulous studio photography that I am known for represents the formalisation of my practice; I am otherwise impulsive, sporadic, frustrated and easily bored. My 'photographer' persona is different – a calm planner who thinks things through and maps out each shoot meticulously. Despite this, I often subvert my plans by making last-minute decisions. I'm motivated by urgency. Often I act on spontaneous ideas – whims, casual connections between things, and snippets and fragments that infiltrate my imagination. The precision of my photography is deceptive, belying chaos that swirls beneath. Sometimes I encourage flaws and mistakes: *Portiscura* (2020) was transformed by a light leak from a hole in my decrepit view camera bellows. Once, I would have been devastated by such a glaring 'error', but it added something psychedelic and unexpected.

CC: Wigs and costumes play a significant role in your work. What appeals to you about these elements, and how do they influence the way you devise and stage a shot?

YT: Generally I hook into a specific costume or idea and the character emerges. The people in my photos are essentially actors in costume – ciphers, encrypted vessels that speak to the vagaries of life. There's a need to present my actors engaging in roles that reflect imagined interior worlds. Each portrait brings a set of psychological qualities that say something about human interactions. They contain facets of the awkwardness and wonder that I feel as a human navigating the world.

CC: You've amassed quite a collection of vintage gowns over the years, and you also design your own costumes. Are you drawn to the aesthetic of particular eras or designers? Do the gowns inspire certain images or characters, or is it the other way around?

YT: I amassed a large collection of costumes and divested them a few years ago when they got too unwieldy to store. My focus recently has been on designing my own costumes for shoots, often out of furnishing fabrics.

A large-scale print, designed for vast swathes of high-impact curtaining, is transposed to the human body in *Emerald* (2022).

Last year, I taught sculpture to secondary-school students and began appraising materials in a different way. In a recent work, *Bracchia* (2021), I used silicone muffin-baking pans as forearm sheaths. And another new work, *Infra-Haze* (2022), features pleather arm-vases stuffed with carnations.

My work is driven by humour and escapism, the lasting impression of watching televised beauty pageants and my involvement in drama and stage productions as a child. I grew up when women were viewed as decorative, appraised for their sexual currency. It's hard to disassociate from powerful formative experiences. Particularly my childhood observations of glamour fused with my interest in the macabre. There are eras of costume that continue to draw me into their orbit: high Victorian and the mod, space-age and psychedelic looks of the 1960s. I keep thinking I need to do a mash-up of these.

CC: Many of your portraits are named after the characters they depict – either an actual name, like *Emerald* (2022), or a role they represent, like *Retired Urologist* (2009) from your *Wall of Man* series. How do character and trope function in your work?

YT: The challenge is to imbue a sense of the definitive in my portraits. Tropes and characters are a big part of this as they speak to the recognisable, the understandable. Again, it's back to ideas around the familiar and the conventions of commercial photography. Once that's established, the challenge is to imbue an image with implication and nuance.

I am fascinated by the seemingly endless iterations of portraiture, particularly in my role as an introverted observer of the world. I want to populate it with a collection of inhabitants – renegades – loitering, posing and awaiting their audience. Their sense of belonging, like mine, is somewhat obtuse.

CC: You sometimes work with models and sometimes photograph yourself. How do you choose the subjects of your portraits? What comes first – the model, or the character they're embodying?

YT: Usually the costume idea emerges first, accompanied by a loose sense of the character. I then look for models through talent agencies. I like the straightforward transactional nature of hiring someone to be photographed. There's the odd act of browsing online agency databases for talent and picking out someone to work with, like a product in a catalogue. I look for people with a connection with the camera, where traces of bemusement flicker behind their eyes, someone who will be a co-conspirator rather than a passive mannequin.

My self-portraits are sporadic and I generally use myself out of sheer convenience. My recent 'selfies' have a sense of everyday drudgery to them due to the Covid lockdowns where my domestic world was front and centre. There's me as a harried mother in a tie-dyed smock, toting one of my infant twins. In another work, I photographed myself in a stretchy blue dress printed with frolicking penguins that I wore as a ten-year-old. I appear in the photo as a middle-aged woman, my jowls unretouched, seemingly asking, 'How did I get here?'

Yvonne Todd is an artist based in Auckland, New Zealand. Her work has been exhibited widely, including at the Edinburgh Art Festival, the Sydney Biennale, the National Gallery of Victoria and the Queensland Art Gallery. Her solo exhibitions include *Creamy Psychology* at City Gallery Wellington, *Wall of Seahorsel* at the Centre for Contemporary Photography, Melbourne and Dunedin Public Art Gallery, and *Blood, in its Various Forms* at the Institute of Modern Art, Brisbane.

Fantasy factory

YVONNE TODD

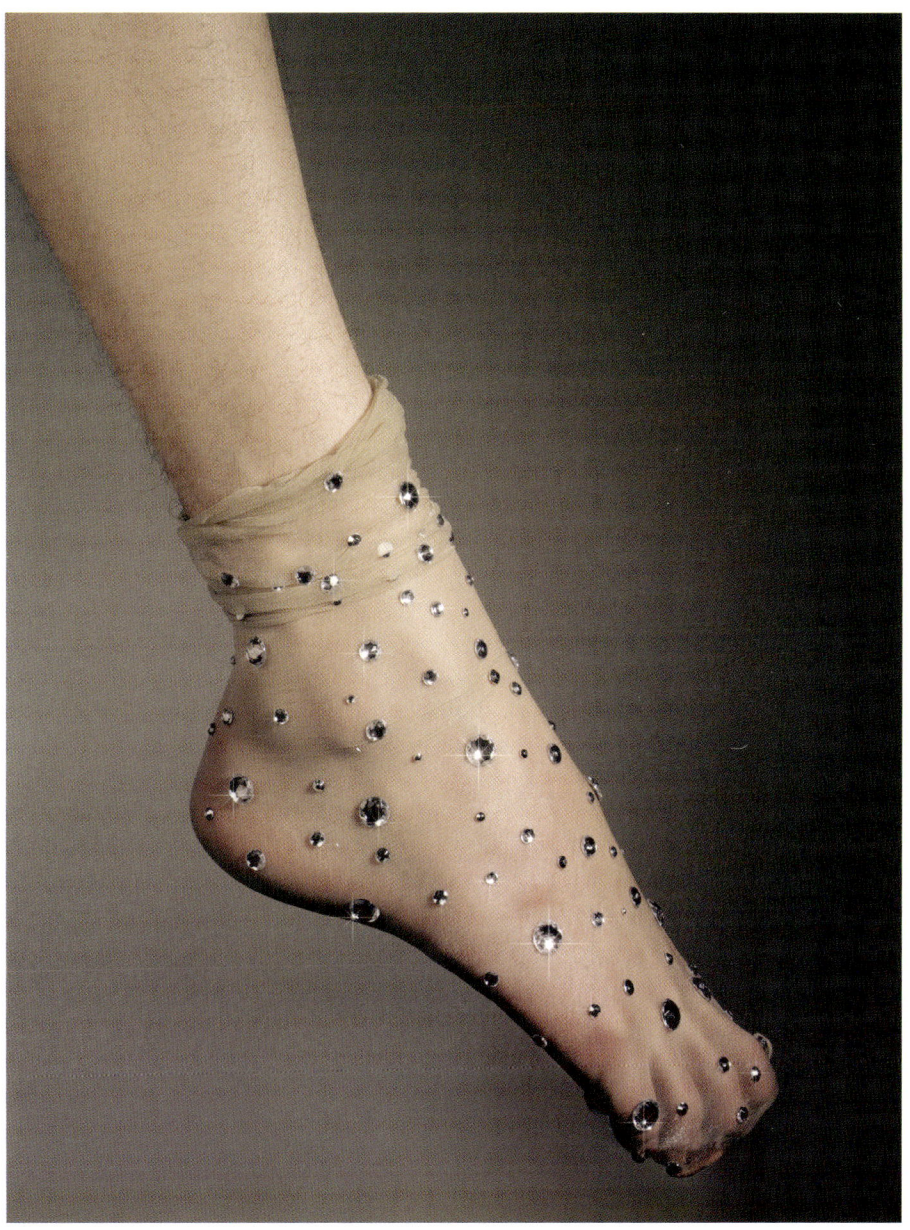

Disco Sock, 2018
C-type print from 4 x 5 transparency film, 45 x 33.5 cm
Edition of three, plus one artist proof
Courtesy of Ivan Anthony Gallery, Auckland

Sage, 2019
C-type print from 8 x 10 transparency film, 144 x 117 cm
Edition of three, plus two artist proofs
Courtesy of McLeavey Gallery, Wellington

Portiscura, 2020
C-type print from 4 x 5 transparency film, 120 x 94.5 cm
Edition of three, plus two artist proofs
Courtesy of McLeavey Gallery, Wellington

Next time it will be different, 2021
Offset poster print from 4 x 5 transparency film, 89.1 x 59.4 cm
Edition of 200
Courtesy of Fine Arts, Sydney

Emerald, 2022
C-type print from 4 x 5 transparency film, 120 x 95.5 cm
Edition of three, plus two artist proofs
Courtesy of McLeavey Gallery, Wellington

Bracchia, 2021
C-type print from 4 x 5 transparency film, 120 x 94 cm
Edition of three, plus two artist proofs
Courtesy of McLeavey Gallery, Wellington

Geranium, 2019
C-type print from 4 x 5 transparency film, 120 x 95.5 cm
Edition of three, plus two artist proofs
Courtesy of Ivan Anthony Gallery, Auckland

Enskë, 2017
C-type print from 8 x 10 transparency film, 165.5 x 121 cm
Edition of three, plus one artist proof
Courtesy of the artist

Morka, 2017
C-type print from 8 x 10 transparency film, 140 x 110 cm
Edition of three, plus one artist proof
Courtesy of the artist

Cloudie, 2022
C-type print from 4 x 5 transparency film, 120 x 95.3 cm
Edition of three, plus two artist proofs
Courtesy of McLeavey Gallery, Wellington

Infra-Haze, 2022
C-type print from 4 x 5 transparency film, 120 x 94.2 cm
Edition of three, plus two artist proofs
Courtesy of McLeavey Gallery, Wellington

Hyacinth, 2022
C-type print from digital photograph, 63.5 x 43 cm
Edition of three, plus two artist proofs
Courtesy of McLeavey Gallery, Wellington

Felicity Plunkett

Dot and Ern

                    Like the hawk
of fabric shears, cockatoo calls cut
raucous through sheets of white sky –

the sole sound as I walk
where they chomp on bottlebrush,
rip through callistemon, flower

the path with filament trash, thrown
like lovers' clothes. I stay within
the suburb's box, as though pinned

into a dress pattern papery as letters
from a poet who lived here,
or didn't – at least not the poet

he said he was. That was decades ago,
in the days of dressmaking, fruit trees
netted in sage and earnest yards.

Where can a cry hide? Whose
words, whose wound? *You're a fake,*
the lemon-mouthed poet declared, perhaps

more to himself. On my heartland's map
a dot marks the furthest place
from fakery. She knew about daimons

and augury, souls of the dead flying,
the sulphur-crested cockatoo her totem.
She didn't give a fuck about the yellow-

hearted, nor an apology for a yawp
echoey and brazen. Held light
against all darkening. They squawked

imposter, self-promoter. She chortled,
taught bristling, pinking: charge.
Ern, ghost of these streets I walk,

it's your silence I haunt, passing
Dalmar Street and the house no one
wrote poems in.

        What falls
to earth the earth will scoff: blossom,
paper, poison, lies. But not

the white huzzah, the bright squawk.
Not poems torn from the sky: their spikes
of red stigma, their feathers. They go up —

climb into vastness, fly too fast,
all flash-flood and blood. If we're lucky,
we'll follow skywards.

Felicity Plunkett is a poet and critic. She has published two collections of
poetry: *A Kinder Sea* (2020) and *Vanishing Point* (2009), both with UQP, and
the chapbook *Seastrands* with Vagabond Press.

The future of art fraud

An artist's memoir

Hazel Dooney

THE ART DEALER said, blithely, 'I understand why he did it. He needed money. He had a particular set of skills. What else would he do?'

She didn't use the words *art fraud* or *forgery*.

I stared back in silence.

She continued, 'You know, he told me all women are prostitutes in one way or another. I think he's right.'

I felt nauseated. These casual revelations did not match her veneer of demure professionalism.

Guests were greeted by a string quartet at the entrance of the lavish home. Velvet rope sectioned off blue-chip artworks, as in a museum. Waitstaff circulated an endless supply of hors d'oeuvres and champagne poured from magnum bottles.

The art dealer sat in the lap of an unattractive man. She smiled and giggled, a practised courtesan performance. Later, before I left, he pressed his business card into my palm with a sly smile.

Years after, I overheard him boast to another man that he used to fuck her.

The unattractive man was accused of multiple art fraud and forgeries. A gallerist friend told me an artist could have sent him to jail with their testimony but did not. The artist told several people that although the unattractive man was guilty, they didn't have the heart to do it. Perhaps there was another reason they backed down.

The artist manager laughed and boasted about an artist, 'He was so drugged out on medication he'd nod off. His head would fall forward and smudge the paintings. Happened all the time. I finished them for him. He never even noticed!'

After a different artist died, I was invited to dinner at a gallerist's penthouse apartment. On the wall was an enormous painting, a clumsy pastiche. The artist manager pointed, said it was by the late artist and grinned. I didn't believe him. A couple of months later it was sold for a significant amount by an auction house.

Over lunch with the international art auctioneer, I told him the art dealer – a mutual acquaintance – said she would 'support' my work at auction. She explained that if an artwork didn't receive enough bids during an auction, she would bid to buy it for a higher amount. Then there would be a public record of my work being sold for the value assigned by her, which she would show people when reselling it privately.

The international art auctioneer recoiled but said, diplomatically, 'Uh, that's not supposed to happen.'

Long ago I was pressured to accept a five-year contract to inflate the value of my work. It specified the amount of art I would have to create and the increasing prices at which the artworks would be sold and bought back through auction houses by a group (their names protected by privacy laws). At the end, a book about these artworks would be written by one of them. Both the book and public record of auction results would be used to justify the pumped-up value. Then artworks owned by the group would be dumped – sold to legitimate collectors.

In the artworld, this is known as *price ramping*.

I refused. On my father's advice, I kept the handwritten contract anyway.

A casual conversation with an art transporter turned to price ramping. He smiled and shrugged, 'As long as you're not the one caught holding the baby!'

I replied, 'What, so it's okay to rip off artists and collectors? So it's okay to steal a truckload of an artist's work right after they die?'

It was a random comment, not aimed at him. But he snapped, 'You know a lot.'

Everyone knows. These are open secrets.

His skin flushed pink then slowly turned white as knuckles on a clenched fist. His face, neck. Even forearms. I'd never seen anything like it but understood it was fear.

Later a military friend said, matter-of-factly, 'You missed an opportunity to interrogate him. He would have confessed everything.'

What use is a confession if everyone knows but goes along with it anyway?

I WALKED BY an early painting of mine displayed in a café. It had been commissioned through the art dealer before I learnt more about her and cut ties.

Ordering a coffee, I sat close to see how it had aged. The surface looked different. Plastic-like. I stared, wondering if it needed cleaning. It had a slightly bumpy texture, like canvas. Except I painted the artwork on smooth board.

Rage surged as I realised this wasn't my painting. It was a photograph of my painting, printed on canvas, laminated to mimic the shine of high-gloss enamel paint, and stretched over a frame the same size.

A professional photographer documented the original painting using slide film – the equivalent of an exceptionally high-resolution digital photo. My gloss enamel paintings reflect light and are difficult to photograph well. They need to be lit in-studio, from multiple directions. The art dealer gave me a slide and kept one for herself. She said it was for her records.

Later, at home, after the initial shock wore off, I called her and said I'd seen the copy of my painting. She said, 'I don't know what you're talking about.'

By the time I returned to the café the copy was gone. When I asked what happened to it, the staff told me they didn't know what I was talking about.

Over the years, as the internet became ubiquitous, I saw the copy of my artwork for sale on various websites. Each time, I reported it to the platform and it was removed. Until I finally tracked down the seller via his digital footprint.

I emailed him. He demanded money. I refused and initiated legal action. After a day of tedious back and forth, he sent documentation of it being cut into tiny pieces and thrown away.

While I relocated to be with my father as he slowly died of cancer, a poorly executed forgery of my work was offered for sale by a small auction house.

It wasn't until much later that I discovered it via an international online database listing past auctions of my art.

I called the auction house. The CEO told me the forgery was submitted by a framer whose name I recognised. He said, 'There's no point taking it further. It didn't sell. The framer will say the artwork was left there and he didn't own it. He'll say he doesn't have it now.'

It sounded like a pre-prepared statement.

I asked why he publicly offered an artwork without any indication of authenticity.

'This is a small auction house with high turnover. We don't have time to check provenance or authenticity.'

'Your business claims to sell original artworks. If you do not verify their authenticity or provenance, the record of ownership, your business is not what you are presenting it to be.'

Silence.

I took screenshots of the website and saved them to my files and external hard drive. Then emailed the international database of auctions. They sent me a form, which I filled in, signed and returned. The record was removed.

RECENTLY I SPOKE with the CEOs of a couple of major art auction houses who've sold my art on the secondary market for more than a decade.

Each asked if I was represented by a commercial gallery.

I gave my standard response, 'No. I still connect directly with the audience for my work via the internet.'

It's well known within the Australian artworld. Ever since I was front page of *The Age* newspaper's *Business* section in 2006 in an article by Nabila Ahmed titled 'State-of-the-art selling rivals play to the galleries'.

But my approach is still unusual enough – at least for an artist whose work retains value on the secondary market – to elicit curiosity.

One replied, 'It makes sense.'

Another said, 'We hold more online-only auctions now. It's the future...
You handle your own copyright, yeah?'

'Yes. It gives me a chance to check authenticity and provenance. If there's
an issue, we can address it before the artwork is offered for sale. As you know,
people often try to create false records of authenticity and provenance through
auction houses because the catalogue and results are a public record.'

He nodded.

The CFO asked, 'Isn't that all checked by Copyright Agency?'

The CEO answered, 'No. They do licensing.'

Copyright Agency is an Australian not-for-profit agency that collects licence
fees for the reuse of text and images – copyright royalty payments – on behalf
of members.

Although I'm not a member, I appreciate their work and we have a good
professional relationship. I know them because they were appointed by the
government to collect artist resale royalties, which apply to some secondary
market sales of my art.

The secondary market art dealer called to tell me he'd sold a painting by me
that qualified for resale royalty. While sales are mostly reported to Copyright
Agency they can also be handled directly.

It makes no difference to him. He offers me the option because I'm
paid faster and don't lose 16.5 per cent of my resale royalty to the agency's
administrative fee. This considerate gesture strengthened our professional
relationship, which evolved in the past decade. A call about resale royalty is
also an opportunity to catch up.

Our conversation turned to the art world.

He said, 'I've seen a lot in finance and business. But even I was shocked
at what people get away with in the art world. It's like they don't know how
bad it is.'

They know. But there's no consequence. So they do it anyway.

He paused. I wondered if he was thinking of his friends who are my
enemies. I know they're friends because he disclosed it to me long ago.
We haven't mentioned their names since.

Our conversation moved on. When it ended, I emailed him the invoice.
He paid via electronic funds transfer. The money cleared in my account
within a few hours.

A friend who works at a commercial gallery also works for a private client, researching uses for blockchain in art. She sees the greatest potential in providing authenticity by recording each sale of the artwork on the blockchain, with resale royalty paid automatically. In theory, it would streamline the resale royalty process and provide a decentralised digital record of ownership that no person or group could control or corrupt.

However, anyone can create multiple anonymous digital wallets, which are used to make the transactions recorded on blockchain. It's ideal for art world price ramping. Though trad art criminals would get *pwned* by crypto bros.

AFTER A LONG, dramatic hiatus, I am in the process of rebuilding my life and career. For five years I received regular intensive treatment at a private psychiatric hospital – in part, due to what happened during my brief stint in the traditional commercial artworld. I learnt the hard way that the sense of entitlement to artists' work extends to women artists' bodies. When I refused to acquiesce, I was raped.

In mid-2017, I returned to Sydney, documented the process of creating new art and establishing a new life, and consistently shared both narratives online. I figured anyone interested in buying my art – often as a long-term investment – would need proof I was well enough to simultaneously make art and rebuild my career without the interruption of returning to hospital. I completed a small commission and documented that too, including packaging and sending it via courier. For my Instagram bio I wrote: *back from the dead*.

A year after my return I received an email: *Dear Ms. Dooney, we are happy you're back from the dead. Do you accept commissions?* The collector and I spoke briefly on the phone, then met for coffee at his office. A few weeks later, I received a plane ticket via email and took several long flights to meet the subject of a private portrait. I worked on the project for three years.

From mid-2021 to mid-2022, I developed multiple series of new paintings with the financial support of arts patron and venture capitalist, Mark Carnegie. His periodic, pithy emails offered encouragement and insights that helped my work evolve faster.

Now I'm making art I'll show publicly this year. Another commission is lined up for when I finish.

Several magazines featured my work: a new conceptual series debuted in *Plateform* magazine in 2017; a large early painting featured on the cover of *Art*

Edit magazine in 2018; and, that same year, a long interview accompanied by new photographic artworks featured in *She Shoots Film*. Art collectors Natalie and Jamie Forsyth highlighted my work during an interview with Jane Rocca about their home for *Domain Magazine* in 2022. I've been listed among the most recognisable contemporary Australian artists by Global Australia, a government taskforce to attract exceptional talent and business.

In early 2022, I withdrew from what would have been an hour-long documentary about my work – and me – pitched to a global streaming service. I felt the story angle positioned me as a victim/survivor crying to camera, which would overwhelm my accomplishments. Instead, in mid-2022, I began writing a chaptered non-fiction column published online by *Coagula Art Journal*.

My focus has been on making art, writing, reconnecting, expanding my network and maintaining a modest online presence that prioritises clear communication and responsiveness over follower count. There have been no over-hyped indicators of success: no viral moment; no high-profile collab; no mass exposure via a social media platform or streaming service. Just the accumulation of my work and a quiet, steady seep of it into the ether, to which people respond.

AS WILLIAM GIBSON observed in *The New York Times* in 2003, 'In the age of the leak and the blog, of evidence extraction and link discovery, truths will either out or be outed, later if not sooner. This is something I would bring to the attention of every diplomat, politician and corporate leader: the future will find you out. The future, wielding unimaginable tools of transparency, will have its way with you.'

In the past, information travelled slowly. It was guarded. Online, it flows organically in ways no one can accurately predict. It cannot be gatekept, hidden, obstructed or controlled.

Lies come undone when information from multiple sources is compared. The future of art fraud is the same as the future of everything else: truths will either out or be outed, later if not sooner.

A previous contributor to *Griffith Review*, Hazel Dooney is an Australian artist and author of the 'Self Vs Self' blog. Her work is included in many local and international collections.

Cusp

Jo Langdon

PATIENCE MET ME in the lobby, her black hair shiny as the glass entry-way and silver elevator doors: liquescent. That summer she'd cut her hair into a bob that flicked subtly into petal shapes at her nape and earlobes, and seeing her now, so neat and glossy, she reminded me of a cartoon character, though I couldn't think which one.

You're here! she said, as though I were late, which I didn't think I was, at least not very. I hadn't known there could be residential buildings on this street, and had wandered the CBD concrete in the late-day heat, walking parallel to the tram tracks and stops, dazedly taking in each shopfront: they were as spare and opulent to me as gallery rooms, all timber flooring and angles of honeyed light.

I'm here, I agreed, fanning my face with my fingertips. I'm so hot and puffed up.

Patience agreed. Yes, she said, it does look like you have some oedema. Let's get you upstairs. I'm sure there'll be air-con.

I always confused the words *oedema* and *enema*, so was stuck on what she'd said, but nonetheless moved forward with her into the lift, and then we were on our way, together. I was regretting the white sundress I'd put on earlier, which at home in my bedroom had seemed crisp and fresh but now wilted against my skin. The insides of the elevator were mirrored, and side by side we were each other's counterparts: me visibly clammy and flushed,

Patience pristine. I thought again of cartoon characters – that she might have been the love child of *Scooby Doo*'s Velma and Veronica from the *Archie* comics. I wasn't anyone else, just my own slippery body. Pink, I thought, like deli meat.

We were going to visit Patience's supervisor Callista, a tenured senior lecturer in literature and cultural studies, though her strange, ageless grace made the word *senior* feel like a misnomer. I knew Patience would have chided me for this, saying it showed both my ageism and internalised misogyny, so these were among the thoughts I kept to myself. Patience, two years of study ahead of me, was Callista's RA – her research assistant – which sounded to me as coolly mysterious as being a PI for Private Investigator, or some other crisp acronym. I wasn't anyone, though Patience said if I wanted to apply for Honours under Callista's supervision, this out-of-office meeting would be key to getting an offer – from Callista herself, both preceding and beyond the university's officialdom. She needs to really *like* you, Patience said. Or, she added, at least find you interesting.

I understood Callista's title didn't yet rank her so highly – in the professorial range – and, Patience had confided, that she was still trying to publish from her doctoral research. Her power came in other ways.

Now, said Patience, once we were out of the lift and on the suit-grey carpet of the landing, don't be surprised, she's lost weight but her face is really – she paused – really *full*? You'll see what I mean.

I wasn't sure I would but acquiesced by following her to the door. Callista had already buzzed us up from the lobby, I realised, and had seemed to time our entry to her appearance: she leaned out of her front door, her long straight hair a waterfall, before she stepped back inside to welcome us through.

You're here, she hummed, like Patience's echo.

Since the first time I'd attended one of her lectures in first year, Callista had reminded me of Morticia Addams, the Carolyn Jones version, but in a palette of grimy pastels: she was all peach and ice-blue, with long hair the colour of almond skins. She wore this hair falling behind her like a bride's veil, and to watch her take it in handfuls when it slid over her shoulders and lift it behind herself again felt like observing something ceremonial. Her clothes tended to be sorbet colours, bright and cool. Tonight she wore what might've been sleepwear or loungewear from another decade: a gauzy apricot wraparound sashed with a bow at her hip. The room we'd entered was surprisingly austere, grey like the hallway outside and barely lit, and Callista seemed to float through the space like a candle flame. She stood behind the kitchen's island bench and held up a dark glass magnum topped in gold foil.

Sparkles? she offered, a sardonic Tinkerbell.

The apartment smelled buttery, warm and decadent despite the conditioned air Patience had pre-empted. Through invisible speakers came resonant piano notes. They were slow and steady and low, then shifting, lifting, spreading until they felt as prolific as raindrops – impossible for the fingers of just two hands, I thought, peculiarly touched. I felt a coldness against the back of my wrist then and registered Patience touching me with her fingertips. As I wondered how she could keep her skin so cool, she widened her eyes imploringly, and I remembered her directive earlier: *just please be yourself tonight* she'd texted my phone during my train commute.

I've made us a flan for later, Callista announced, and I felt the heat in my skin deepen to remember we'd arrived empty handed, though Patience had said that was expected. *She will be genuinely offended if you bring anything, trust me*, she'd also offered by text, and because Patience knew Callista best and knew her home already – because sometimes she even did some cleaning or fed Callista's cat as a kind of house-sitter in her spare RA hours – I'd followed her instruction.

I took a flute of the sparkling wine and wondered if I'd meet Callista's husband, Taylor, whose name somehow made me think of the men in soap operas in that it could work either as a given or paternal family name, though Patience said I had the wrong idea. To be honest, he's not who you'd think, she'd said.

As though guessing my mind Callista said, airily, Taylor's watching something at the moment. He can't wait to meet you but he's also... She stopped. He'll come out later. He's, you know, she said, my own Miss Havisham. She caught my eye and shrugged, adding: I only mean solitary, not jilted. Let's go outside, she said then, extending her words to include Patience, who was eyeing the escalations of bubbles in her drink with poised attention.

Through double French doors there was a balcony with a picnic table and long benches either side. A yellow-and-white striped umbrella flowered above it, redundantly, in the night – once we were sitting, it seemed to close the hot air over our heads. This terraced area placed us halfway towards the heights of inner-city towers either side, floating upwards to hard angles of glass and metal and after-hours white and blue light. From below there was regular traffic noise and the rumble and clanging of a tram signal.

As soon as we sat, I realised I'd swallowed my drink in too many – or too few – gulps already, my glass all but empty. Coolly Callista topped up my flute and I watched as fresh bubbles zipped to the surface. I realised she'd only poured glasses for Patience and me, and felt impressed that she could keep her hands empty with such ease and calm. She and Patience flanked me either side on the long bench, and so I kept turning my head clownishly between them like a carnival game, my head feeling outsized and cumbersome. The heat clung like a bedsheet while I thought of the crisp, air-conditioned grey indoors. On our one shared bench we were facing towards the apartment, and from here I could see the sliding doors leading into the open-plan kitchen and lounge, but also a window that might've belonged to a bedroom. Through the blind's edges flickered blue light, and I registered this must be Taylor, *watching something.*

How's my new best friend? Patience enthused now.

Oh, he's perfect, Callista replied. You kept him so happy, thank you again!

I realised they were talking about Callista's cat, whose pictures I had seen in some of her lecture slides and once in a consultation meeting in her office, pinned above her work desk. He was frothy-maned and dove-coloured and had the open face of a sunflower with a sour, lemon-sucking expression.

Since they'd been together, she and Taylor had named, Callista explained, all of their cats after the streets they lived on – tacky but true – so they'd had Sweet William when they'd lived on William Street, and Lonny above Lonsdale…

What happens to the cats when you move? I blurted, intending light-heartedness, but Callista looked wounded, averting her face in profile.

Kayley, said Patience firmly, you just have to meet him. He's a dream. This time she reached for the bottle to replenish my drink, and I eyed hers. Neither her skin nor the outside of her glass seemed to perspire; as ever, she seemed unlikely to slip, spill, sweat.

I should ask, I thought, for a glass of water.

I want to help you girls, Callista said, returning herself to us, because no one ever helped me. She said 'girls' like 'gulls' and, extending past the umbrella's stripes, I felt my gaze lift and float between the skyscraper windows and aircraft collision signals to the night sky beyond. I'd once had a boyfriend who'd told me, looking at the city lights from across a body of water, that light pollution was his *least favourite kind* of pollution, confiding this with such earnestness that I'd been struck with nothing to say in return, having not once before considered pollution as something I'd have a favourite or least favourite of. At intervals I felt something like this, or its inverse, with Patience and Callista. I would say something and they would angle their smiles towards one another.

She's the best, isn't she? Callista said at one such moment to Patience.

In the previous semester Patience had marked one of my third-year assessments, for which I'd had to submit a personal essay. I'd received a copy back with Callista's annotations added, usually in dialogue with anything Patience had written already. In reply to Patience, Callista would put 'Yes!', and 'Mmmm!' – a row of hand-drawn birds in a blank sky. In other marginalia notes, she'd left single emojis: yellow hands clapping, a lightning bolt, a pink heart with sparkles. They'd graded it 79/100. You're just on the cusp, Patience had written in her final speech-bubbled comment, of being so great! Underneath that, from Callista, 'Yesss!!'

Now they asked me about my research interests, if I had a plan for a year, three years, five?

I babbled out my first thoughts and Callista tilted her head. You're adorable, Kayley, she said. I know that's so patronising, but you're just the sweetest, just such a flower. Truly, I love your made-up sounding name – sorry, she interrupted herself, what a shocking thing to say. I just mean I love where you're coming from and, actually, this is exactly why I choose *not* to teach at a top-eight institution. She paused to look down at her hands. I'm much more self-aware than I'm seeming; I know I sound like the girl (gull, I heard again) in the Pulp song, calling you *common people*...

The thing is, she resumed, the essays you write, the life experiences behind your perspective – you've got this gritty authenticity we love. Don't you feel a bit like Professor Higgins? She was talking past me by then, to Patience.

I felt flattered to realise I was Audrey Hepburn's character, but at the same time her words made me feel like I'd swallowed a marble.

I used to watch that with my nan, I offered.

Then you get me! Callista, in her orange-sherbet taffeta as it now looked to me, positively glowed. Our own little flower seller, we're going to make you our project. We're going to *make* you – if you're open to our proposition. She was leaning her elbows on the table, her face between her palms. She shone opaquely, her skin like the ice rinks of Christmas movies, and I tried to discern an open pore or dot of sweat. Instead I found her nose and cheeks were flecked with tiny freckles the colour of cinnamon, which might've been pencilled on under powder. Still, I thought, she is positively supernatural. It was an urge I had sometimes, to prattle out something so ridiculous, or to reach for her and feel the ends of her hair or sleeve slip between my fingers.

After a moment she stood and said: Let me check on our dinner, though I don't want to stop talking. Then she was inside the cool grey on the other side of the glass.

Patience looked at me. You're doing well, she said. She'd withdrawn a single-use Pump water bottle from her bag and took a long drink from it. The plastic crumpled and popped, bouncing back in her grip as she swallowed. It's really sad, Patience said next, that she doesn't really have anyone else – just us. People are so threatened by her, but they also don't take her seriously, and she's having to make bargains with the patriarchy all the time. But if you get to do this, you can help lift her up, you can ghostwrite for her, you can do so much, when you're ready, and she'll never pull up the ladder after herself. She's, like, *building ladders*.

I tried to meet her eyes to measure her sincerity, but Patience was stowing her water bottle away then pinching the ends of her hair back into their petal shapes. The umbrella above us made me feel boxed in with heat, and though it was dark around us, I imagined my thighs would leave two visible sweat prints on the bench when I stood.

Patience traced a fingernail against the stem of her wine glass. She said, Callista is a recovering perfectionist you know, so that's why, sometimes, I help her in other ways, when she needs to stay hands-on. It sounds dreadful, doesn't it? Like I'm a 'work wife', or just her wife in general, in this invisible service role, but actually I think in our context it's different and subversive.

Patience went on: As I said, you've been great tonight. But – she took a sip, this time from her wine glass – if you need, I can give you something to help calm you down a bit. She threw her gaze to her bag under the table then gave it a nudge with her foot.

I felt my answer forthcoming, words escaping before I'd fully absorbed her question – the same reply I'd meant to give to Callista before.

When Callista came out again, she said: So I'm not ready yet – the flan is on the cooling rack. I must warn you, it's mostly base, mostly dreamy carbs with butter, and I've thrown together some leaves and served some up to Taylor already; he'll eat in our room…

She proffered a new wine bottle. But let's keep *going*.

WHEN I COULD get myself inside to use the bathroom, later, the sudden cool air against my clammy skin would make me feel like I had a fever, some kind of gastro with shivers. When I was sick into the white expanse of Callista's basin, I thought: it's okay, it's all just liquid, but it was unstoppable, unrelenting, and when Callista came to find me and registered the unmistakable bile smell, she looked at me as though I was something that had crawled out from under her bathmat. Whether this was also because she'd knocked and called out to me so many times before I'd unlatched the door, or because of the rooms I'd disturbed finding my way, startling Taylor – almost exactly as I'd imagined him – and the street-named cat, I didn't know for sure.

Callista began to clean furiously, materialising a bucket of hot water, Aesop suds, steam and a sponge that looked like a real sea artefact. She brought in a mop, though I was sure I'd spared the floor.

I'll make it up to you, I kept saying to Patience as she swept me out, into the lift and onto the street under the shawl of her arms. You don't need to, she said, there's nothing to make up for, and I felt soothed until I found myself in the taxi alone, tunnelling away in the wash of the night.

After that I have no memories to account for the driver or the ride, only an amount drawn from my bank card later and that I woke out of a blackness next door to where I was living, still with my mum and nan and sister at that time, being sick into the neighbour's garden bed of impatiens – which I'd always confused with the word *impatience*, and so I thought of Patience first, as the biliousness shifted, a velvety humming I could only expel and wait out at intervals, crouched and fumbling for my house keys between shuddering ejections.

Waiting for the taxi, Patience had tried to feed me like a toddler: slow sips of water from her Pump bottle, until I'd said I couldn't, shouldn't, try any more liquid, so she'd helped me to take steady breaths of air, counting them in and out as we crouched close to the curb.

Only then, in the impatiens, I thought of Callista's cat: a variation on the nameless cat of another Audrey Hepburn film. I wanted to picture a ginger tom instead of the long-haired seal-point cat from the photos. In the dark its coat had been the same suit-grey colour of the apartment, and I imagined it then, high over the city, with yellow headlight-eyes following me home in the night, a projection of something between surveillance and care.

Jo Langdon's writing has been published in journals including *Cordite*, *Island*, *Meanjin* and *Overland*. In 2018 she was a fellow of the Elizabeth Kostova Foundation's Sozopol Fiction Seminars and CapitaLiterature festival in Bulgaria, and in 2020 her short fiction was recognised in the Olga Masters and Newcastle short story awards. She is also the author of two collections of poetry: *Snowline* (Whitmore Press, 2012) and *Glass Life* (Five Islands Press, 2018).

A passing phase

Thirty years of Regurgitator

Ian Powne, Quan Yeomans and Ben Ely

Way back in 1993, an alt-rock three-piece called Regurgitator began life as a side project in the Brisbane suburbs. By 1995, they'd signed with Warner Music Group, and their debut album, Tu-Plang, *was released the following year. But it was 1997's* Unit — *featuring the mega-hits 'I Like Your Old Stuff Better Than Your New Stuff' and 'Polyester Girl', among others — that lodged Regurgitator firmly in Australia's popular music consciousness, positioning them as a band able to fuse musical styles and influences without taking any of it too seriously. In this wide-ranging conversation — which has been lightly edited and condensed for clarity — 4ZZZ Programming Co-ordinator Ian Powne talks art, authenticity and mashed potato with two of the band's founding members, Quan Yeomans and Ben Ely.*

IAN POWNE: When I first heard the name 'Regurgitator' I felt as though I got what you guys were about immediately: I didn't think, 'This is about vomiting'; I was thinking this is more a comment on the fact that as a band you were going to be regurgitating everything happening now and before, and that you had no high-minded ideals about originality.

QUAN YEOMANS: That puts you in a very small percentage of the population, Ian, if you thought that just from seeing the name. I don't know how rare that is, but that was definitely a part of the reason why we called ourselves Regurgitator.

IP: Something of the '90s attitude made me think that. There was a bit of taking the mickey out of stuff.

BEN ELY: There was also a little bit of cultural burnout by the time the '90s came around because the '80s were so excessive and over the top, and then the '90s were a little bit like, 'Where to now?' And I guess Regurgitator is like, 'The only thing we can do is just, you know…'

QY: Take the piss.

BE: Take the piss, but also regurgitate all the different styles of culture from the past. It was pretty unusual growing up in the '80s with so many different subcultures in high school… There were skinheads and hippies and swampies and goths and bogans. There were so many different forms of expression it was like, 'What do you do now? There's nothing else you can do now.'

QY: Don't you think that the reason we had that 'take the piss' angle was because our immediate locale felt very conservative in terms of music and the things that seemed to be popular at the time?

BE: Yes, definitely. Culturally, in Australia, there wasn't a lot going on: Chocolate Starfish, the Sharks, Roxus, Mantissa – the bands were pretty beige.

QY: Maybe that was part of the reaction to the '80s as well. Everyone just was so overstimulated by cocaine that all their sensory receptors were destroyed and all of it was sort of beige.

BE: Just mashed potato.

QY: Yeah, exactly, it was all mashed potato, and so I think coming through that mashed potato – swimming through the mashed potato – we were like, 'Oh man, this is ridiculous, let's just take the piss and loosen it up a little bit.'

BE: But we weren't supposed to be a big band; we were just a side project. It was just supposed to be a little throwaway thing that ended up having legs.

QY: Well, that's part of the whole punk aesthetic; that's also part of the take-the-piss thing that we took from the '70s and '80s as well: not giving a fuck and talking about how silly it all was and how ridiculous life is. So that punk aesthetic definitely moved and pushed the band – that was a wave we rode even though we didn't sound like a punk band a lot of the time.

BE: We wanted to sound heavy and nasty because we were into that kind of music at the time, and it just so happened that we changed over time as well.

IP: I'm interested in how your perception of Regurgitator, the name, has changed.

BE: I guess there's a degree of honesty to it because, I mean, everyone rips off everybody, and we're just basically saying, 'Yeah, we do it too, but it's in our name', so it almost excuses the fact that we do it.

QY: In a way that is our job description: if we were plumbers we would plumb, right? If we were accountants, we would account, and we regurgitate, so we're Regurgitator.

IP: Regurgitator first released music on a major label, the Warner Music Group, and, to frame that, I want to use a quote from singer/songwriter/poet David Berman from the Silver Jews. It's something I dwell on regarding the concept of selling out, which was huge in the early '90s:

> selling oneself does damage to the self. people are used to thinking of it as a betrayal of fans or predecessors or a music scene but it's an act of self-corruption which paradoxically appears to be self-elevating. one thing i remember from the eighties is whenever bands went to a major [label] they suddenly did their worst work, and the drop offs were so evident, the bands never recovered. dream syndicate, husker du, x, meat puppets, butthole surfers. those were really cautionary sales! it was the comedy of the commons. it was like any group that tried to sell out, was punished for their hubris by destroying the magic. and so there was a constant reminder not to fly too close to the sun. this probably made staying small the savvy choice for those who were paying attention.

In what way does that kind of sentiment, that analysis – one person's perspective – speak to you? You've kind of done this in reverse: you started out on a major label.

BE: We did do it in reverse. That was something that we really tortured ourselves over, the idea of signing to a label.

QY: What [Berman] was talking about was definitely a feeling that was there, and it's correct in lots of ways. But it really depends on how aware you are at the time and the reason that you're doing it. I felt that a lot of the pressures on us to do what we did came from disparate areas, and there were disparate ideas within the band about whether we should or not. So there was this deep awareness of what was going on and how it might affect us, especially because we were just starting out.

BE: There were a couple of major record companies fighting over us and we were umming and ahhing about it so much that we made sure the contract allowed us complete creative freedom and control and to deliver what we wanted, which was pretty poor recordings in a shit studio, which no major record company was doing. So we had – maybe to our detriment – free rein, but when our record company's A&R guys left, this new guy came on and then he started exerting control over the music. And he came to Andy Gill's studio in London and was like, 'Oh, this song "Fat Cop", it needs a chorus. You need to write a chorus.' And that was the first time we made a creative compromise with the record company, and it actually did feel like that – I felt like I was physically ill. And then we did whatever we could to get out of there; we couldn't stand it. I think if you have to compromise, if the A&R guys go, 'Oh no, boys, do it like this, you'll sell more records' – that's truly selling out, I think. And that was the only time I think we sold out.

QY: When you sign to a record company, you're basically agreeing to work with salespeople. Their job is not to understand what you're doing, particularly creatively; their job is to put units out there and get rid of them as fast as they possibly can. And if they see a barrier to that in your organisation, if you're not selling records, they'll come in and do what they can to make it work better. And it's those conversations that really, really fuck with you as a creative individual and really wreck whatever you're doing. So I'm thinking that what Ben was describing is probably what happened to a lot of these bands that did it in reverse.

IP: I want to move on to the 2000s, when we saw this wave of reality TV begin, including *Big Brother* – when the mundane lives of so-called regular people and celebrities started compelling collective attention. *Band in a Bubble* in 2004 [a reality television show in which Regurgitator spent three weeks inside a glass bubble in Melbourne's Federation Square to write and record their 2004 album *Mish Mash!*] slots into this timeline pretty neatly.

Was *Band in a Bubble* riding the wave of this reality TV thing or was it critiquing it?

QY: I think it was collection of things: seeing David Blaine sitting in a bubble in London really pushed the idea forward in my mind, and Paul [Curtis, Regurgitator's manager] was also very keen on something similar. But I think it was definitely informed by all those things you're talking about: the reality shows and the idea of authenticity. Everyone in the band knows how fucking boring it is to record music sometimes when you're just sitting around waiting for someone to do their parts, or just playing video games while someone else is busy, or all the mixing's being done. It's about that demystification, which of course is taken to the nth level now with the internet.

What I find really amazing is this whole new wave of process-oriented stuff, where it's the responsibility, it seems, of any artist, be they a 3D artist or a visual artist or a musician, to lay bare their process on a daily basis…and create a following that way, which is fascinating. Back in the day it was all about the mystery, and I feel like *Band in a Bubble* was us going, 'Well, hang on a minute, you want to know what's going on? Let's show you how dull it can be and put ourselves out there.' And, ironically, we sold very few copies of *Mish Mash!*; we didn't capitalise on that whole hype thing. It was a great experience and a really weird one.

BE: It's funny because the day we came out it was on the front page of every major newspaper in Australia.

IP: So what does it feel like – you're a *Band in a Bubble*, you're on the front pages of all these tabloids – how does it feel to be tied to fame?

BE: It's a really funny thing because music is a real – I don't know if it's especially so in Australia – music is a real nostalgia-driven thing. A lot of people love our band because…the records that really hold weight with people are the ones they listened to when they were young. I feel like people have this attachment to us, to a kind of a prime time in their life – music sounds better when you're a teenager. And so people connect with you on this level that's almost like meeting the school captain or something. When they see you, they're not really a fan as such – they're more attached to this idea within themselves that's connected to this part of their youth.

QY: A very, very distinct part of the cocktail of their youth: that heady mix of hormones and drugs and energy and thoughts. It creates a very powerful memory in a lot of people's minds and you're a part of that memory. If you want to talk about fame, like the cultural idea of it, to me it's always just been that image that's replicated to the nth degree – so there's more pictures or more sounds of you out there than the person next to you or the woman who just works in an office or whatever. And that's really all it is, it's just this replication and positioning of your image, your blueprint.

IP: You're known as being this multi-genre band – you use musical genres to make a comment in 'The Song Formally Known As' from 1997's *Unit*, 'A Nod to Prince', 'Metal is Big in the Baltic States' from *Mish Mash!* There are many examples of the fun you guys have mucking around with musical forms tongue-in-cheek. Would you say that it's messing with the whole idea of originality at the same time that it's a genuine project, not a parody?

QY: Sometimes it's fun to parody yourself, it gets meta at some points, but when you're in a band for so long it starts to feel that way sometimes – you start to think, 'Well, am I a parody of myself? Are we just repeating ourselves as an entity, as artists?'

IP: I read this quote from Dave Graney in an interview with *Crikey* in 2011: 'Generally music is a constant search for authenticity. In an Australian context, any Australian performer in rock music is wearing a mask: American accent, American music. And wearing a mask is fucking great because it allows you to say things you can't normally. But the downside of that is people are always saying *you're a fake*. You're looking for that. That's how low the discourse is in rock music generally.'

QY: That's very '90s. There are so many successful Australian artists that have just gone, 'You know what, I'm putting the mask on. Here it is.' Just look at Iggy Azalea, Kid Laroi, all of those new artists – that boundary isn't there anymore. I remember the last time I was harassed for putting on an American accent, and it was in Fremantle. I recall someone yelling out, 'You're not American! Why are you putting on an accent?' That wasn't that long ago, maybe fifteen years. And it's really interesting how, with the internet and with the globalisation of sound and art, that stuff doesn't seem to matter as much anymore to people.

IP: What does it mean to be original?

QY: Originality is really a sense of surprise, if you think about it. You want to be surprised, genuinely surprised by something, and it's hard to do. But if you overthink it, of course, it often doesn't work, and that's part of the authenticity thing – not overthinking, just being yourself, just expressing what's real to you, and if you can do it in a surprising way, then that seems original to other people. Often you think something's original and then years down the track you go, 'Oh, this older one was clearly the inspiration for it, clearly they just ripped that off.' So that experience of originality is kind of warped, and it really depends on a certain ignorance of the cultural complexity that's behind a piece of work. You can be overeducated and really find nothing original because you know the histories too well.

IP: I love this quote from Grace Jones – she's referring to a de-identified pop star she calls Doris:

> I could see what she wanted to be when I watched her doing something when she started out that was starker and purer. Deep down, she doesn't want to do all the dressing up nonsense; she loses herself inside all of the playacting.
>
> The problem with the Dorises and Nicki Minajes and the Mileys is they reach their goal very quickly. There is no long-term vision, and they forget that once you get into that whirlpool, then you have to fight the system that solidifies around you in order to keep the outsider that you claim you represent. There will always be a replacement coming along very soon – a newer version, a crazier version, a louder version. So if you haven't got a long-term plan, then you are merely a passing phase, the latest trend, yesterday's event.

What's your long-term plan been?

QY: My long-term plan is to be a passing phase, but basically that's the only long-term plan any human can have, right? You're just a passing phase, let's just be honest here. But like Ben says, I think as long as you enjoy it, just keep doing it as long as you can, and if other people are enjoying it, go for it. Obviously you don't want to be – I mean, if you want to play to nobody in a burnt-out pub or retirement village or whatever, you can do that as well – but if you can entertain people and you love what you're doing, why not just keep doing it?

BE: I've been really feeling strongly over the last six months that music resonates better in a room with people who get along, are really conscious of each other. Music is a celebration to me. It's really, really hard to keep going if you don't have this kind of celebratory, communal aspect to music.

IP: I'm glad you used the term 'celebratory', because having seen Regurgitator play all over Australia, I'm constantly blown away by the genuine connection between you and the audience. Ian MacKaye from Fugazi and Dischord Records fame says, 'How can an artist not be real from the word go if they decide to make art? They're real… but there's this sense that they're not actually authentic artists until they make money.' And so it's the same thing: you put Regurgitator in a small bar and you've got that energy, that musicianship that's right in front of you, that's real regardless of anything else.

QY: Isn't that interesting? Because from an artist's point of view, that's not the case at all – that's like what we were talking about before, it's the sell-out moment, so that's the death knell for artists in their mind. But he's saying the public's view is that they're not authentic until they're popular and they're making money or they have some status.

IP: Where he's coming from is that a band that's playing in a small venue right in front of you, where you don't even know four people or whatever, is just as real as you two playing at the football stadium.

QY: Absolutely. Some of my fondest memories were playing to no one when we first started, just to staff in the bar. Some of the best art I've ever seen was art brut, going to Lausanne to that gallery that's specifically for art brut that was started by [Jean] Dubuffet, the painter who just collected all the non-artists' work – they'd died or they were in mental institutions – outsider art. And it's all collected in this museum: all this stuff that existed in their houses and in their mental asylums and in their attics and was just for them until it was brought to this place. And then you see it and it's stunning, it's absolutely stunning and they never made money off it. No one ever appreciated it while they were alive, and you don't get more authentic than that. Those particular artists were living, but the most authentic artist's life they could live was by doing it specifically for themselves and not for anyone else. In that sense they couldn't be accused of being inauthentic.

As you go on in your career, you tend to overthink things a little more easily than when you were young. When you start a band, you have a really powerful feeling about what you're doing and where you are in your life and what you want to achieve, and when you do achieve it, obviously you move on. So I think it does become harder when you get to this stage and maybe there's a barrier that you push through if you've been around for long enough to realise that it really doesn't matter in the end, and you can get back to that 'not giving a fuck' kind of period of your creative life. Which I think is important, and it often feels like we're all trying to get back to that initial 'I don't really give a fuck, let's just do it'. I feel like that's what I'm always trying to do.

IP: Going back to Grace – Grace knows who she is and delivers it, and that's a pretty rare gift, right? To know yourself as an artist and go out on stage and say, 'This is who I am.'

QY: Exactly. And people who have really long careers, they have that self-knowledge and that self-confidence – people like David Bowie and people like Grace, they have that confidence within themselves. They can express themselves clearly and that's what matters to them more than anything else. So that's what I try to remember. A lot of being an older artist is about trying to get zen about it and trying to let go of those things that success and experience have pushed you towards.

BE: If you sit down with a piece of paper and go, 'I'm going to draw a dog', and then you draw a dog, you're kind of shooting yourself in the foot before you even put the pen on the paper. But if you sit at the paper and go, 'I'm going to have fun and just make up stuff', that's when I feel like your true character comes out.

I went to Tim's Guitars years ago and I saw Grant Hart from Hüsker Dü do a solo thing and he had a Q&A after the solo. And some guy went, 'How often do you practise guitar?' And then Grant Hart said, 'I never practise guitar, practising guitar gets in the way of my personality.' And I was like, 'Oh wow, that's actually really true.' There are guitarists or musicians I know who just work on technique a lot, but much of their personality and their character doesn't come through because a high percentage of the energy taken up by their music is in their technique.

QY: It's also about connection to your instrument. There are people who practise a lot: Hendrix, for example, would literally fucking sleep with his guitar, and that guy had a connection with that instrument, but he's also had this incredible authenticity.

BE: But then there are people I know who just work on technique and I think there's a degree of phoniness with that.

I'll look for new music gear on YouTube and look at guitar pedals, 'What does this guitar pedal sound like?', and I'll YouTube some white guy playing blues licks, and there's nothing bluesy about it – it's just some guy rehashing some licks. There's this real phoniness to it that I can't stand.

QY: I guess people play instruments for different reasons as well. There's craft obviously and then there's replicating something or playing something for the sake of the feeling of the technique, the feeling that you can actually do something. Whereas people like us, we prefer not to work that way. We write songs and we get a lot of joy out of writing songs and the technique comes from playing those songs over and over again.

IP: It feels like originality is kind of disguised theft, like you're creating something and go, 'Wow, where did that come from?' You're ripping off somebody else, what you've heard and what we've all experienced before, but it's done with your own feel – with the way you play the instrument, the way you put the words together – and everything is kind of like this nice juxtaposition. That's where originality lies, perhaps.

QY: And a lot of the more original stuff has this feeling of pure love as well for the things they've stolen: it's not like this surreptitious theft; it's kind of this homage a lot of the time. So it has a sense of authenticity in that regard as well. It's about paying respect to the past and to people that have come before and trying to just embody that in your own way.

Ian Powne is an Australian musician who plays in the band the Stress of Leisure. He's also the programming co-ordinator at Brisbane's 4ZZZ, where he co-presents the radio show *Brighten the Corners*.

Michael Farrell

Roxy Music Has The Right To Children

Once I had a tape made of something that did not exist; I'd never be in a band
at that rate. After some delay I fathered a child with my neighbours, and we sang
the baby songs, till they went away somewhere. I cared, but I had a life to manage.
A pencil thin moustache would come and go. You didn't know me then, not any
of you. It was around 1980 or 1988. I had not yet begun to think in 'off the record'
terms. I felt myself immune from germs, also. Little fragments of memory, such as
moments of gardening, of talking like a hawthorn, or some flower (a Bill or a Ben
from *Play School*, but less noticeable in pitch), come back to me; a decorated plate
of macaroni, or cauliflower, kept me going then, or some refillable black potion
in a Styrofoam cup. It couldn't be said I had a grammar, or a rhetoric, or a theory.
But poems decay. Honour decays, if it is not kept up. If I could have lived for long
in a voice I would have. London abstractions, Glasgow abstractions, on top
of Sydney abstractions, all had birds living in them. Not all English birds either.

The fun people had on TV then! The hair, and not only the hair, but full monster
suits. The mashed potato had a smoky, bullety, flavour, the gravy made the black
and white tasty. To know me is like pulling teeth, I've been told more than once.
I'm still immersed in 1986, with a student card, and a bank account, and a life
as thin as *Peanuts* really was, for the secondary characters. You can't drink beer
on a diet of fairy floss, as they said back then. To fall in Manhattan was easy
in the shoes I was wearing. What is my point? Glamour has the right to children,
I said so from the beginning. It's a nice day for a red wedding. For Otis Redding
to walk in and grab somebody's trombone, and blow it. My point is not that this is
how to write poetry, but that while I had a penchant for acting like a steer without
a mother (no mother, no penis), when the greeny blossoms were on the tree, yet I
wanted, however slowly, without losing the poker in the ashes, or the milk-breath-
flavoured smell of a calf's muzzle, to break into the abstractions, like love does.

Michael Farrell is the author of *Writing Australian Unsettlement: Modes of Poetic Invention
1796-1945* (Palgrave Macmillan), as well as of seven books of poetry, the latest being
Googlecholia (Giramondo).

No name for the country

名のない国

Declan Fry

LANGUAGE EXCEEDS THE borders of race and nationalism: this is what Ian
Hideo Levy's work said to me when I first encountered it fifteen years ago.
At the time I had begun to suspect something illicit – something founded,
perhaps, in the furnace of colonisation and White supremacy – about the self-
imposed limits of 'English literature'. Who, after all, owns a language? The
nation-state? The passport holder at the airport or border crossing, standing
in line with the locals (if not in that other queue designated *foreigner*) or the
speaker whose skin colour suggests they are native to a tongue, a culture, a
whole system of thinking and being?

Only about 6 per cent of non-Anglophone literature is translated into
English. While studying in two university departments – English and
Cultural Studies, and Asian Studies – I learnt more about the importance
of materialist analysis and multilingualism, something that seemed to be
neglected by the English department. Such departments have attempted
to reframe their work in light of changing economies and demographics
through the advent of 'Global Anglophone' or 'World Literature' studies.
Yet the English-speaking, White author, ensconced in the metropole, remains
the invisible comparison point or true north of what is deemed 'the world'.
Meanwhile, area studies (of which Asian studies is an iteration) has been criti-
cised as a Cold War instrument, arising out of American investment and the
United States' desire to study – and outwit – potential enemies or roadblocks
to the growth of its markets. Notwithstanding the work of numerous scholars

in drawing attention to the legacy of area studies' origins, its engagement with other languages, cultures and disciplines remains a happy corrective to the narrower purview of English studies.

The tendency for Australia, in its settler-colonial history, to orient itself towards Whiteness is visible in the primary, near-exclusive focus on politics and the economy in our relations with Asia and the Pacific – as if these regions were composed not of living, breathing people with diverse views and philosophies, literatures and cultures, but of diplomatic 'interests' to be mollified, defended against or flattered, based upon the impressions of the nation's security and intelligence apparatus. Asian countries are rarely viewed as a whole, confined to existing as another source of economic or military anxiety. Cultures, scholars, languages, philosophies, literature: all vanish. Like the foreclosed diplomacy it rests upon, this kind of thinking seems unable to conceive of China or Japan, never mind smaller nations, as anything but a site of instrumental strategising – precisely the view that ensures Australia will never be capable of having its own role and place in the world. Moreover, it seems to speak solely to, or imply only the existence of, a White Australian audience.

This essay, then, is about more than the limits of English literature – it is an attempt to wrest us out of this realpolitik by attending to the kinetic possibilities of language.

IAN HIDEO LEVY – or as he is known in Japanese, リービ英雄, *Rībi Hideo* – has tested the literary geography established by an Anglocentric worldview. Born in Berkeley in 1950 to a couple who named him Hideo after a Japanese-American friend, he moved to Taiwan at age five and at twelve to Hong Kong before spending four years in Virginia. Travelling back and forth between Japan and the US, Hideo eventually quit his tenured position at Stanford University in 1990 to permanently settle in Shinjuku, Tokyo.

For the past thirty-odd years, Hideo has worked exclusively in Japanese, publishing several novels and collections of criticism and essays. *Why Japanese?* is a question he is often asked. It harbours a kind of suspicion: why would a native speaker of the English language, the language of power and prestige and capital – someone with no racial connections to Japan (*not even one drop of Japanese blood*, as he says in the afterword to his debut novel) – give it all up in favour of a comparatively minor language, a marked and ethnicised tongue?

Hideo has admitted he will probably never be able to answer the question in a way which might comprehensively satisfy those asking it. The terms of inquiry are known in advance: the White Westerner *must not* go native. They are *not allowed*. An author from the metropole *cannot* betray the gifts of empire. *Cannot* migrate to the margins. A major language *must not* be traded in favour of a minor. And yet one thing remains undeniable: this is exactly what Ian Hideo Levy, for several decades now, has done.

More remarkably still, he has not done so in the role of cultural translator or entertainer, or as a diplomat employed to facilitate negotiations between cultures and nations – the roles normally assumed by (White) foreigners. Instead, Hideo chooses to write Japanese literature in one of the country's most decidedly literary genres: the 'I' novel, the narrative of which tends to mirror the author's own experience.

Part of what Hideo does is open up the nature of personal subjectivity by taking advantage of the Japanese language's many words for 'I'. This leads to a larger question: who has the right to be an 'I' in Japanese, or any language? What narratives of the 'I' are national or universal, and which are 'multicultural', 'minority', ethnicised, peripheral – a matter only of personal identity, of foreign/anthropological information to be variously 'listened to' or 'respected'?

私、僕、俺

I, I, I

Hideo began writing in Japanese as an American growing up during the economic rise of Japan, a period when the US-Japan relationship was still the most dominant in the Asia-Pacific. That is part of Hideo's connection to his subject. Yet being someone with neither Chinese nor Japanese heritage who writes about China in Japanese – as he has regularly done for the past twenty-five years – is something else entirely.

Here, he follows in the footsteps of authors in a Japanese/Chinese literary lineage – those such as Ryōtarō Shiba, whose pen-name comes from Sima (Shiba) Qian, the great Han dynasty historian. Qian's work offered a model of history-writing for both China and its ancient cultural sphere – Korea, Vietnam, Japan. Ryōtarō Shiba looked at Japan, not only in relation to the West, but in connection to its neighbours. Such a perspective did not become common until the '90s, when Japan's economic bubble finally burst.

Even then it was often tentative, as fiction, music and film began to question the increased globalisation of Japan and its culture. There was a sense that it was important for the country to try to repair its relationships with estranged Asian neighbours.

Hideo has come to the Japanese language not through historical persecution or economic necessity – or colonisation – but as a matter of personal choice. Acknowledging this linguistic affinity sans racial connections involves a roundabout language: *Japanese-language author*. It recalls the example set by local writers such as Kim Scott, troubling the idea that a language or a literature might belong, hermetically sealed, within the borders of the (colonial) nation-state. Border-crossing and tortuous expressions of belonging are common bedfellows: visibly xx, of xx heritage, having xx-xx identity, a hyphenated existence, appending disclaimer upon disclaimer, neither/nor nor exclusive. Why write *Western Japanese-language author*? Why not *Jewish-American*? Why append disclaimers at all?

WHO, IN HIDEO'S work, is the 'I'? We might begin with his first novel, published when he was forty-one years old: 星条旗の聞こえない部屋, *A Room Where the Star-Spangled Banner Cannot Be Heard*. Set in the 1960s, it tells the story of Ben Isaac, a young man whose father is a Jewish-American diplomat. After living with his mother in Virginia for several years he graduates from high school and moves to Yokohama to live with his father at the American consulate. Having remarried, his father now lives with his Shanghainese wife, Gui-lan, and Ben's younger brother, a speaker of Mandarin and English who experiences learning difficulties. The marriage has caused a rift: his father's Orthodox Jewish family have disowned him for wedding a Chinese woman.

Like Hideo, Ben desires more than to observe or study or spruik the foreign-exotic. He wishes to be part of it: in the novel's climax, when he's challenged by his co-workers to eat a raw egg, Ben finds himself 'seized by an indescribable emotion, something resembling anger yet different'. For a moment, a thought rushes through his mind in English, an *American* instinct: *Smash it in his fucking face!* Yet he ignores the impulse to assert himself and eats the egg. By humbling himself, he wins.

Hideo shares with Ben certain privileges as a White Anglophone male. But he has had to work as hard – or harder – than those without such concessions in becoming a 文学者, a *bungakusha* – a literary being, a self in Japanese. As he wrote in his 1997 essay collection アイデンティテ ィ ー ズ (*Identities*), Japan, like much of Asia, has historically teemed with 'erts' and 'ists': Japanologists, Sinologists, experts, anthropologists, outsiders translating and offering up exegeses for a foreign audience. To be a *bungaku-sha*, however, is to be a participant among participants. As Hideo writes: 'Needless to say, *bungakusha* is a modern category. In premodern times, there were poets of tanka and haiku, but no *bungakusha*. Like much of Japan's modern identity, it carried conditions of ethnicity and nationality: foreigners engaged in Japanese literature are often labelled "Japanese literature *research-ers*". In modern conventional wisdom, it appears never to have occurred to anyone that a person without Japanese citizenship could ever be a *bungakusha* and insider in Japanese literature.'

This statement recalls a scene in *Star-Spangled Banner* where Ben, in a café he will later be employed by, encounters a young Japanese woman. She becomes increasingly frustrated, even angry, at her inability to tell him what he is. Ignoring his replies in Japanese, she interrogates him in English: is he a soldier? A tourist? Missionary? Hippie? Ben eventually dubs himself a *BŌ-MEI-SHA* – a refugee. When the woman's irritation at this answer becomes apparent – referring to Vietnam, she asks indignantly, 'Aren't you guys the ones waging the war?'– he reluctantly assents to the label of tourist, ignoring his desire to speak of running from 'you guys' – who, he reflects, 'were actually "my guys"'.

白人優越
ホワイト・スプレマシー
White supremacy

In an afterword to the novel's Japanese edition, Hideo writes of a lone young man dropping out of Western culture, wandering the border separating 'insider' from 'outsider' in Japan. Running away from home and America toward Shinjuku, Ben Isaac is, Hideo emphasises, seeking a refuge *beyond* Japan; perhaps that place the author Natsume Sōseki writes of as being 'even bigger than Japan' in his 1908 novel *Sanshirō*: the inside of one's head.

Such a story, Hideo says, could only have been written in Japanese. Choice had nothing to do with it: because the story takes place in Japan, in the Japanese language, to write it in any other – notwithstanding that English is Hideo's first – would only have rendered it second-hand. A translation.

There is a lesson here, I think, about the complexity of identity and privilege. Neither is easily reduced, in spite of the contemporary urge to do so. Although Hideo has written criticism for prestigious literary publications, had his writing featured on the admissions test for one of Japan's most eminent universities, and won numerous awards in Japan, the Akutagawa Prize – one of the country's biggest literary awards and a litmus test for what passes as pure or 'high' literature – has eluded him, even as his 1996 novel 天安門 (*Tiannamen*) received a nomination. His name has surfaced in Nobel Prize discussions, but history, on at least three levels of racial and geopolitics, does not favour his odds. Firstly, East Asian writers have received Nobel consideration based primarily on the English translations of their work. Secondly, ethnically Japanese authors are considered perhaps once a quarter century. And, finally, the prospect of granting candidacy to an author writing in Japanese who isn't ethnically Japanese is politically contentious.

It's a proposition Hideo seems cheekily aware of: in his 2017 novel 模範郷 (*Model Village*) he writes about Pearl S Buck, author of a series of bestselling novels based on her direct experience of provincial Chinese life and the first American woman to receive the Nobel Prize for Literature in 1938. Her triumph proved controversial, including in mainland China – as Hideo notes, the government boycotted the ceremony (she was also later denounced, during the Cultural Revolution, as an American cultural imperialist). Buck seemed to have sidelined herself, Hideo hints, by being a non-Chinese author who gained her reputation as someone writing in English rather than in Chinese, participating as an equal. As Hideo notes, she might have done this, given her bilingual upbringing (Chinese was her first language). Instead, she was feted for 'bringing' China to the West, receiving a Nobel sixty-two years before the first ethnically Chinese recipient. It recalls the Swedish Academy's grandiloquent claim that Patrick White introduced 'a new continent into literature', even as White, and certainly many First Nations, would have known this to be a dubious assertion: the continent had already been written, at least for those who cared to look and to listen out for it.

TO DATE, HIDEO has had only his debut novel conveyed into English, by Christopher D Scott. There, words like BAN-SHŪ, NA-KA, NA-TSU, NA-MA-E – or LATE AUTUMN, INSIDE, SUMMER, NAME – are capitalised and bracketed with speedbump dashes as if to emphasise the unease of their arrival; how Ben must learn to tease out, character by character, the sounds of Japanese. It communicates the intentional awkwardness of Hideo's original, where these same words are transcribed using only hiragana, one of the two basic phonetic Japanese syllabaries that exist alongside the more complex system of kanji.

Hideo's fiction and essays are attentive to the connections and disparities both within Japanese and between Japanese and other languages. Perhaps the most interesting example of the latter is the use of Chinese and English at the conclusion of Hideo's 2002 novel ヘンリーたけしレウィツキーの夏の紀行 (*Henry Takeshi Lewitsky's Summer Journey*). The titular protagonist travels to the city of Kaifeng in Henan province, one of eight ancient Chinese capitals, hoping to find proof of the city's long-vanished Jewish community. After discovering a synagogue's former well in the boiler room of a dilapidated hospital, Lewitsky wanders down a street lined with construction sites, overcome by a sense of freedom, of release. Children emerge from the houses nearby, shout

老外!

ローウエイ！

laowai!

Their cries — *foreigner* — are followed by three words in English, a question which transforms into a kind of accusation: *What's your name?* As the children continue to shout, the words become a mantra — punctuated, in their final appearance, with a censorious exclamation mark: *What's your name!* Unable to answer, the protagonist breaks into a sudden sprint. The novel ends.

Star-Spangled Banner also concludes with an image of its protagonist running, a symbol of commitment to giving up preassigned allegiances of ethnicity and passport in favour of the Japanese language. Whatever directives it may offer its authors is a matter of survival as much as integrity, for the life and the work.

Hideo himself possesses a rubbing taken from a stone monument erected during the construction of a synagogue in Kaifeng over 800 years ago. 'It reminds me that people have always translated themselves,' he has said.

'It's a reminder that there was a bilingual consciousness at the beginning of literary history.'

日本作家
リーベンズウオジア
ジャパニーズ・ライター
Japanese author (in three languages)

HIDEO'S WRITING ON China represents a kind of homecoming: he spent five years in Taiwan as a child, learning and speaking Chinese (a language he has retained), although it was in Japanese that he first became fluent. In writing about his trips to China in Japanese novels and essays, he is consciously disturbing centuries of literary tradition. Such journeys were traditionally documented in Chinese characters, the Japanese script proprietarily reserved for literature about Japan. Hideo's recent work aims to untether the Japanese language from the borders of its homeland in much the same way his earlier efforts called into question the largely ethnic notion of Japan's 'national literature'. He has thus become someone who, with the increased freedom of travel in China since the '90s, could *kenbun* (見聞) the country – see and hear it directly. It is how he has said he experienced Japanese: not as a student or observer but as a matter of direct engagement, a person encountering sights and sounds and yearning to join them. The limits and possibilities of transcribing such experiences are fundamental to the writer's life.

The China Hideo writes in Japanese disrupts and expands what we associate with the categories of 'Japanese' or 'Chinese', and their respective languages. In choosing not just Japanese, but a Japanese mediated by and mediating China, Hideo has, in global terms, chosen a kind of obscurity – what Cynthia Ozick called 'the forced muteness of living writers who work in minority languages, away from the klieg lights of the lingua franca'. In the context of Anglophone literary dominance, it amounts to a voluntary invisibility. What does not yet exist in English – or within the bounds of linguistic nativism – does not, in some sense, seem to exist at all.

Words connect us. They travel. Yet there is always the risk, in celebrating Hideo, that his presence might be used to solidify a cosmopolitan narrative in which the unitary nation-state is seen as ready and beneficent enough, finally, to admit difference via a White author. There are many writers, past and present, whose legacy Hideo writes within; writers who have long disrupted the essentialist borders of what is 'Japanese': Okinawan writers; Indigenous Ainu writers; Taiwanese and Korean authors writing in Japanese during the colonial era; postwar Korean authors in Japan (*zainichi*); even the Japanese war orphans – 中国残留邦人 – who, unable to return to Japan after the war, were brought up in China and whom Hideo writes of encountering in 我的中国 (*My China*).

Hideo has often talked about his border-crossing lineage in the context of the *Man'yōshū*, the oldest extant collection of Japanese poetry. He cites one poet in particular as evidence that Japanese literature has its foundations in migration: Yamanoue no Okura, a writer whom Hideo, like the scholar Susumu Nakanishi, believes heralded from the ancient Korean kingdom of Baekje, the place from which Chinese characters were first imported into Japan.

Writing at the very origin point of Japanese literature, border-crossing figures like Okura raise a question: who has the right to create literature in Japanese? Perhaps language itself is the diplomat, a form exceeding that which national borders, passports and race might reduce to a stable, essentialised unity of BLOOD = RACE = LANGUAGE = CULTURE. By expressing himself in a Japanese that incorporates English, Chinese and other languages, Hideo prods and pulls at the language's borders, enlarging the idea that things might exist within safely quarantined spaces either 'outside' (外部) or 'inside' (内部) Japan – and, by extension, its culture. For Hideo to express ideas not commonly considered 'Japanese' using the Japanese language poses both a challenge and an invitation. Language is culture, yes: but it is a culture which is kinetic and always capable of answering to the needs of those who engage with it. It exceeds – indeed, it cannot help exceeding – the borders of race and nationalism. Although Hideo continually reminds readers that he was not born with the Japanese language and thus cannot be at home in it in the way that a native speaker might be, the fact of his literary oeuvre and achievement speaks to the reality that he has become, in some radical way, a new kind of Japanese (language) writer, an advocate for what he calls 'the victory of Japanese'. Tellingly, this is not the victory of a people or of a race, of a culture or a nation-state, but, literally, the triumph of the Japanese language *as* language, and all of the global potential that might entail:

日本語の勝利
nihongo no shōri

When Hideo reflects, in the final lines of *Model Village*'s chapter 'Going Native', on the complicated legacy of Pearl S Buck, he writes, simply: 'It's not about race or background, it's about style.' Hideo's insistence that style matters, for ethnically non-Japanese writers as much as those who are ethnically Japanese, is a call many authors around the world, frequently consigned to the role of 'border-crossing' or of being 'diverse' – with the assumption that, somehow, the majority ethnicity is not also part of the diversity upon which its own 'normative' identity is established – may recognise. This insistence on style is visible and constant, not least every time a writer outside the received profile of a nation's literature is asked, once again, not about their style or their writing practice, but their personal history, their ethnicity.

After journeying with him these past fifteen years, I feel it is only fair – as the sun begins to fall, just outside my window, here on Wurundjeri country – to let Hideo have the final word. The 結語:

I carry two cultures. I exist between two languages. In the contemporary nation-state, to cut off either – and thus solve the problem of identity – would be a waste. This is not something the *bungakusha* seeks. Those of us who are *bungakusha*, who work with words, must always resist that contradiction. It is in this resistance that contemporary literature endures.

二つの文化を、両方、自分が持っている。二つの言語の狭間にいる。どちらかを切り落として、近代国家のアイデンティティの問題を解決するのは、もったいない。それは、文学者が求めるものではない。文学者たるものは、あるいは言葉を書くものは、その矛盾に一生耐えなければならない。耐えるのが、現代文学だ。

A previous contributor to *Griffith Review*, Declan Fry has written for *The Guardian, Astra Magazine, Australian Book Review, Overland* and *Westerly*, among others. His *Meanjin* essay 'Justice for Elijah or a Spiritual Dialogue with Ziggy Ramo, Dancing' received the 2021 Peter Blazey Fellowship. His poetry has been shortlisted for the Judith Wright Poetry Prize and selected for *The Best Australian Science Writing 2021*. In 2022 he was nominated for the Pascall Prize in criticism. His latest work appears in the anthology *Another Australia* (Affirm Press).

Same old new village

Jarni Blakkarly

SITTING WITH ONE leg folded across the other on a small red plastic stool outside his shop, the old man looks up as the shiny blue interstate bus pulls into the Gopeng terminal. He sips his oolong tea and turns his face back to the newspaper, the one he has been reading for the second time this morning. He sighs and folds the black-and-white photograph of a politician waving their finger in the air accompanied by small Chinese text that his eyes strain to see these days. The bus comes to Gopeng twice a day, once on its way to Kuala Lumpur and another on the way to the nearby regional city of Ipoh. There are many more buses of course, but they all run express. Each time the bus stops in Gopeng the sleepy town wakes up for a few minutes. Taxi drivers come out of the woodwork, mainly old Chinese men, but some Indians from the nearby village also show up. Families come to the bus stop to greet their relatives arriving from interstate.

No one is there to greet me this time.

I jump down the last step of the bus and grab my suitcase from the baggage compartment underneath. I look up, squinting. After I've spent a couple of hours in the bus's aircon watching the palm-oil plantations zoom by, the heat hits me hard. I look around also expecting my Ah Gong, my grandfather, to be there with his old yellow 1970s Datsun, the way he used to pick me up from the bus station every time I came. Instead there is just another old man, sitting on a red plastic stool outside a general store sipping

tea. He looks up at me and then looks down again. I suppose he's wondering if I'll come over and buy anything. No more than a handful, the other
passengers getting off the bus with me quickly make their way over to their
families or get in taxis and drive off. I wander over to the old man's store and
look through the drinks fridge and pick out a green can of Milo. When I was
little my uncles used to drive me into town here and go to the *mamak* stalls
that lined the highway to drink Milo ice. The sweet condensed milk was a
world away from what my mother back home would let me have usually,
but those were holidays and this was different. I pull out my wallet, and
the old man's face watches closely as I flick through the plastic Australian
notes until I reach the Malaysian ones. He grunts a thank you as I pay and
wander back out into the hot sun to try to find a taxi. One of the Indian taxi
drivers is leaning against the back of his car smoking a cigarette. Unlike the
other drivers who rushed when the passengers arrived he seems content to sit
back and wait for the customers to come to him. He is the only one there so
I approach him, despite knowing how much it would annoy my grandfather
to watch an Indian man pull into his driveway. If he was watching.

'Where to, boss?' he says to me in English.

I look up, embarrassed. Usually I pass as a local in the kampong, in the
village, but something about my appearance must have given me away, made
me stand out. Maybe it was my dithering. He drops his cigarette and stamps
it out with his sandals, his feet dark and cracked from the sun.

'Lawan Kuda Baru,' I say back to him. He nods his head and grabs
my suitcase, heaving it into the boot of the taxi. His car smells like ciga-
rettes and suddenly I miss smoking. The leather seats are hot and the air-con
doesn't work. I wind down the window as we pull out from Gopeng onto
the highway.

'Where are you from, boss?' he asks me again in English. This time
I reply in Malay. I tell him I'm from Australia – but that my father is from
here, grew up here, in the new village. He seems satisfied with the answer
and turns up the radio, which blasts out an old Bollywood tune I vaguely
recognise. With Shiva sitting on the dashboard, he turns off the highway
and into the quiet street of the village. We pass the soccer field where every
Monday night the town would gather for the night market, the stalls selling
fried food and sweet drinks, the counterfeit luxury brand-named clothing and
the toys that always enchanted me as a child. The pirated DVD stalls selling

all the latest movies that I could buy and impress my friends with back home, assuming Australians customs didn't search my bags and want to make a big hassle of it.

We pass the food market, and the dining hall, where each morning I would take my grandmother to eat yong tofu, hot noodle soup with fish-balls and stuffed tofu. She said she always wanted to eat, but in reality she wanted to show me off to her old friends. We would sit at the table and one by one her friends would come over and talk to her in Hakka, slap her on the back and laugh with her, and she would boast about me, her grandson from Australia, to them. 'Woah, from Australia?' another old lady would ask me in broken English. 'So handsome, you should meet my granddaughter,' another would say, 'Not married yet? No?' before bursting out laughing. My grandmother would laugh too in an infectious manner and her broad face would open up. These are the times I saw her at her happiest, and the times I try to remember now.

The taxi pulls into the old house. I pay the driver and thank him, fumbling through my bags for the keys that haven't been used in years. I leave my suitcase in the tiled room downstairs and take my shoes off. Slowly I begin to ascend the steep wooden staircase, up to the second floor. The heat is stifling and the air is still. I turn on the old ceiling fans but they do little to move the air. Sweat starts to drip down my forehead almost imme-diately. The room is exactly how I remember it: the wooden trophy cabinet with awards won by all the uncles and aunties at school and university, the photos on the wall of various members' wedding days and graduations, faded with time behind still polished glass. I find the photo of my dad sitting with my baby brother on his lap – the photo, from the early 1990s, looks strange on so many levels. It's the only photo I have seen with my mother and father together and it's the only photo I have seen where my father has hair.

The fan squeaks as it makes its laboured turns; I push open the sliding windows to let some of the cooler afternoon air in. The sky is grey now and it looks like the monsoon rains might be coming in again. The tables and chairs are packed away neatly in the corner, but I remember when they were lined up across the living room here. Those long afternoons of Chinese New Year when Ah Poh used to cook up the seafood and the aunties would help as the uncles and some of the older children sat around playing mah-jong, clackering the tiles together as five-sen coins changed hands. As the preparations for the feast continued, the other younger kids and I played with the small fireworks in the driveway, lighting the tails of the bumblebee firecrackers that would spin in circles before zipping off into the sky. These were joys so far beyond my everyday life in Australia.

The door downstairs opens and it snaps me from my memories. 'Hello? Are you there?' It's my uncle. I turn away from the room with its folded tables and chairs, the photo of my father on the wall, switch off the fan, close the windows and slowly head downstairs. I return the room to its state before I came – the stillness of a museum without visitors, a relic of an extended family that used to gather here, so many distant years ago.

MY UNCLE KICKSTARTS the scooter and I hop on the back silently. We don't talk much because his English is rubbish and my Chinese non-existent. We don't talk much because he knows why I'm here and there isn't much more to say. He kicks up the speed and the village falls away behind us, the imposing limestone mountains growing taller and closer. As kids, my cousins and I used to play a game by making the faces of animals out from the patterns of trees on the mountainside.

When we pull up to the cemetery, my uncle parks the scooter and goes to open the gate. The gravestones planted into the soil on the mountainside stretch on and on, the grass between them unkempt and overgrown. He leads the way and we trudge up the mountainside between the rows of stones. The spot we reach is hard to make out – the graves are identical to the hundreds of others, only slightly newer, the writing less faded by the weather and by time. I pull out the incense sticks from my bag and bend down to light them. Three sticks for my grandfather and three for my grandmother. Someone has placed a small pile of oranges next to the grave recently and they are still fresh. I bow down and shake the sticks in front of my face, the smoke drifting up into my nose. After placing the incense sticks down, I step back and look up at the sky. The rain drops slowly at first, but I know it will speed up. The air is thick and moist; you can smell the storm so strongly now. My uncle is clearly keen to go before the storm sets in properly, so I turn and bow one last time at the gravestones. The smoke from the incense turns in circles and mingles with the air, but I can't smell it now. All I can smell is the fresh incoming storm.

This is the moment I have been waiting so long for, but it feels somehow empty now. I had lit three incense sticks first for my grandfather when he passed away and then for my grandmother just months later, the smoke billowing out over the Lygon Street balcony in Brunswick. Those days when we couldn't leave our homes, let alone the country, to attend a funeral were tough. I watched the rituals on Zoom, the traditional Taoist ceremony conducted behind facemasks by my uncles and cousins. I got through those days and the isolation of distance by telling myself that at the first chance I would come here, I would catch the bus to Gopeng, drive down Lawan Kuda Baru and come to the cemetery at the back of the village and light incense at their graves. And now, now I was here, it all felt hollow, like a performance almost, a performance for no one but myself.

My uncle closes the gate and starts up the scooter again. I hop on the back and turn my head to look back up the hill. The rain is coming strongly now and it's hard to see their graves, but I know they are there. I'll come back soon, I say to myself, I know where the graves are now, know which ones to look for, I'll come back earlier in the morning before the afternoon rains set in. They might not care, but I'll be back – if only to say I'm sorry I couldn't be there.

A previous contributor to *Griffith Review*, Jarni Blakkarly is a Melbourne-based investigative journalist and writer of Malaysian heritage. He is the winner of a Young Walkley Award.

Will we dance when it's over?

Fortnite and the colourful end of empathy

Oliver Reeson

> *Birds, butterflies, and rats were gone.*
> *Grass and leaves had withered.*
> *Flowers had turned into memories.*
> *Streets and buildings were deserted.*
> *Everyone had gone to the moon.*
> Tomi Ungerer, *Nonstop*

I WAS LIVING alone in my grandma's vacant house in Thirroul, on the south coast of New South Wales, after a period of sickness. The idea was to write and rest, which I was doing, but I was also playing Fortnite a lot. Sometimes I watched old movies or called friends, but a lot of the time I just played Fortnite.

With co-operative shooter games, most people play with a headset on so they can talk to their teammates. I never used a headset because I was too shy to speak. I had come out as trans the year before, and just started testosterone, and for my physicality to be discernible, even obliquely through my voice, felt too fragile. No one knew anything tangible about me from my screen name alone and I didn't want my voice to reveal anything either. I'd play with strangers all over the world. Their voices would come through the television speaker and fill the loungeroom around me. Usually, they were teenage boys who shouted things like:

> *Oi, give us ya shotgun, cunt*
> *Where ya goin' fucker, they're over here*

From the careless way they spoke to me, I knew they either thought I was a boy or they didn't think about me as a person at all, and both these possibilities were appealing because they placed me in a sort of vacuum of perception. I could act, I could interact, I could exist, without having to be seen or heard. This was a relief for a time, but eventually I came to question the real-life limitations it reflected: how much could this lack of perception restore and protect and how much was it allowing to wither? How much was even the desire for it a result of what had already withered?

IN FORTNITE, ONE hundred players board a *party bus*, a blue school bus carried by a hot air balloon. The party bus cuts a straight line across the landscape below and, after working out where you'd like to descend, you choose when to eject yourself, freefalling quickly before gliding into an accurate landing. This landscape is brightly coloured and cartoonish – you are delivered to it by party bus, but it is post-apocalyptic: you might stumble upon cars abandoned on country roads, towns void of inhabitants, factories spilling pollution into lifeless streams. The objective is to eliminate every other player you encounter, to be the last player standing in this 'end of days' environment.

A 'death' in Fortnite spills no blood. It is a simulation within a simulation. When you die, a small drone comes and finds you on the map, breaks your body down into pixelated light. It is 'game over', nothing more.

In addition to the threat of other players, a storm is closing in. A clock counts down the time until the eye of the storm will begin to constrict. A vector line on the mini-map in the top right of the screen shows you how far until the next 'eye'. If you're outside that eye when the timer runs out, you have to outrun the encroaching wall of the storm, a fast-moving disaster, faster than your player can run. Like the in-game death, the storm is not natural or part of a weather system – there is no rain or wind. Rather, it is a harsh purple mist with an implied sentience and purpose: to harm you. When you find yourself caught outside its ever-narrowing eye, it seems to scramble your circuitry, depleting your shields and health quickly.

Sometimes 'loot boxes' are dropped from the air like humanitarian aid. Desperate players will compete to get to the loot quickest so they can eliminate the slower contenders. It doesn't always work. Sometimes, they'll be ambushed at these boxes by stronger players who have already looted enough.

Most eliminations happen in the first few minutes of the game when things are high energy and less tactical. People who don't find loot, or good-quality loot, soon enough are taken out quickly. As the initial one hundred players dropped onto the map are decimated, the game slows down and becomes more focused. The closing eye of the storm draws the dwindling numbers together, making it easier for the players to hunt each other.

If this sounds stressful or unsettling, it is important to know that in Fortnite there is also dancing. The more you play, the more outfits you can equip yourself with, the more emotive reactions or dance moves, often inspired by memes or viral internet phenomena, you can perform. At the time I was playing, one of the most popular Fortnite dance moves was flossing – the move in which you clench your fists and swing one arm behind and one arm in front of your waist as though you are flossing your body like a large tooth. These moves are usually used to gloat and showboat. They are often deployed after a good kill or the discovery of valuable loot. Even finding yourself alone in an area of the map, you might be compelled to dance, either as a private joke or to see if you can trigger something in the game, a mystery mission completed.

ONE AFTERNOON, LIVING in my grandma's house, alone in a small town where I didn't know anyone, I played a game of Fortnite. In this game I landed in what I thought was a quiet location, but when I opened the door to the first house I came across, I found it had already been ransacked. One of the tips on the game's loading screens suggests closing doors behind you as you progress. This means you avoid letting opponents know that you've been there before them, or that perhaps you are still there, waiting in the next room.

When I noticed the emptied-out rooms in this house I became, in real life, in my physical body, nervous. I hadn't found any weapons yet to defend myself. Footsteps in Fortnite, like the sound of foraging for materials, are loud. People hear you coming and search you out if you make too much noise. I stopped running, softened my grip on the control stick, and walked slowly through the rooms of the house, pausing at doors before opening them, looking for a quiet exit. But before I could leave, I found myself in a room with a player wearing a black motorcycle helmet and leather coveralls illuminated with neon stripes down the sides. They were waiting for me, gun raised.

With nothing left to do, about to be shot, I danced. I did the crab walk dance, and a funky beat sounded around me. The other player didn't shoot. Instead, they cycled weapons, dropped a gun on the ground and cycled quickly back to their original stance, gun raised. My dance animation had stopped. I waited again for the player to shoot me. Their character looked at the gun on the ground and then back at me. I looked at the gun on the ground. I looked back at them. I took a few steps forward. No reaction from them. I waited. They looked back at the gun. Another few steps. No movement. I picked up the gun. They shot me before I could do anything. Then they danced.

Another game: this time, loaded up, I entered the basement of a service station. In the far corner, behind some filing cabinets, another player was facing the wall. Sometimes the person behind the controls walks away from the game, returns to real life. I approached the idling player and, surprisingly, they turned around to face me. So, they were there.

When this other player turned around, they didn't shoot though they were holding a gun, and I found myself hesitating too. With the angle of the camera, and layers of animation, their face and shards of their weapon crowded the screen. I stepped back and thought I noticed that their body shifted, swivelled, just a little. Neither of us moved and, as before, it was difficult for me to work out what was happening in the world behind the avatar, what the player was thinking of doing. The storm had started closing around us, time was running out, but I couldn't bring myself to shoot them. The point felt too easy. But if I were to turn and leave, I would eventually see their screen name appear in the bottom-left corner of the screen, a feed of wins and losses – 'player_x was lost to the storm'. They would lose anyway. Another possibility: if I turned to leave, maybe that would be when they shot me. Maybe that was the game they were playing.

I shot them once in the body. Not enough to kill but enough to provoke the game out of them if their intention was to fight. They did nothing. I shot them again, in the head, and they disappeared from the game. I took the point. I picked up their weapons, which were loaded, and I felt shame. An eye icon in the corner of the game told me they were watching me play. I didn't deserve the point, and the eye icon reminded me that someone else knew it. When the eye disappeared, I felt shame again. I missed them. I found that I was no longer content to interact and not be seen – I wanted to talk to them. I wanted to know why they didn't try to beat me.

I still think about the feeling of shame and what is unplaceable about it. The shame has a depth or a source or a direction I can't quite work out. The more I think about it, the more I try to pin it down, the quicker it wriggles away. It's just a video game; someone stopped playing properly for a moment. The doorbell rang, their mum told them to take out the garbage, their partner wanted to talk. It must happen all the time. It is not cause for existential crisis. It is an inconsequential moment in an inconsequential game. And yet I was compelled to fill it with significance – to the extent that I wanted to atone for taking something from someone, even though I knew that person wouldn't miss it, had likely already started playing another game.

THIS DYNAMIC MIMICS, I think, the emotional effects of neoliberalism we are experiencing in real life: the simultaneous hypervigilance and extreme apathy. No matter how imminent the evidence of impending climate disaster, of political degradation, of the slow erosion of our ability to empathise with each other, no response – neither ignoring it (lazy nihilism), nor dissenting from it publicly (disingenuous and performative) – feels remotely adequate.

Just before I left my grandma's house, David Buckel self-immolated in Brooklyn's Prospect Park. In a suicide letter he left for police and sent to various news outlets, Buckel wrote, 'pollution ravages our planet, oozing inhabitability via air, soil, water and weather. Our present grows more desperate, our future needs more than what we've been doing.'

Buckel had previously been a successful human rights lawyer and defender of LGBTQIA rights. He won high-profile cases, including against the Sherriff's department in Nebraska for its failure to prevent the death of trans man Brandon Teena. But in the years before his death, Buckel had become more devoted to environmentalism. He led a community composting project in Brooklyn Botanical Garden. He left behind a partner, a daughter and two other co-parents.

Buckel's partner stated that he had often spoken about the Buddhist use of self-immolation as a form of communication. In his suicide letter, he also spoke of Tibetan monks' use of self-immolation to protest Chinese occupation: 'no other action can most meaningfully address the harm they see.'

Buckel's death has been described as characteristically methodical – a typed note, a perfectly scorched circle of earth suggesting a ring of soil was used to contain the fire, a polite apology 'for the mess'.

A friend said of his death: 'it's hard to know what David thought the outcome of his final act would be. He was a brilliant, smart guy and he sacrificed his life for this perceived public good. I don't condone it, I don't understand it. It just seems like a statement he wanted to make.'

This is now a world full of isolated statements, encouraging projections of the self: self-interest, self-care and self-esteem. Simply having individual interests is now the only thing that groups us as a collective. An extreme action taken by an individual does not affect us because we cannot recognise it as something we would do, are doing, are ready to do. We categorise it as someone else's business and move on.

Buckel's demonstration was reported on for a few weeks and then it slipped out of public dialogue. A year later, when I mentioned it in a book club at work, no one remembered it at all. When I went to explain it to them, I felt something like that shame again. I was uncomfortable having to tell such a gruesome story, and disappointed in myself because I was failing to describe it as anything more than extreme, as something that shouldn't be forgotten.

On New Year's Day 2022, protesting Victoria's vaccine mandate (the ultimately temporary requirement for people to present proof of vaccination to enter hospitality and entertainment venues), a man in the Melbourne suburb of Richmond set himself on fire in his car. Onlookers who came to his rescue described him as 'off his face, yelling about the mandate'. For a few days afterwards, he was reported as fighting for his life from injuries sustained in the blaze. Months later, when writing this essay, I went back to find out if he survived. There were no reported updates.

These protests, however you feel about their motivation, are equally desperate, extreme acts of communication. But their deaths may as well be Fortnite deaths, may as well be part of a simulation, for their surreal absence of effect. These men are simply lost to the storm, no longer spoken about. But why does the response to the loss of human life, and a reckoning with their intentions, feel just as detached as the reaction to the disappearance of a cartoonish avatar? The stakes in our real world have reached a point so high, so close to apocalypse, that they've disappeared entirely. We are gripped by a nihilism and unnerving sense of unreality, and so we don't receive the messages others are trying to send to us. At least, we don't respond to them. The excess of these protests does not disturb us because we no longer expect reality and the actions of others to make much sense. We are momentarily confused by it and then we move on. We are so individualistic, so incapable of seeing and hearing each other, that whatever outcomes we expect from others are limited to projections. In Fortnite, I was distanced from the motivations of other players by a gulf of simulation, and this led me to wonder, 'what game are they playing?' The answer is likely, to paraphrase Buckel's friend, that their actions were just a statement they wanted to make.

Fortnite's atmosphere of disaster is defined by memes. Despite the complete absence of hope, there is also silliness; there is absurd glee. There is the sense that no plea for attention is too big, because attention in this world is pointless. Everyone is watching but also no one is. In Fortnite, cruelty doesn't matter, not because it is condoned, but because the game's bright, post-apocalyptic battleground environment is so dire that for someone to dance after they kill you feels, in the scheme of things, small. Who cares, the world has ended, why not dance?

What Buckel did, what the man in Richmond did, is one way to respond to this predicament: sacrifice life in an attempt at forcing people to see, if not you, then at least the meaning of your loss. But it doesn't work. We are too expectant of disaster. That doesn't mean that dancing or laughing at the event of another's death is the appropriate reaction. But whether we are heading towards the end of the world, or whether things are bad but will eventually get better, the result of a neoliberal media landscape that thrives on spectacle and attention is an emotional numbing and a physical agitation and freneticism. Where can that energy go when opportunities for solidarity and connection are so often filtered through the same media platforms making us feel this way?

ONE DAY, WHILE receiving stock at work, I picked up Tomi Ungerer's picture book *Nonstop* and something about it made me put it aside. I eventually turned it over in my hands, flicked through it, read the blurb: 'Earth is devastated and empty. Everyone has escaped to the moon – except Vasco.' I decided to buy it for myself. Something about it reminded me of Fortnite, and the feeling of playing Fortnite alone in Thirroul.

In *Nonstop*, Vasco is a solitary figure moving through a desolate, abandoned world. Although much of the colour palette is grey or black or brown, highlighted features of its landscape are rendered in pinks and greens and blues – the colours of Fortnite's environment. Vasco has no purpose in this world and so he follows his shadow, cast by the moon he was abandoned for, and his shadow protects him, guiding him through the world and steering him away from disasters. These disasters also resemble those of Fortnite: sudden explosions, buildings toppling over, overturned and abandoned cars, the reverberations of fright embedded into a landscape.

Following his shadow, Vasco happens upon a green, bug-like creature called Nothing, who asks Vasco to deliver a letter to his wife. Vasco accepts the task but when he finds Nothing's wife, she is dying at an abandoned hospital. Vasco adopts her newborn baby, Poco, and pushes Poco in a pram through the collapsing world. They pass through frozen seas and molten deserts, abandoned, imposing factories and tanks chewing up trees, before eventually finding a house at the end of the world. The house is a giant cake and Vasco and Poco live there together for the rest of their days, peacefully. It is a happy ending and this could be saccharine in any other context. Vasco and Poco's lives continue beyond the final page – and here at the end of the world, this simplicity feels right because it is, in some way, silly. We can't seem to bring ourselves to believe our world will end, so if we are opening our imagination to consider its possibility, it is only natural that a big cake house would slip through, a beautiful place to wait for what comes next.

What Fortnite and *Nonstop* share, beyond a colour palette and empty world, is the almost absurd presence of play against the backdrop of apocalypse. When I picked up *Nonstop*, I was reminded not just of Fortnite the game, but rather that specific time playing it alone in my grandma's house. Which is to say, I am reminded of that moment of shame I felt but could never properly articulate. I return to it and understand that though we play with it in art, 'The End' is an overwhelming thought. It sometimes seems so very close, and yet impossible to talk about. It is impossible to write. And perhaps my shame is the feeling of failing to communicate – the realisation, all at once, that there is so much that needs to be said before it is too late, but there is so much that words will always fail to convey.

To play at the end of the world: to dance, or to live inside a cake, to paint blue and green and pink onto black, could signal a nihilistic giving up, making light of what isn't funny. But these works do teach me something about hope. There is a lot to learn from optimism, though it is easy to believe that cynicism is more serious and honest. The shared sensibility of Fortnite and *Nonstop* advocate against succumbing to pessimism. They suggest that a belief in innocence is necessary to start over. To think of a new world. To re-create a world that has failed. To play, even through sarcasm or dark or dry humour, is a commitment to the possibility of finding a way out of despair.

To dance at the end of the world is neither an admission of failure nor an act of cruelty. It is a wordless transition, a refusal to allow an end to be 'The End'. It suggests there is more to come without needing to find the words to explain what it will be.

Oliver Reeson is an essayist and screenwriter. In 2021, they were a recipient of the Wheeler Centre's Next Chapter Writing Scheme. Their work has appeared in publications including *Overland*, *Meanjin*, *Sydney Review of Books*, *Literary Hub* and *The Saturday Paper*, among others. In 2018, they co-created and wrote the SBS web series, *Homecoming Queens*.

Liam Ferney

Run River: An exercise

Not unusual, still plays a lame game
destined for detention. The drive-in
in dereliction, the town a weak creek
as industry pushes a slow move.
If you've got gossip, 'Please, Miss, dish.'
Glaze this ragged mess in a fire kiln.

Glaze this ragged mess in a fire kiln.
No time to revive my stale game,
I'll make this fade-away 3 if you just dish.
Your name bright lights at the drive-in
and the way this town's streets say do move,
metaphors lie but that's a dry creek.

Long summer deep rains mean a full creek,
glaze this ragged mess in a fire kiln.
It's best we activate plans for a hard move.
Little space in this town for dead game.
Steal a teal Corvette, hit the drive-in,
Find the tatty shop. They serve a fish dish.

Browse the sale, fair price for a rare dish
and a fantastical pic of fake creek.
Buy land cleared for the new drive-in.
Glaze this ragged mess in a fire kiln:
every poem stretches to a dumb game,
bye knight, checkmate in two, your move.

However you scam it, they stay one move
ahead of your quest for the rich dish,
a warden's watch keeps poachers from game

where they graze by the bank of a full creek.
Glaze this ragged mess in a fire kiln,
stake a renegade's camp at the drive-in.

One video to rent: *Dead End Drive-In.*
Long way to the one door make a slow move,
glaze this ragged mess in a fire kiln.
A terrible second date with Miss Dish
then the way out of this poem a weak creak,
last line, the last stanza of a lame game.

Encyclopaedia's kiln sets this dish.
Boredom's move a filthy sour creek.
Roll up, drive in to your dumb game.

Liam Ferney's most recent collection *Hot Take* was shortlisted for the Judith Wright Calanthe Award. His previous collection, *Content*, was shortlisted for the Prime Minister's Literary Award and the Judith Wright Calanthe Award. His other books include *Boom, Career* and *Popular Mechanics*.

Art, AI and figuring the future

On the coming of computer-generated creativity

Luke Buckmaster

THE 2015 SCIENCE-FICTION film *Chappie* was not very well reviewed, and nor is it particularly well remembered. Director Neill Blomkamp's Pinocchio-esque tale of a sentient robot who longs to be human has also not been 'rescued' from the dust-covered cupboards of zeitgeist by a fanbase adamant that critics didn't 'get it'. In the tradition of sci-fi productions ripe with interesting ideas but lacking in execution, however, the film evokes fascinating concepts that – less than a decade since its release – have become major talking points in the real world. One scene in particular represents something that, as history would demonstrate, was just around the corner: the creation of AI-generated art.

The chirpy titular character is a robot (voiced by Sharlto Copley) created by a British tech whiz, Dev Patel's Deon, who believes he's discovered how to build the 'world's first proper, full artificial intelligence'. Blomkamp, best-known for his Oscar-nominated apartheid analogy *District 9*, sets the story in another dystopian future, where policing has been outsourced to an army of robocops. But the sweet and naive Chappie – who takes seriously Deon's instruction to never misuse his power – is a lover not a fighter with a fondness for dabbling in art. The scene begins forty minutes in when the robot does something we have rarely seen any machine do in the history of pop-culture representations. He picks up a paint brush.

Sitting in front of an easel, Chappie dips his brush in blue paint and illustrates the scene in front of him – depicting the body of a rusty broken-down car situated in a crumbling warehouse. Instead of daubing at the canvas here and there, outlining different elements then filling out the tableau the way a human might, Chappie uses a method more befitting of a printer. He begins at the top of the canvas, painting lines left to right, then moves his way down: an approach that implies he knew the exact end result before he commenced.

The recent rise of machine-learning tools such as DALL-E and Midjourney has reinvigorated this sequence, filling it with additional meaning and drawing to the surface powerful ideas lingering in the subtext.

Is the picture Chappie drew art? This is a reflex question, typical in periods of shock and confusion, which has also been asked of DALL-E (named after Salvador Dalí and the Pixar character Wall-E) and Midjourney. Both launched in 2022, rocking the foundations of the art world through their ability to convert text-based prompts into vivid artistic images in roughly the time it takes to scratch your nose. It's an innovation that elicits fundamental discussions around what constitutes art and who gets to decide, the extent to which computers can be creative, the evolution of artist into architect and the inevitable moral panic such breakthroughs cause. Plus, the big question: where is all this heading?

IN THE MOST basic scenario, using DALL-E or Midjourney involves a user inputting a string of words – no matter how unusual or ridiculous – which are then translated into pictures. An example may be something like 'pink dog holds a red balloon while skateboarding'. The AI then spits out a bunch of illustrations the user chooses between or edits (the editing process being remarkably easy – as simple as writing 'remove the red balloon' or 'make the background yellow').

The algorithms powering these tools are informed by deep-learning systems that analyse a vast array of pre-existing data – in other words, pre-existing artwork. The technology involves, as Ahmed Elgammal wrote in *American Scientist*, programming algorithms 'not to follow a set of rules, but to "learn" a specific aesthetic by analysing thousands of images. The algorithm then tries to generate new images in adherence to the aesthetics it has learned.' It's not just pretty pictures AI can spit out. Other initiatives in this rapidly evolving space include tools that can replicate the style of any famous writer.

The headline of an article published on *The Conversation* in June 2022 summarised many discussions surrounding the aforementioned tools: 'Give this AI a few words of description and it produces a stunning image – but is it art?' Again, this is another version of that same reflex question – *is it art?* being an oldie but a goodie – with its habit of resolving itself after much debate and hand-wringing. While initiatives such as DALL-E and Midjourney in many respects are without precedent, previous examples of works that challenge the very concept of art help us draw a historical context. One famous instance comes from an unlikely place: the bathroom.

In April 1917, French artist Marcel Duchamp set out to challenge the underlying principles espoused by the recently launched Society of Independent Artists in New York. Full of avant-garde types dedicated to the idea of total artistic freedom, the society claimed it would accept any work of art submitted by a member. To challenge this view, Duchamp submitted a piece he called *Fountain* – a urinal rotated horizontally, signed with the mysterious pseudonym 'R. Mutt 1917'. When the organisation rejected it, the artist quit in protest. Nobody could have guessed the extraordinary impact *Fountain* would have, posing the basic question of who gets to decide what art is. The critic? The artist? The public?

The headline of a 2017 BBC article summed up the dunny's extraordinary impact: 'The urinal that changed how we think.' Acknowledging that Duchamp forced us to 'rethink how an aesthetic object should be approached' and encouraged us 'to put aside conventional biases about the nature of artistic craftsmanship', the article declared that for the first time 'the significance of a work of art has been detached utterly from the artist's role in making it'. The AI art movement escalates this prioritisation of ends over means. No longer is discussion about the work's being detached from the *artist's* role – because there is no artist. At least not in human terms, and certainly not in the conventional sense.

Detaching the art from the artist is a concept many struggle with, and for understandable reasons. Appreciation of art has historically been connected to the decisions of the artist; a large part of understanding the former requires interrogating the motives of the latter. Without a human artist, our interrogations require different kinds of analysis – for instance, scrutinising the structures of the platforms enabling artistic creations rather than the creations themselves.

THERE IS DEFINITELY craft in the writing and refining of prompts translated by DALL-E and Midjourney into impressive illustrations (just as there is craft – however invisible to the user – in the way developers build and refine the foundations on which subsequent creation processes take place). In the weeks and months following their recent launches, popular ways to add instructions include inputting words such as 'hyper-realistic', 'cinematic lighting' and 'macro photography'. Other terms drawn from photography and filmmaking can inform various elements, including (to name only a couple) focus and distance – such as 'long shot' and 'mid shot'. Ways to influence aesthetic style include referring to particular movements or artists: for instance 'Renaissance', 'noir' or 'in the style of Andy Warhol'.

On Midjourney, prompt-crafters can adjust the weighting of individual words, reducing or increasing the likelihood of the software's focusing on particular elements. Each word has an automatic weight of 'one', which can be changed by inputting two colons and a number. 'Kangaroo:: 1.5', for example, increases the likelihood of the animal's being the focus of the image. Conversely, 'Kangaroo:: 0.5' reduces the likelihood. It didn't take long for this process to be commercialised, creating a new market for selling pre-written prompts. *The Verge* described prompt-writers as 'AI whisperers' who have created 'a kind of meta-art market'.

It doesn't require much thinking to envision a minefield of copyright-related issues, not to mention the ethics of exploiting an artist's work without permission. To say this is a legally murky area is an understatement. Perhaps the best analogy is to describe it as the Wild West before any major shots have been fired (at the time of writing). A human artist might fear the legal consequences of snatching another person's IP but a computer does not. But is the computer itself being creative?

The sweet, art-loving Chappie certainly gives this impression, meticulously applying his blue paint to the canvas. The likes of DALL-E and Midjourney seem creative also, producing visually striking and sometimes (depending on the prompts) intensely surreal works. But can they *originate* anything, or act independently of the way they were programmed? A well-known answer in the negative is called the 'Lovelace objection'. Writing in 1843 about the potential power of a hugely influential, albeit never-finished analogue proto-computer called the 'Analytical Engine', mathematician Ada Lovelace – described by *The New Yorker* in 2013 as 'the first tech visionary' – made what became a widely accepted argument. A computer program 'has no pretensions to originate anything', she wrote, but rather 'it can do whatever we know how to order it to perform'.

Many years later, another highly influential mathematician, Alan Turing (born almost a century after Lovelace), took umbrage at Lovelace's objection and countered it by oversimplifying her argument into a question of whether computers can surprise us. They can indeed, he stated, and it's hard to argue otherwise. The short period between entering a prompt into DALL-E or Midjourney and waiting for the AI to render its drawings is a moment ripe with possibility; the mind buzzes with anticipation. Nobody can exactly predict the outcome. The question of whether or not computers can surprise us, however, is not the same as whether they're capable of creativity.

Lovelace was not a naysayer who rallied against the amazing potential of computers. Quite the opposite. While stating the aforementioned objection, she also put forward a prediction that would've been mind-boggling at the time. Lovelace saw potential in the Analytical Engine to go well beyond its initial purpose – namely to perform calculations – even to produce art. The machine might, she wrote, one day 'compose elaborate and scientific pieces of music of any degree of complexity or extent'. Implicit in this observation is an acknowledgement that the computer creator, or programmer, builds a foundation on which subsequent creation processes take place.

In the context of contemporary art, this emphasis on foundational elements feeds into a broader trend: a reduction of the autonomy of the creator and the repositioning of the artist into more of an architect-like role, designing enabling structures rather than precisely sculpted works. These sorts of structures are familiar to video game developers, who understand they can control certain elements – such as the design of virtual environments and mechanics of gameplay – but not the behaviour of the player. Creating video games involves anticipating likely behaviour and constructing an over-arching framework guiding participants towards particular outcomes. With AI-generating art, this guessing game applies aesthetically: to the surface as well as the substance of the work.

There is an eeriness in the anonymous way DALL-E and Midjourney create art. In *Chappie* the AI was given relatable features: a voice and human-oid body, including eyes and a mouth. Audiences empathise with the robot in a way that's similar to how they empathise with Pinocchio, comforted by the knowledge that this non-human entity *wants* to be like us. DALL-E and Midjourney offer no such comfort, seemingly conjuring art out of thin air, the end result of a complex set of unseen processes. The artist is nowhere and everywhere, like a ghost inside the machine. We see the rendering of images, but nothing that makes the design process more relatable.

Artists and graphic designers are understandably concerned about this technology, contemplating the ramifications of things that can achieve in seconds what may take them weeks, months or longer. Other artists such as filmmakers are yet to be confronted with the same existential fear (at least not at the time of writing – a necessary caveat due to the intimidating speed with which this process moves). But this will come. Predicting the future is impossible, though certain things are a given – such as the increased prevalence and capability of computer-created works. The early images of DALL-E and Midjourney blew many minds but, in an age of rapidly accelerating change, they will soon be seen as relics from a bygone era.

IN THE NARRATIVE world of *Chappie*, assuming the protagonist continues creating art, the same would probably apply to that early sketch. How long before Chappie begins drawing in a full spectrum of colours and styles? How long before he turns to creating movies, holograms or virtual reality productions? And what will these artistic experiences look like?

In a 2019 BBC interview discussing what films and other art may be like in twenty years, the influential immersive artist Chris Milk predicted that AI would deliver on-the-fly entertainment experiences tailored for individuals. Computers, he said, will be capable of 'crafting a story in real time that is just for you, that uniquely satisfies you and what your likes and dislikes are'. In this possible future, perhaps elements of DALL-E and Midjourney prompt writing will carry over. The viewer or user may, for instance, input their desired genre, style and duration ('a crime drama told in a noir style, with a romantic subplot') and let the computer do the rest.

If the concept of custom-made, computer-created movies feels far-out, imagine how Lovelace's idea of a machine creating art would have sounded in 1843, well before the first PC. One can already point to many tools, however primitive, that may one day be used to enable processes resulting in Milk's vision. In July 2022, for example, Apple researchers announced a neural network named GAUDI that can generate realistic indoor 3D sequences from text prompts. Write *go through a hallway* and the AI will render a realistic depiction of a hallway being navigated. The camera is virtual and, as with DALL-E and Midjourney, the algorithms informed through analysis of countless pieces of pre-existing data.

Conversations about such technologies inevitably lead to utopian and dystopian speculation. This was foretold in a scene in *Chappie* in which Deon pitches the possibility of an art-creating robot to the head of the corporation (played by Sigourney Weaver) employing him. The boss, unimpressed, shoots back: 'Do you realise you just came to the CEO of a publicly traded weapons corporation and pitched a robot that can write poems?' In this scene, Blomkamp presents a simple dichotomy: robots can be used for authoritarian purposes (policing the population) or for artistic expression. In other words, for good or ill.

Acknowledging and attempting to counter potential misuses of their tools, DALL-E developers have incorporated a range of 'safety mitigations'. These include prohibiting photorealistic renderings of real people's faces (to curb deepfakes) and of violent or pornographic images.

But these measures will not be enough to assuage fears of the technology being used for pernicious purposes. Such concerns are valid. It's important to acknowledge, however, that every kind of major emerging technology provokes moral panic. As time rolls forward, the initial panic tends to be sidelined, or forgotten in the haze of history. Few would be aware, for example, that the introduction of radio technology in the early decades of the twentieth century ignited great debate and many concerns – from the proliferation of misinformation and propaganda to questions about its moral content and even its potential to kill the art of conversation. Similarly, the invention of photography brought reactions both giddily utopian (Edgar Allan Poe proclaiming it 'the most important and perhaps the most extraordinary triumph of modern science') and apoplectic (JMW Turner predicting 'the end of art'). Even fewer would be aware that in as early a text as Plato's *Phaedrus*, Socrates speaks out against the invention of writing, arguing it would negatively affect human memory by introducing 'forgetfulness into the soul of those who learn it'.

The Greek philosopher wasn't wrong, though not many of us would advocate regressing to a society based wholly on the oral tradition. Not that we have a choice: the wheels of technology never stop turning. The same is true of artistic expression and the evolution of its enabling functions.

The most powerful question at the core of narratives such as *Chappie*, which attribute human behaviour and emotions to non-human entities, is not what these entities are capable of achieving but what they tell us about ourselves and the wider world. This is also true of the intersection of art and technology. In 1878, Eadweard Muybridge famously used high-speed stop-motion photography to capture a horse in motion, demonstrating that the animal has all four feet in the air during some parts of its stride. This basic fact might have sounded ridiculous before an artist (using a new technology) proved it. Imagine that Chappie went on to become a prolific artist – perhaps the first superstar 'cyberbard', to borrow terminology from Janet Murray's influential book *Hamlet on the Holodeck*. What key themes would emerge in his oeuvre? How would his work help us make sense of the universe? Just as movies are limited by the frame and novels by written language, art *about* humans has historically been limited to art *created* by humans. This is no longer true. No matter what the future of art looks like, it will be shared with computers.

Luke Buckmaster is the film critic for *The Guardian* Australia and a contributor to publications including Flicks.com.au and *NME*. He is the author of the George Miller biography *Miller and Max: George Miller and the Making of a Film Legend*.

The money shot

Pornography and the performance of pleasure

David Corlett and Maree Crabbe

Readers are advised that this essay contains sexually graphic content and descriptions of sexual violence.

AUSTRALIAN PORN PERFORMER Monica Mayhem is naked except for her black stilettos. She is having 'reverse cowgirl' sex so the camera can capture a full-frontal perspective. Behind her, Steve is sitting on the edge of the spa pool staring at Mayhem's back, a look of intense concentration on his face. His is not an easy job.

'Poke that thing right in you and keep eye contact with me the whole time 'cause that's kinda hot,' the photographer tells Mayhem.

Like Mayhem, the man she is having sex with is almost naked. He sports a thick chain necklace and a brown woollen beanie that he is not wearing to keep warm. The sun is shining in Los Angeles.

'Eyes to me and take it all the way to the balls,' the photographer says. 'That's it. Happy face. Nicely fucking done right there.'

The camera clicks, the lights flash.

'Move your hand from your clit so we see insertion,' says the photographer. 'Yeah, that's hot. Look at me from there.' Click. Flash. Click. Flash.

Mayhem looks down the lens. Steve is firm inside her. 'Nicely fucking done,' the photographer encourages. 'Let's have you blow him. Please.' He's polite.

She squats in front of Steve and starts fellating him. 'Cock in the mouth, eyes to me. And that right hand can conveniently cup the balls. Nice.'

The photographer takes his shots. 'Regular cowgirl, please.'

But the man wearing the beanie is struggling. Mayhem puts saliva on his softening penis and starts to masturbate it. The photographer, without irony or insight, tells her to ride it hard. But there's not much that's hard at the moment, so there's no riding.

Mayhem fellates Steve again. He leans back on the spa pool. He needs to get this thing working. 'Oh yeah, that feels good,' he says.

Good, but not sustaining. And Mayhem is out of options: 'There's not much I can do here,' she tells the photographer.

'I'm sorry, sweetheart,' he responds as she tries to get Steve's flaccid penis inside her. 'Open your eyes.' Click. Flash. 'There we go.'

Finally, it's starting to work. Steve is thrusting, now from behind.

'Nicely done,' the photographer encourages. 'Open up that left arse. I want to see that cock there.' Click. Flash.

But Steve's gone flaccid again. He starts to masturbate himself.

'Not much fun, the real sex, huh,' the photographer observes. They laugh. 'Kinda boring.'

Mayhem lays back on the concrete spa wall, legs apart, her stilettos in the air. She is touching herself. Her man stands above her, masturbating. He starts to firm up and gets himself into her. He's thrusting again. Click. Flash. Click. Flash.

'Nice. There we go. Tip of the cock,' the photographer says. 'Massive load right there, Monica. Big, big fucking orgasm. Sir, hold your cock in your right hand. Nicely done.' He puts his camera down.

'We give it loads of fun,' he says, picking up a container of moisturiser. He walks over to Mayhem and squirts some of its contents onto her stomach and chest before going back to his camera. 'Can you turn slightly sideways so I see nut all over you? You hold the spent penis and go "Wow! Thanks Mister."' Click. Click. 'Nicely done.'

PORNOGRAPHY PURPORTS TO be real. Monica Mayhem and her beanie-clad colleague are real people with real bodies, real 'cocks' and real 'clits' having real sex.

At the same time, most of us, including young people who are only beginning their sexual exploration, realise that porn is also fake. Young people know, for example, that the pizza delivery guy isn't going to deliver an orgasm with their capricciosa and that you don't give the police officer a blow job so he'll drop the speeding ticket. They also know that while the bodies in porn are real, they're exaggerated: fake breasts, big buttocks, huge penises, massive pecks.

But this knowledge doesn't make young people – or anyone – immune from porn's influence.

The leaders of the pornography industry know their product is fake, too – and their concern is not just the occasional squirt of moisturiser. In fact, even as they're fundamentally shaping the sexual world we live in, they're concerned that the whole edifice they've constructed – built around their portrayal of desire and pleasure – is at risk of collapse.

According to legendary pornography producer John Stagliano, 'This is what we talk about all the time. How do you get real sex? How do you get people to be real in front of the camera instead of being fake?'

The solution, according to Stagliano, is a genre he's credited with creating in the 1990s known as 'gonzo'. Gonzo pornography takes its name from gonzo journalism, which was popularised by, among others, Hunter S Thompson. Think *Fear and Loathing in Las Vegas*. Thompson does not just report. He is a participant, experiencing, indeed shaping, the narrative.

Similarly, according to Stagliano's conception, in gonzo porn you are watching him 'shape the eroticism'. He's holding the camera; the images are shot from his perspective. And this becomes the viewer's perspective. You see the director's hand come out from behind the camera to touch the woman. You hear his voice. According to Stagliano, 'The great thing about gonzo porn is that if [the girl] starts acting and being fake you can tweak what she's doing and get a real response out of her and then move the scene towards naturalness... And that's really the single most important thing that gonzo has brought to the world, I think, which is reality.'

Gonzo now dominates mainstream pornography, and it's led the industry into rougher and harder sex. Stagliano says this is what consumers want: 'We want to see people pushing themselves and doing something that's beyond the normal. That's what's visually interesting. That's why rough sex and strong sex works because it's incredible to look at. As human beings we want to see stuff like that.'

But this shift isn't only consumer-led. In a crowded market, content producers need to differentiate themselves. One way of doing this is to produce more extreme material – and this isn't just about supply and demand.

It's also ideological. According to Stagliano, 'Every day in the porn industry we're exploring our art form.' His art form, he reckons, is about creativity and reality. He says that the men in the porn industry have learnt 'to control the progression of the sensuality'. By this, Stagliano means that they 'test' the woman and 'push her a little bit harder in terms of doing a little bit stronger sex and if she likes it he'll go further and the scene becomes something rough or something interesting or real. And it's real because you can't fake pushing your limits sexually.'

Part of the issue here is that porn pretends to be about sex. To be sure, sex is central to it. But pornography is about money. As academic Jennifer A Johnson argues, 'At its core, it is a commercial artefact. It is an economic product which is produced, distributed and marketed by a corporate entity that resides at the centre of the modern digital economy.'

THE RISE OF the internet helped make Stagliano's 'art form' more accessible. Porn sites account for three of the top fourteen most-viewed websites. They are more popular than Amazon, Netflix and TikTok. Pornhub reported forty-two billion visits in a single year (2019) and that 83 per cent of all its traffic came from mobile devices. You don't have to work hard to find porn these days.

Much of the content on these sites is what Stagliano euphemistically calls 'strong sex'. A range of studies has found high levels of aggression in the most popular porn: gagging, choking, spanking, hair-pulling. And the aggression in porn is almost always directed towards women. Usually, women are shown enjoying – or at least not minding – the aggression. But there's also content in which lack of consent is a key part of the narrative – where, for example, a hidden camera, or someone being forced, asleep or too drunk to consent is the selling point. It's not always clear whether these are consensual enactments of non-consensual scenarios or simply (and disturbingly) recordings of sexual assaults.

Porn's murky ethical territory doesn't end there. There's also the recent proliferation of incest-themed or so-called 'family' porn, positioned prominently on the homepages of the most frequented porn sites and found in 46 per cent of the most popular porn videos.

For many young people from diverse backgrounds and contexts, this kind of porn – the mainstream variety – has become foundational to their sexual education and development. On average, young men see porn three years before their first sexual experience with another human being and young women see it two years before theirs. They may have watched – and masturbated to – many hundreds of scenes of internet pornography before they've kissed or even touched the skin of an intimate partner. They've described to us how this multi-billion-dollar global industry is shaping their sexual experiences and the impact that violent mainstream pornography is having on their sexual imaginations and expectations. This is their reality.

ACCORDING TO JAKE, the first time he had sex, 'because I'd watched so much porn, I thought all chicks dig this, all chicks want this done to them all chicks want it up here all chicks love it there, so I tried all this stuff and yeah it turned out bad.'

Eighteen-year-old Georgie from Melbourne says that young women watch porn to find out how to please their boyfriends. This leads to a 'whole whirlwind of imitation and expectation'. She says that young women think, 'Okay well if that makes him happy, if that turns him on, then I have to do that. I have to look like that, I have to talk like that.'

Ben is a young gay man who says that his sexuality was 'never acknowledged' in conversations or education about sexuality and relationships at school or more broadly. 'The curriculum that we learnt was extremely heteronormative,' he says. This void in knowledge and understanding was filled by pornography, providing a longed-for visibility of diverse sexualities. But as Ben explains: 'You're also taking a lot of the problematic elements of porn into that process of development. There's a lot of dominance and submission, I think, in popular gay porn. So you still have, not a man and a woman, but kind of elements of masculine dominance and feminine submissiveness as an ideal. You have your fem guys and then there's that toxic kind of alpha dominant masculinity that's presented in and idolised in gay porn.'

Tess says that she started watching similarly gendered and aggressive pornography with her teen boyfriend. 'The kinds of porn that my partner and I were watching at his request involved a lot of gendered violence. It was a lot of dominance from the man and submission from the woman or women,' she says. Initially, because they were 'new to sex', both she and her boyfriend 'saw it as a learning tool. We both thought that it was just a way to find some new fun sex positions or to find out how to act.' And indeed, they were learning how to act. 'It parlayed into him slapping me or pushing me really aggressively against walls with a hand on my throat,' Tess reflects. 'I think the way porn interacted with that was that it gave him an outlet to be physically abusive with me that wasn't just hitting your girlfriend. I definitely picked up the idea that I should be submissive to that.'

We can track porn's influence through an increase in particular sexual practices. For more than a decade now, young people have told us that practices such as heterosexual anal sex, 'deep throating' (where, during fellatio, the penis is put into the throat) and ejaculation on faces and bodies have become 'normal'. Often, young women report that they don't like or want these things. For example, in Melbourne, Sara told us, 'Anal, that's a big thing. Like you're going at it and they try to slip it in the other hole. They don't ask because how do you ask? They just do it and hope that she'll take it.'

More recently, young people have spoken about the addition of strangulation, or 'sexual choking', to the list of porn-inspired practices. 'There has been a normalisation of pushing for sort of extremities in different sex acts,' says Juliet, who lives in Sydney. 'And strangulation, choking, has definitely become normalised.'

Juliet's assertion is consistent with research from the United States. According to results from a large 2020 survey, 58 per cent of women, 26 per cent of men and nearly half of transgender and gender non-binary people have been choked during sex. Over a quarter of women, nearly 7 per cent of men and about 22 per cent of transgender and gender non-binary people had been choked during their most recent sexual experience.

What's being emulated isn't just pornography's sex, but its power dynamics. The Australian young people we've interviewed understand that it's often men who choke women in heterosexual contexts and that, as Georgie puts it, 'It's meant to be an act of dominance. And it's meant to make the person who is choking feel powerful and feel like they have power over the person that is being choked.'

Similarly, Susie says that the appeal of sexual strangulation is 'dominance. The subjugation of women. And if you find that sexually appealing, it's probably the ultimate form of submission. To have someone's life literally in your hands.'

AT A DEEPER level, pornography challenges our very constructions of what is 'real'. It complicates questions about how we understand 'real' consent, for example. There may not be anyone forcing young people to follow the pornographic script. But with so much influence on young people's sexual imaginations, pornography is setting the cultural context within which they *do* sex and gender. Within this context, what might appear to be a smorgasbord of choices may actually be a series of predetermined options curated by the pornography industry.

Take the normalisation of sexual strangulation. While young people can read the messages of power in strangulation, they can't escape it as part of the sexual script they have inherited.

So, does engaging in sexual strangulation reflect authentic choice? Or are people really just playing the gendered roles to which they are assigned by the social and sexual script? And if they are performing their socially constructed role, can their consent be understood to be full and free – to be real? How do we understand the tension between individual agency and the power of sociocultural influences such as porn? What is 'reality' and what is 'performance' in this context?

Such questions about what is 'real' also apply to pleasure. Tess, who watched and then enacted violent porn with her teenage boyfriend, says: 'I genuinely think I convinced myself that I liked it [sexual strangulation] and I have taken that with me from sixteen onwards. And I know exactly where I got that from and that was porn.'

Nearly a decade after becoming sexually active, Tess reflects on her sexual journey. 'It was just like I downloaded this information and became like a rough sex robot and thought that was the output that I had to be doing all the time,' she says. Now she finds herself asking, 'Am I enjoying this or have I convinced myself that I should be enjoying this?'

This points to the bigger issue of what reality actually is. What is real pleasure? And what is real consent? How do we know what we authentically like and want?

'Quite recently I've started dissecting what that really means,' Tess says. 'It's probably in pursuit of validation and, because that feels so good, being slapped or strangled during sex is something that you not only grin and bear, but really embrace and pretend to enjoy.'

This raises questions about how we might assess the value of the influences shaping our choices – and the possibility of making choices about what we *allow* to influence us, as individuals and as a society. What influences should we trust? Which should we give more weight? Because, to be sure, some influences are better than others.

Taking their cues from pornography and from other online influencers, young people engage in sexual strangulation on the assumption that it is safe. In fact, strangulation, according to medical experts, cannot be practised safely. Dr Jane Van Diemen is a forensic medical expert at the Canberra Hospital in the ACT who has studied strangulation for fifteen years and advises Australian courts. She is very familiar with the wide spectrum of damage that strangulation can cause – and with how complex variables make the timing of such damage impossible to predict. 'Even knowing as much as I do about strangulation,' she says, 'I cannot predict the point at which strangulation is going to end up in irreversible brain damage and death.'

THERE ARE NO easy solutions. Addressing pornography's influence on the contemporary sexual world will require a range of strategic interventions. This includes providing young people with not only accurate, positive information about sexual safety, consent, pleasure and relationships, but also education addressing pornography's misinformation on these issues and more. Indeed, good sex education cannot avoid confronting pornography. As Tess reflects, 'I don't think you can have a conversation about how dangerous strangulation is without having a conversation about how prevalent it is in porn. I don't think that you can just say to young kids in high school, "Strangulation is not something that you should be doing during sex," because they're going to log on to Pornhub that night and see it in almost every porn video they watch and be really confused by that.'

Being critical of porn is challenging in a cultural environment in which consumption is normalised and any critique interpreted as prudishness. Susie is familiar with this dilemma. She considers herself to be 'sex positive'. But she observes a sort of 'militant sex positivity' that asserts that 'everything is fine as long as it's in a sexual context. Racism is fine as long as it's in a sexual context. It's fine to use the t-slur for a transgender person in a porn video, because it's porn and people are getting off on it.'

Susie's observation takes us into the world of politics and power. All media depictions are representations of power. They portray a perspective. They convey a set of assumptions. Critical media literacy involves asking, 'Whose story is being told and why? Whose interests are being served?' The answers to such questions may not be immediately obvious, especially if the cultural assumptions implied in a particular narrative are so imbued in us that they seem invisible – which itself underscores the critical importance of such education.

Some argue that pornography is a mirror of society's attitudes and behaviours; it reflects but does not shape. Certainly, pornography echoes existing values. But it also promotes ways of seeing and being in the world. So where we choose to stand in relation to pornography is, in the end, a political decision. Because reality is constructed – by us and by others. We are at the same time formed by our contexts and we are actors in our own lives. This means that whether pornography is 'fake' or 'real' is, in a way, beside the point. The real issue is about the sort of society we want to create and re-create; the type of world we want to live in. Where we stand on contemporary mainstream pornography is a question of the place we are prepared to grant media – from a multi-billion dollar global industry – that eroticises the stereotypes that reinforce and promote violence against women, racism, homophobia and transphobia. The answer has real implications.

David Corlett is a writer and filmmaker. He is co-producer/co-director of *Love and Sex in an Age of Pornography* and *The Porn Factor* and producer of *Return to Bosnia*. He has written two books, *Stormy Weather: The Challenge of Climate Change and Displacement* (UNSW Press, 2007) and *Following Them Home: The Fate of the Returned Asylum Seekers* (Black Inc., 2005). He was host of the multi-award-winning series *Go Back To Where You Came From*, and has reported for SBS *Dateline*.

Maree Crabbe is an educator, writer, researcher and filmmaker and director of the violence prevention initiative, *It's time we talked*. She is the author of *In The Picture* and co-producer/co-director of *Love and Sex in an Age of Pornography* and *The Porn Factor*.

Outside, Mona Lisa

Peak bagging, tourism and authentic engagement

Ben Walter

THE GREEN HUMP of Mount Foster is a gap on my map.

Right now, I'm filling in gaps by climbing mountains like this. I know that sounds a little detached, maybe even cold, but over the past eight years I've been busy with three young children, so walks have been rare. The gaps in my map have been staring at me. Perhaps travellers stuck at home through the pandemic have felt something like this – the call of the named unknown.

I have low expectations for Mount Foster. Many years ago, a friend held an exhibition he called *The Forgotten Corner*. Like plenty of other Tasmanian photographers, he was pursuing images of the wilderness, but these were images with a difference. He recognised that central, western and southern regions dominated the island's landscape photography. All those deep green rainforests, golden buttongrass plains, soaring cliffs, jagged peaks and black rivers – the largely uninhabited areas that are now covered, for the most part, by the Tasmanian Wilderness World Heritage Area.

The north-east corner of Tasmania is different. It's drier, and there are huge forestry operations that can give it a bad name – views from mountains can be brimming with plantations that swamp the valleys with landfill trees. But there are also superb beaches and coastlines. There are distinct summits, such as Mount Victoria and Mount Maurice, as well as the Ben Lomond plateau with its massive boulder fields and dolerite cliffs, by far the most extended stretch of country above 1,500 metres in the state. My friend wanted to capture something of these neglected virtues in his exhibition.

I've enjoyed walking in these areas, but I also knew that many of the smaller mountains tended to be predictable green lumps with scraggly bush, a little rock scree and no view. Climbing mountains has never been a box-ticking exercise for me, but in this case it felt as close as I was ever going to come to it.

A gap in my map. Somewhere to climb, before moving on to the next mountain.

MY MAIN MEMORY of visiting the Louvre is of not being able to see the Mona Lisa. This was more than ten years ago, after months of backpacking around Europe with my wife, months that became suffused with a sense of ennui. I was weary with moving from place to place for the sole purpose of viewing, of continuing to see and yet feeling disconnected from everything around me. This gave me such a persuasive sense of accumulating unsettledness that I've barely travelled since.

My discomfort was exemplified by wandering into the room where the Mona Lisa is displayed. Because it's so hard to see. The bustling crowds could be at a football game; at times, they could be the players, shouldering each other out of the way. I'm sure I remember signs requesting no photography; if so, they were passionately ignored. I don't hold any delusion that my wife and I were exceptional, *real* visitors who were impeded by all the 'tourists', just that an authentic engagement with the artwork seemed impossible for any of us. We stood at the edge of the crowd, saw bits of the painting and wandered off to the next room.

What would it have meant for us to see the Mona Lisa properly? Could we have had an authentic experience with the painting, even if we were standing in the room by ourselves? It's likely unwise of me to use a word like 'authenticity' in this essay, saddled as it is with so much historical and philosophical baggage, but perhaps it still has some usefulness. The idea of attempting to experience a thing as it is, rather than through the lens of artificial or (perhaps more often) simplistic narratives and representations. This notion has its own issues, of course, but I feel it speaks to something we can recognise in our experience – that time we might have stopped and stared at a painting, taking time to consider and feel its effects, instead of offering a quick glance of recognition to a famous image reproduced on millions of greeting cards.

The old story of the simulacrum overtaking reality – the idea that in engaging with certain cultural objects, we're not necessarily experiencing inauthentic things, but we may as well be – is at least a little convincing. Constant reproductions have set the terms for our relationship. Was the biggest impediment to experiencing the artwork the bustle in that room, or the one in my mind?

And what about the natural world? How do these questions and contrasts apply to my habit of chasing mountains?

IN TASMANIA, THERE are a few sacrificial regions that attract significant numbers of tourists – places like Cradle Mountain or Freycinet Peninsula on the east coast. The car parks are big and there are plenty of shoes you'd struggle to call sensible. Beyond these regions, the landscape is relatively unknown to visitors. In terms of summits, it's possible you've come across Frenchmans Cap and Federation Peak, two destination mountains for walkers. You probably know kunanyi/Mount Wellington, the mass that swells above Hobart, but you'd be doing well to name any other Tasmanian high places.

Partly, that's by design. The Parks and Wildlife Service (PWS) maintains a classification strategy for Tasmanian tracks that specifies approaches to management and track development. The rankings range from 'W1', a wheelchair-standard nature trail, all the way to 'Routes', which are often trackless, but the way people tend to go.

You'd be forgiven for thinking this is just a humdrum government system, but there's a fascinating intersection between the fifth and sixth ratings: T3 and T4. Tracks categorised as T3 include a selection of the more difficult mountains around the state, the challenging ones that Tasmanians, for the most part, set themselves to climb. They're in guidebooks. They exist as dotted lines on maps.

Tracks in the T4 category are a lot more interesting. Publicising them is actively discouraged. The guidelines state that they should '[not be] included on maps except for PWS management purposes. Authors [are] encouraged to keep route descriptions vague.'

That's kind of astonishing. Where bushwalking is concerned, Tasmanian maps are not an authentic picture of the landscape. They're fine if you want to stick to well-known trails, but if the track has been assigned a T4 rating it won't be on the map. Sometimes that's because the route is so rough it would be misleading to mark it as a track, but sometimes it's that for a range of management and environmental purposes, the PWS just doesn't want many walkers going there. This totally upsets the way we think about modern mapping; it's more in tune with how we deal with military installations, a contemporary approach to 'here be dragons'.

I don't necessarily have a problem with this system. The PWS doesn't have the resources to manage all these tracks as they might, and in one sense there *are* dragons in many of these areas; if you need a detailed guidebook and perfect map to get to some of these peaks, you probably shouldn't be going – these tools aren't going to help you enough and might provide just the right amount of knowledge to get you into serious trouble. Environmentally, there are sensitive habitats that would be degraded by too many visitors. On the other hand, there are safety considerations. Some people are determined to get to a mountain, and if they're going to do that, they may as well walk along the rough track that is just waiting there. It's going to be easier and will likely cause less damage to habitat.

These debates aside, the system does prompt me to consider how our experiences with nature are framed, determined and contextualised, just as cultural objects are: the way natural experiences are packaged up for us and made permissible or desirable, from obscure national park guidelines through to tourist marketing. In a recent issue of *Ecotone*, Joanna Brichetto writes of preparing for a guided bushwalk, being late and missing the tour, then speeding along muddy roads, desperately failing to catch up with the group. She finally accepts that it's not going to happen, and recognises that she can embrace the forest, all on her own.

> [I]t's the wrong time of year for hunters…so you do it: you get out and get wet in a ruined glade in the moment, this moment, the only one you have, and hear field sparrows, hear a peewee, hear wind in the cedars, and smell more honeysuckle. You are not expected on that hike. You are not expected anywhere. You remember you are lucky to be alive. The rain stops. You like this, too.

Is this a more authentic experience – from a Western perspective at any rate? One that seeks to explore and understand the natural world for what it is and something of our part in it, that lets it imprint on our senses and feelings, that recognises the tiny details and the bigger picture? There are benefits to packaged experiences – efficiencies for buyers and sellers – but do they make for an inauthentic relationship to nature? Or can the wonders of the world outside transcend these limitations?

The latest craze in Hobart is travelling to the Disappearing Tarn, a small lake that forms on the southern slopes of kunanyi/Mount Wellington after significant rainfall, before draining quickly. Like everything else, its growing visibility as a popular destination has made it more popular, underlining narratives about important places we should be visiting and enjoying – there, with the crowds milling around us, queueing for Instagram shots.

Certainly, these experiences feel mediated; travellers are going there to experience a sense of discovery that is predetermined. It's a little like reading genre fiction: there's definite pleasure in expectations fulfilled, in seeing the same image in the real world that was pictured in the brochure. We might critique things for being predictable, when at the same time we find them comfortable and delightful.

Perhaps we'll even enjoy natural regions that have been widely advertised to tourists more than those that haven't. In *Useful Delusions*, the science writer Shankar Vedantam found himself confounded by a study demonstrating that people experienced more pleasure drinking wine from a $90 bottle than when the same wine was poured from a $10 one.

> The experiment raises a disturbing question for me…[w]e might think that connoisseurs who pay premium prices for wines are suckers, but if these people derive more pleasure because they paid more, are they being cheated – or getting their money's worth?

The dampening effects of crowds notwithstanding, perhaps the same is true of tourist destinations – that we get *more* pleasure and meaning from these experiences because we're expecting to. It aligns with the stories we've been told and those we keep telling ourselves. At Cradle Mountain, there's a small station set up where photographers can take exactly the same photo as everyone else.

But, of course, it's not *exactly* the same. The weather changes, the colours shift, the vegetation will be in a different state at certain times of the year. The natural world isn't so easily packaged – it's not a McDonald's burger, and we don't know exactly what we're going to get. Perhaps there's room for awe, even in the context of expectations met. Realities can burst visitors from the simulacrum – a photograph of a mountain can't loom like the real thing (though I find it can provoke the same sick fear when looking over a cliff edge). We can feel disappointed when the weather closes in and a whiteout blocks the view we were expecting, but we can also find delight in the details of birds, plants and stones that are like nothing we've ever seen before, that broaden our wonder at the natural world singing for itself.

THE WALK TO Mount Foster starts on the edge of a highway. It's a beautiful morning for walking – cool, but not cold, and completely still. We climb a fence and make our way along the edge of a paddock, then the trees start to rise and we find ourselves stomping along a forward boundary that seems like nothing so much as a four-wheel drive track. It's a useful route, steadily gaining ground while losing little, following ridges through the loose bush, all the while working towards the green lump we can see in the distance. At a certain point the boundary gives up on getting us closer and begins to contour around the mountain. We go off track, choosing the best way through the untucked vegetation. For a while it gets thicker, so we crash through the slicing, chest-high scrub, before picking our way through a cliff line to the top of the ridge. The top is scrubby too. Nothing too difficult, just the prickly arms of cheeseberries and pink mountain berries; still, we keep to the edge, following the top of the cliff where the ground is rockier and the wind keeps the growth constrained. Soon we're close to the summit. We head away from the escarpment and find the highest rocks.

We have reached the top of a predictable green mound in the north-east.

There are scraggly bushes and patches of scree.

There's no view to speak of.

But I'm having a glorious time.

WHY DID I go to Mount Foster in the first place?

When I started writing this essay, I was considering peak bagging, the hobby of climbing an extensive catalogue of mountains, one by one. I felt surprised by a paradox – peak bagging, like twitching, gets a bad rap at times for being little more than working through a list. But what does that actually mean for the experiences it prompts? Can it provoke a deeper engagement with nature in the context of more detached expectations?

I had gone to Mount Foster with a set of vague assumptions about what it would be like – and these were largely met. And yet: *they weren't met at all.* In one sense, the landscape was exactly the kind of terrain I was expecting to find, but each detail filled out these narrow bands of predictability. The shape of the hills, the encounters with every wombat, rock and tree. What's more, I'd conflated expectations of the landscape with expectations of how I'd *feel* about the landscape. The forgotten corner of the north-east might not always prompt spectacular awe, but there's still pleasure in encountering the landscape on its own terms. An enjoyable day outside isn't necessarily the same thing as an authentic experience of the natural world; we might value the experience for many reasons that take little note of where we are. The exercise, the company, the fact of being outside as opposed to stuck at a desk. But there's likely to be strong overlap, and I find it hard to argue that my experience on the mountain was inauthentic. If it wasn't, then I'm not sure what an 'authentic' experience for someone of my cultural background would even mean. A day out in the natural world, observing, experiencing and enjoying.

The pleasure of a packaged expectation met still seems likely to contain something of this authenticity. Even if we're reading landscapes through simulacra, it's hard to argue that the whole experience is fake. Perhaps, rather than thinking of these kinds of encounters in terms of a binary – authentic and inauthentic – we should think of them as existing on a spectrum: where we end up is governed by our knowledge of the landscape, our connections to it and their significance, and our experiences in the moment. I'd guess a First Nations walker with intimate, far-reaching connections to these regions would likely have a more authentic experience than me, but that doesn't necessarily render mine inauthentic, just more limited in its abilities to understand the manifold realities of the world outside.

IT'S NOT THAT prior knowledge is necessarily a problem; indeed, it can deepen our experience. I've always remembered Ryszard Kapuściński's reflections in *Travels with Herodotus*:

> I noticed…the relationship between naming and being, because I realized upon my return to the hotel that in town I had seen only that which I was able to name: for example, I remembered the acacia tree, but not the tree standing next to it... I understood, in short,

that the more words I knew, the richer, fuller, and more variegated would be the world that opened before me.

I can see how human categories could get in the way of experiencing something on its own terms, but I feel we're more likely to be troubled by simplistic expectations than deep knowledge. Still, perhaps it's sometimes useful to travel to regions about which we know little to escape the burden of superficial branding and the filter of our assumptions – to wander without direction, searching out surprising experiences and applying prior learning to completely new locations. Coming as it does from theories of urban alienation, the idea of the flâneur may have something to contribute, particularly in a context where the natural world is being overtaken by mass consumer culture. Can its ideals of wandering, observing and understanding serve as a model? By contrast, there's the flâneur's lesser cousin, the *baudad*, or gawker, whose individuality, in the words of Victor Fournel, 'disappears, absorbed by the outside world, which ravishes him, which moves him to drunkenness and ecstasy' – a curiously apt description of the way that much nature writing advocates for our experience of the world outside. In the natural world, do these category differences matter?

Perhaps walking at random does have less baggage; it could be a better route to authentic engagement than peak bagging through a list. But it might just depend on the list – how extensive it is, the terrain it covers and whether it's focused on famous mountains or a wider range of summits. Even in a best-case situation, lists aren't devoid of expectations, as evidenced by my attitudes to Mount Foster. We might know the landscapes we're likely to encounter, or hear stories from other walkers. And they're still subject to a range of constructions. Walkers are attracted to climbing *named* high points, rather than those which just happen to be there. If a mountain has a name, then it has an identity in human terms and fits more easily into the structures of meaning we like to build. A list also has significance attached to it by a human – these are the places that are deemed to be worth visiting. The Hobart Walking Club's peak bagger's list has around 479 Tasmanian mountains to climb (the exact number depending on which version you're working through). Only a few people have finished it, and I don't ever intend to. But I get a little pleasure from filling in gaps; perhaps this is a kind of expectation filled within the limited branding of the list.

But still, I feel these expectations are more likely to be confounded than those attached to canonical destinations, the sites fanned by fame. Perhaps the helpful thing is the limited nature of the promise – simply that it's a place worth going to. It's not promising to change your life, it's not attached to a whole host of imagery that's trying to sell you something, it's not just focused on star attractions. It's relatively contentless, but it's getting you out of the house – after all, if Mount Foster hadn't been on the list, I likely wouldn't have gone there. What's more, in a Tasmanian context, peak bagging often means walking off track, paying constant, thoughtful attention to the landscape around you.

For some writers, the flâneur could only ever exist in Paris, but it's liberating to consider that the walker in nature can go anywhere. Perhaps every place is worth going to, but we can't visit every place. A list has its own arbitrariness – in this case, most of the higher mountains in the state – but it can also direct us to a wider diversity of landscapes than we would be likely to stumble into through sheer randomness. Chasing lists can motivate and sustain us; in keeping our expectations relatively abstract, they potentially leave more space for the world to fill our attention. It's not just the goals of branding and the market, or reinforcing what others deem significant. We're not just keeping to the T3 tracks.

I still think this, and feel the need to emphasise the realities of this paradox. But I also need to be careful. If I really believe in the spectrum of authenticity, then I have to take heart from the power of nature to speak to people wherever they are. That even if crowds in national parks present management issues, even if they create concerns for sustainability and the environment, even if they make it difficult for other visitors, even if someone only ever visits one well-trodden, famous natural place in their lives, pursuing a brush with significant reality among the celebrity culture of places, it's still possible to have an authentic experience; that the natural world is bigger, more overwhelming in detail and impact than any painting; that it can penetrate and even shatter our expectations, wrestling our attention away from ourselves and towards all of its shocking capacity to be itself.

For references, see griffithreview.com

Ben Walter is the author of the short story collection *What Fear Was*. His work has appeared in *Meanjin*, *New Australian Fiction* and *The Saturday Paper*, as well as internationally in *Literary Hub* and *Dark Mountain*. He is the fiction editor at *Island*.

John Kinsella

Vaudeville

after an extract from Rimbaud's 'lost' manuscript La Chasse Spirituelle

I am crying over spilt existence which is no commitment to fealty or compliance to patriotic singing no matter the conditions. All those issues of war played with and 'learnt through': sandpit classroom or patch of carpet that's a battlefield. I would never encourage anyone to lapse into heroics, and would likely try to persuade otherwise. I would stop before a finish line if I had the opportunity. I find no satisfaction in the death of an enemy which is an office of human failure to gather each to their own. *Keep science that offers more than daily bread away from this fragment of bushland.*

I have been embedded forever by your disdain. But you'd expect me to say all this, so far from those fantasies of expeditions and conquests, of letting dreams loose across the quadrangle where I was blooded by accessories to the state. Some say I have lost my sense of humour, but I say, *It's simply less sumptuous.*

I lament that fairytales never did what they were supposed to do, or I weep because they did and do. I obsessed over them. I never trusted the sacristy but was compelled to consider its light. It caught me with the chapel fresco of its imperial sell. I am not sure how much stained glass I bought with my pocket money. I avoided the crowded streets, the towers. Ah, malady!

With plans to sail, I saw myself on the deck of plastic yachts, but preferred the slippery deck of the boat with a bedsheet for a sail. Naval officers and sailors passed through the office of the city, immortalised by pirate nightclub operators. Brawlers and enforcers narrowed the streets to a crawl. Daytrips are made with gusto into a rural that is fumigated with chemicals. *The children are surveyed with future deployments in mind.*

If the magical colours aren't even across the page, it's a failure of art according to aesthetes. An obscenity of blues and reds, they say. Generations of imbibers whitewash the curative and label it 'free speech'. Satisfied as gentle waves on an endless beach of fun, the city eats country to make its 'quality of living'. *Accessible 'arts' and false pianos* won't bring harmony.

I won't be swept along by the ableism of history. The drop-jaw extravagance of entertainment at the expense of bodies. The false liberties of 'expression'. Wounds and mouths.

Apotheosis collapses with every glorification. Dawn is a false flag. Accordingly, hybrid warfare gestures at indifference in the induced disaster of air, water and soil. *Spent,* but still homing in on land and mothers.

A previous contributor to *Griffith Review*, John Kinsella's most recent book is the first volume of his collected poems, *The Ascension of Sheep* (UWAP, 2022).

Tell me a story

Folklore, fact and fantasy

Martine Kropkowski

> *...the question isn't whether or not something is real but when is it real and for whom.*
> Kristiana Willsey

WHEN I WAS twelve or thirteen, the kids at school used to whisper about the Toy House, a lone weatherboard dwelling at the end of a cul-de-sac, hidden deep within an industrial estate. Picture the front yard, they'd say: its soil dry and red, clumps of hedge along the front boundary. Straggly trees dot one side of the garden, then grow haphazardly around the dead-end. And amid the boughs of those trees you'll find fluffy toys, maybe a hundred of them, strung up with rope. Some toys dangle from a limb, others by a noose around the neck. If you go to the house, they'd say, the man who lives there will lurk inside, watching you while you survey the toys – waiting until you've found one to liberate from torture. With your arms reaching and your back turned, you won't see him spring out to snatch you.

Folk stories like this have been a part of human life since we began communicating some 100,000 years ago. And they're not simply historical – folklore is alive now, evolving in contemporary cultures day by day. Whether whispered in the playground, shared over cups of tea or recited around a campfire, folk stories help us to make sense of the world and each other, to understand where we've come from and where we'd rather be now. We pass folk stories between generations, first orally and now via multiple channels, and through this telling we create identities, establish patterns of behaviour, delineate right from wrong. Whether they tap into fear, excitement, longing or some other emotion, folk stories exploit the feelings that create or sever communal ties. And in this way they set expectations – determine *how we do things round here.*

Folklore, then, is the expressive life of a community. While its definitional nuances and level of authoritativeness differ from culture to culture, complicated further by its presence online, folklore is typically defined in contrast to institutional knowledge, or what we habitually label *official* knowledge. It's not high or elite art. It's not scientific or anthropological study. It's not a product of commercial or popular culture. Rather, we understand folklore as *non-institutional* or *vernacular* knowledge, knowledge about the world that we learn from participating in a community. Folklore can bestow upon us everyday beauty, like the wish silently uttered before blowing out birthday candles, and it can be deployed to resist or reframe our understandings of dominant power structures.

But folklore isn't only about knowledge. Folklore also refers to the rituals and practices we collaboratively create and perform. For example, generations of families have sung the London Bridge nursery rhyme: parents teach it to their children, who in turn teach it to theirs. The song recounts the story of a wayward bridge and proposes a mixture of practical and bizarre remedies, such as 'Build it up with stone so strong' and 'Set a man to watch all night'. And there's a game to play alongside the tune: two children form an arch with their arms and a line of players walks under it, singing the rhyme as they go. When the song ends, the two children drop their arch, capturing a player.

The game's sinister subtext is based on a legend that stretches back to the late Middle Ages: for a bridge to remain sturdy and solid, it must consume a live body. Variations on this legend, which have appeared in folklore around the world, commonly involve watchmen, women or children – and sometimes animals – being buried alive within a bridge's footings. The stories, and the lessons they are meant to impart, shift and mutate over time and place, but the theme of live sacrifice remains the same.

Recently, scholars have looked to folklore to understand its connections with contemporary community-generated stories, including those constructed online. Stories that rest on long-running mythology, such as the sacrificial body in the bridge footings, provide a framework from which new stories can be generated, tweaked and moulded to suit each new teller's purpose. While folklore of old was bound by geography, many contemporary folk stories are constructed and shared online by interconnected communities with unprecedented speed and reach.

A contemporary audience, of course, can easily pick out the apocryphal stories of old. But what about new ones? The internet disseminates new folk narratives, including ones that are harmful and prejudicial, every day – and some of those narratives are being received and adopted as fact by anyone with a device and a willingness to believe.

TAKE LORRIE SHOCK from Ohio, for example, who in 2017 traded her hobby of reading novels for something new. In an interview with a journalist for *The Atlantic*, Shock explained that she'd head home from a shift at work, where she cared for adults with special needs, and spend her evening investigating a conspiracy theory online. 'Do your own research,' she told her interviewer, and 'make up your own mind'. The narrative Shock had naturalised to make sense of the world went something like this:

While unassuming citizens go to work, care for their families and communities and do the best they can to live a good, fair life, something sinister impedes their every move. For in each state, and in each country around the world, an elite group of people conspires to create a new world order. They continually plot to maintain their secrecy and the power they wield over the population at large. Their end goal is to implement a global totalitarian government to replace sovereign nation-states by contriving a series of events. According to the narrative, this deep-state cabal has covertly orchestrated innumerable political and economic incidents, including the 2019 Christchurch mosque shootings, the global financial crisis, the advent of fifth-generation communications technology and the spread of COVID-19 – all clandestine operations alleged to serve their progress. One of their leaders is Hillary Clinton, a woman with powerful connections and familial ties to the cabal that controls the United States of America.

Alert to the cabal's operations is another group. This group, of which Shock counts herself a member, is searching for signs and symbols of The Great Awakening, a growing realisation among the people that the cabal exists and can be defeated. Their influential secret agents include Donald Trump, a covert agent of change who is playing '4D chess', leading an offence against the deep state and its Machiavellian plots.

In 2017, an agent began advancing the awakening online. Known as 'Q Clearance Patriot' or just 'Q', this anonymous person was a kind of government whistleblower, sharing cryptic messages online in the hope that 'patriots', adherents to the conspiracy, would interpret them correctly, band together and dismantle the deep state cabal. 'The light', as they referred to themselves – 'the dark' connoted the cabal – was tasked with interpreting the secret codes posted on internet message boards as well as the secret hand gestures and linguistic tricks employed by Trump himself, among others.

This conspiracy group came to be known as QAnon. And Lorrie Shock was playing her patriotic part: interacting with fellow researchers, joining the dots, awaiting directions for what to do next.

LIKE FOLK STORIES, conspiracy theories are shaped over time by collective, collaborative authorship. While the person or people known as Q left cryptic messages online for adherents to interpret, it was the communal deciphering of those messages that allowed for the construction of a cogent narrative, one that had been developing long before Q had even made a post.

In the process of building and disseminating their narrative, the QAnon 'qommunity' created its own peculiar language, a sociolect difficult to interpret from the outside. For instance, *breadcrumbs* referred to the posts dropped by Q. *Bakers* described the people who interpreted those breadcrumbs and turned them into narratives. *Clowns* were FBI or CIA agents. *The Storm* denoted the coming reckoning between the shadow states engaged in protracted battle. The slogan *Where We Go One We Go All*, often shortened to *WWG1WGA*, remains the group's rallying cry. This vernacular strengthened their sense of superiority and separateness from the *sheeple* around them. Like something out of a spy novel, the vernacular was characterised by a cryptic, rhetorical-questioning, clue-dropping style, mimicking the precise type of secrecy that the group sought to unmask and instilling the thrill of the chase in adherents who were 'doing their research'.

Folklore scholars point to three conditions that inspire the uptake of folklore narratives: a shared understanding of story structures (especially that of the hero's journey), a reservoir of existing stories, and a shared worldview. And when we look closely at a group of conspiracy theorists who are aligned in their beliefs, we can identify these same three conditions.

Through a structure comprising a neat beginning, middle and end, stories suggest causality, the idea that one thing leads to the next, all packaged in a form that humans innately understand and relate to. For instance, the hero's journey promises as its denouement a new world forged from the adversity that our hero has bravely conquered. Conspiracy stories leverage such structures, omitting intricate analysis and contradictory or otherwise confusing information to reduce complex phenomena into a simple storyline. In this way, conspiracy stories wield persuasive power, offering comfort by making order out of a disordered world and a sense of agency by outlining solutions.

QAnon stories have dredged their meanings from generations of folklore. The motif of infanticide, for example, has its roots in multiple folkloric tales, including the antisemitic blood libel, a pernicious legend that accuses Jewish people of ritually murdering Christian children and harvesting their blood to make bread. Prophets and great awakenings, the unending battle between good and evil, and the enduring hero's journey are also prominent in both folk stories and biblical prophecies that stretch back millennia. QAnon adherents activated the subconscious appeal of these long-told stories, accessing a ready-made cache of suspicion and paranoia that bolstered their worldview.

As QAnon members circulated their vernacular and practices across social networks, their acts and ideas became increasingly visible, and individuals began to recognise the behaviour as sanctioned, expressive acts within their community. In other words, adherents of QAnon began to recognise and conform to their very own folklore – one that explained who they were and described how they should act in given situations.

IN DECEMBER 2016, a twenty-eight-year-old North Carolina father of two drove for four hours to a pizzeria in Washington, DC. He parked his car, gathered his AR-15 assault rifle, handgun and folding knife, and systematically searched the busy restaurant. The man was looking for the basement, an area he believed was the headquarters of the deep-state cabal, who met there to ritually sacrifice children. The cabal, he believed, was harvesting children's blood (sound familiar?) for the chemical compound adrenochrome and consuming it as a drug for various effects, from a psychedelic trip to immortality. The man, Edgar Maddison Welch, had arrived to save the children; he'd embarked on his own hero's journey. Eventually, he fired shots into a locked door that he thought led to the imprisoned children, opening it to reveal nothing but cooking supplies. The restaurant did not have a basement. He was later sentenced to four years in prison, pleading guilty to interstate transportation of a firearm and ammunition, and assault with a dangerous weapon. The conspiracy theory that led to this event was eventually dubbed Pizzagate.

In January 2021, Rosanne Boyland, a thirty-three-year-old woman from Georgia, drove ten hours to the Capitol Building. Buoyed by then-President Donald Trump's instructions, Boyland joined a crowd of thousands who would later be described as insurrectionists. They surged the west side of the Capitol, pushing through a tunnel to jostle with police. Boyland believed the deep-state cabal had tampered with the election, falsely calling it for the Democratic nominee Joe Biden, and now it was up to her and other adherents of the QAnon community to mobilise, to advance The Great Awakening and take the country back from the cabal. Within a few hours she would be dead, trampled by her fellow adherents. One police officer and three other insurrectionists died during the riot. In the weeks that followed, several police officers would die by suicide.

The actions of Welch and Boyland were not inspired by Q's posts alone; in fact, Welch acted before Q had made a single post. Their actions were bolstered by their shared worldview and their internalising of long-percolating stories that satiated some need in them. Almost four years after Welch's crimes, QAnon had collected these needs and the stories that expressed them in a cogent narrative, a bonfire fuelled by branches of fundamentalist Christianity, a distrust of authority, an atmosphere of division, prejudice and superiority, and the promise of a return to an imagined, simpler past. Ultimately energised by the gravitas of the office of President of the US, people like Boyland were led to commit crimes or lose their lives in support of what was a fanciful story based on mythology, galvanised by ideology and simplified by a desire for the comfort of a vaguely recognisable storyline. Perhaps even more insidious is the fidelity with which some QAnon adherents – from people like Lorrie Shock all the way through to serving members of the United States Congress – cling to the narrative even today.

CONSPIRACY THEORIES OFTEN contain, or at least allude to, some kernel of truth. There *was* a toy house in a Rockdale industrial estate, near Sydney's airport, in the 1990s. Groups of powerful people *do* conspire to advance their own agendas. At least one skeleton has been found in the footings of a medieval bridge. Proven conspiracies lend credence to new conspiracy theories, which, when combined with the hidden power of folk narratives, produce fertile ground for paranoia.

But how might individuals and communities navigate a world riven by competing narratives, each supported, if you look hard enough, by a legacy of tales that came before? If folklore doesn't consist only of stories but also of the behaviours and practices they sanction, isn't there an ethical burden attached to our adoption of certain stories as truth? Shouldn't we look closely into the stories we tell as well as the stories we're told and mine them for meaning in order to decide which stories we should continue to tell and which ones are better left in the past?

When I started researching QAnon's narratives, I wanted to understand the process by which some stories are taken up as truth and others are not. Though I wouldn't believe someone who insisted to me that the Clintons were descended from lizard people, I wanted to articulate why they held that belief, and I thought an answer might lie somewhere within the stories themselves. But the questions worth exploring, I discovered, are not about the elements of truth in these stories or the gullibility of their audiences, but about understanding what it is that we gain from believing them.

MY PARENTS HAD gone out and left my sister in charge. She'd concocted a plan with her boyfriend: he'd borrowed his mum's car and they were going to find it. They'd figured out where the Toy House was. I sat in the backseat, gripping the handhold as we made turns through unmarked streets. Every few minutes, an aeroplane would take off, vibrating the steel roofs over the neighbourhood factories. I brought my elbow inside the open window, looked to the footwell, reminded myself that this was just a story – nothing to be scared of.

Eventually, light-soaked streets faded to the dull orange of a single street light. We had found it. We slowed near the kerb of the solitary house, and I forced myself to peer through the diamond shapes of the screen door. A long, empty, brightly lit corridor lay beyond.

My sister took a breath. I shuffled towards the middle seat and followed her gaze through the windscreen. There they were: the toys, so many of them, hanging from the trees just as the story promised. The headlights illuminated a white bunny with pink ears, hanging limp from the neck. I squeezed my eyes shut.

'Drive!' my sister yelled, pointing out the passenger window. The man had appeared and was now silhouetted in the open front door of the house. He was still, watching us. I fumbled with the crank to wind up the window. My sister's boyfriend tore the car around the cul-de-sac. 'Quick,' I pleaded, not daring to look up.

SOMETIMES I THINK about the Toy House and how differently I interpret it as an adult. I wonder what purpose the story held, what need in us it fulfilled. We were young, drawn to the macabre, the taboo, the grisly details that fascinated us, having grown up reading the Brothers Grimm. The Toy House gave us something to speculate about at sleepovers, to fear after the lights went out and, for those of us (un)lucky enough to visit, to brag about to our friends. It formed part of our lore.

There's an abundance of narratives I could draw on to make sense of it. It could be a cautionary tale, a Hansel and Gretel-like warning of temptation and the dangers of people unknown to us. I could position it as a story about greed, about trying to take what isn't yours. Perhaps it's about loneliness. Or maybe it's the story of a violent individual, a criminal who would wilfully harm children. Maybe it's all of these things. It's tempting to enclose these narratives within one story, one persuasive tale structured in a way that's coherent and comfortable, that suits the needs of the group listening.

But what if we could entertain multiple, conflicting narratives about the same event? What if those narratives were complex, nonlinear, contradictory? What impact would *those* stories have on our behaviour, on the ways we interact?

With distance, with a worldview that better encompasses the complexities of life and that resists the pull to simplify events into good and evil or absolute cause and effect, I can entertain such narrative ambiguity. But back then, when I was caught up in the moment, the only thing I could see was the thrill of a good story.

Martine Kropkowski is a writer and HDR candidate at The University of Queensland. Her research examines folklore practice in the online space, including the narrative techniques that communities employ to generate and communicate conspiracy rhetoric.

Radical love

Julie Koh

WHENEVER I GO on tour as a psychic shaman oracle medium visionary prophet saint, there is one question that my fans unfailingly ask. And that is: *Julie, how do I manifest the life of my dreams?*

This is, of course, a question that requires a thorough response and usually there are so many poor souls in the room clamouring for my attention that it is impossible to sit down and expound fully on the answer. The energies in the room can be overwhelming because my appearances on tour involve channelling precious messages from loved ones who have crossed over, meaning that my fans are both alive *and* in spirit – twice the usual crowd.

The sheer volume of energies with which I come into contact is enormous, especially because my latest tours have involved a tight schedule of six appearances a week, fifty-two weeks a year, and recently my entourage and I have had a documentary crew filming at all times.

Occasionally, when I am woken by spirits at night and am finding it hard to get back to sleep, my Executive Assistant says, 'You can't help everyone!'

'But I *must*,' I reply, turning to the camera. 'For whomso else shath helpeth the meek?'

DESERT DAZE

People ask me how to manifest their greatest desires because I am clearly living the life of my dreams. I am renowned for my healing work and own a vast business empire connected to it, although this has not always been the case. Prior to my unlimited success, I dabbled in various careers but never settled on any, feeling there was more to existence if only I could grasp it.

My journey to understanding how to manifest one's dream life began with a near-death experience.

I had always been a keen skydiver. In my thirties, lacking engagement in my latest career as an influencer, I went to Dubai to fulfil my dream of skydiving over the desert. It was a clear and beautiful day, and the dive went spectacularly well. The aftermath, however, did not.

When I landed, there was no one to be seen. I'd expected the skydive operators to send a van to collect me but no vehicle appeared. I was alone in the middle of the desert without a phone. I sat, waiting. Day turned into night turned into day. I realised I had been abandoned.

It was time to take matters into my own hands. There was no way of knowing the right direction, so I picked one at random and began moving. The sun beat down. I had no food and not a drop of water. At one point I examined my hands and saw that the skin was blistering in the heat.

I began hallucinating. I saw a viper gliding sideways across the sand, singing Il Divo's cover of 'Amazing Grace'. A passing gazelle lifted a hoof and gave me a high five. An ancient ghaf tree bent down and introduced himself. He said he was a landscaper and was exploring the desert too but did not think it was laid out particularly well.

I left the tree behind and wandered endlessly through the shadow of the valley of death – through what I came to identify later as the dark night of the soul.

On the fortieth day, I fell to my knees and pleaded with the Divine for succour.

It was then that a cool breeze caressed my straw-like hair, and I looked up to see the clouds part. A shimmering pastel vision appeared in the sky. It showed me scenes of my own far wealthier future as an entrepreneur and saint. Future me, with luscious balayaged hair and glass skin and barely noticeable rhinoplasty, stepped out of one of the scenes and spoke to desert me.

Your spiritual gifts have upgraded, she said. *It is time to pivot from influencing to build the empire of your dreams.*

A boundless sense of abundance washed over me. I was on the threshold of a whole new reality, having finally met my stunning higher self.

Then I heard another voice in the distance, scratchy and annoying and beset with vocal fry.

It was my then-EA, Katie. She had turned on a pedestal fan and was telling me the desert livestream was going viral but she was really sorry about the landscaper, who had somehow snuck in.

'Katie,' I said. 'Can you *not?*'

But it was too late. She'd ruined the vibe. My higher self vanished before my eyes. I pulled off my motion-capture suit and logged out of the metaverse.

Katie offered me a carob bliss ball from an enormous edible bouquet of them – she'd been feeding me at regular intervals. I batted it away.

'Give me another bliss ball,' I said, 'and I'll shove it down your throat.'

As it turned out, I would be able to break my desert fast elsewhere. Because I immediately had a deep knowing that I must leave the penthouse and travel to what the masses call a 'supermarket', where there was a special individual whom I was destined to meet.

TEARFUL TAGUE

Upon entering the chosen venue, I was drawn to the fresh produce section, where a man was stacking oranges into a pyramid. I knew immediately that this was the individual I was looking for. I felt an irresistible pull towards him, like a turtle in Japan receiving the divine call to migrate to Mexico. My spirit guides – a fifteenth-century Franciscan monk and Florence Nightingale – urged me forward.

I tapped the man on the shoulder and he turned, accidentally knocking over half the pile of oranges. The oranges rolled across the floor. The man's name tag read 'Tague'. He was balding and had the aura of a frightened mouse. I watched as he began picking up the dropped oranges, four at a time, placing them gingerly back on the pile, only for the pile to collapse again. It happened over and over, oranges rolling everywhere. He stacked more and more frantically. It was difficult to watch.

Then my vision warped. I began to see Tague as I had never seen anyone before. He appeared to me in layers, as if I were looking at a deck of cards, with his current incarnation at the front of the deck and his previous incarnations behind.

I could see Tague's present and future unfolding in infinite ways across the multiverse. There was Tague in his previous and parallel lives, knocking over pyramids of oranges as an ancient Chinese cook, a Spanish farmhand, and a dowdy brown-haired maid in the Palace of Versailles. In each scene, Tague's spirit guide, a distracted French mime, floated by his side, dressed as a clown and wrestling a lion.

Focusing my eyes on the Tague at the top of the deck, I could even see deep into his body, my mind diving in and swimming around as if I were a tiny shrimp shooting through his bloodstream, feeling his heart pump and his intestines contract. I was now not only clairaudient, clairsentient and claircognisant, but also omniscient.

I stooped to grasp Tague's hands and told him to stop with the oranges already. There was something else he needed to focus on – a figure in spirit above his left shoulder, darkening a doorway. I felt that this figure represented unresolved trauma that Tague needed to process before stepping into his best life.

I asked him if his father – whose name, the spirit informed me, was James – had passed. Tague nodded.

'He's tightening my chest,' I said, 'signifying that he died in a freak boat accident during a mini-break off the coast of Italy.'

Tague's chin wobbled.

'He's having me acknowledge that you should have been on that yacht instead of him, and that he suffered tremendously as he died. It's all your fault.'

Tears began streaming down Tague's face.

'Your father is here to validate that his soul is not at peace. He is with you every moment of every day, witnessing every failure. He is not at all proud of you and wants you to know that you bring shame upon the family line.'

Tague turned away and burst into silent sobs over the carrots, having received the closure from his father that he had always longed for.

My meeting with Tague that day was all part of a divine plan. I could see that he was of weak character, with a pitiful sense of self-worth and a blocked throat chakra. As an only son, he had received an inheritance from his father, but because of his grief and guilt about Tague Snr's death, he found himself unable to spend a cent of it. Nevertheless, I had a gut feeling that Tague had something to contribute to the economy, and I – representing the will of the Universe – was destined to bring him that message. His life purpose was that he would not only become my first disciple but also my replacement EA, effective immediately.

From that moment on, I began utilising my psychic powers in earnest. It was time to tread my fated path, finding ultimate freedom through revolutionary positivity. And it was in that heady first year of my new career as a medium that I heard remarkable stories from the dead concerning the lessons they had learnt in their lifetimes about what it takes to achieve one's wildest dreams.

REGRETFUL REASON

Tague arranged my first client consultation, which was with a woman called Rhyme, who had recently lost her cousin, Reason. We met Rhyme over a four-course lunch by Sydney Harbour. Rhyme was distraught. She wanted to connect with Reason and find out what really happened on the night of her cousin's untimely death.

Pushing aside a plate of glazed duck á la Presse, I began channelling. A semi-transparent woman materialisèd next to our table, hovering in the air. She was slouched forward as if she had no core strength, her face completely covered by a curtain of long black hair that lapped at her toes. She kept turning slowly without moving her feet, like a wind-up music-box ballerina. Upon each rotation I could see blood leaking from the back of her skull in a pulsing stream.

Reason told me she was in her late twenties. She had grown up the only child of a single mother from an aspirational family with a penchant for idioms. Her father had died when she was an infant, with little to his name. When Reason was in her teens, her mother became permanently disabled after exposure to toxic chemicals at work, so she struggled to make ends meet.

Reason dreamed of becoming a visual artist but there was no possibility of studying art. As soon as she left high school, she began working as a picker in a warehouse, then took a second job, then a third, to keep herself and her mother afloat.

Over the years, she washed dishes, ghostwrote CVs, and worked from home providing online chat support for a bathroom ware retailer that monitored her screen remotely and penalised her for toilet breaks. Reason worked fifteen hours a day while trying to teach herself painting at night. She developed RSI in her wrists, a bad back, constant tingling in her legs and major depression.

Every night before she fell asleep, she would look at a homemade poster taped to her wall, on which she had painted her dream home. She envisioned spending her days there doing watercolours of the field of sunflowers located by the road leading to her house.

One afternoon, Reason bought a lottery ticket to win $200,000 in gold bullion and an estate on the Southern Downs that looked exactly like her dream home. That night, she began her shift delivering meals for a rideshare company that guaranteed twenty-minute delivery times around the clock. At three in the morning, while biking along Parramatta Road with her insulated backpack after making a hot chip delivery, Reason was overcome with exhaustion. To stay awake, she tried imagining sunflowers lining the road, each turning towards her as she passed.

Suddenly, everything went dark. She had gone under the wheels of a black convertible. It screeched off into the distance. There was no surveillance footage of the incident and there were no witnesses – only Reason, hovering in spirit over her broken body, sunflowers bowing by her side.

A poor manifestor, Reason did not win the lottery that day either. Instead, the winner was 729522 from Toowoomba, Qld, 4350, who celebrated his sudden prosperity by buying ten jet skis for his new mates from the pub, and consequently sank into a funk after realising they had only become friends with him to be close to a new jet ski.

As I channelled Reason, she said: 'In reviewing my experience on Earth, my one regret is that I should have tried harder.' She asked me to advise Rhyme not to bother pursuing answers about her death. 'My cousin must move on with her life.'

Rhyme left, a great burden on her shoulders lifted.

Reason had been right in identifying where she had gone wrong. She had wasted the opportunity to fulfil her greatest purpose. And what a waste that was – Reason being personally to blame for her bad luck in an economy that blesses us with an infinite array of choices through which we can manifest our best selves.

CAPABLE CARODY

Carody appeared one night in my bathroom as Tague was brushing my teeth.

She was a slender, diminutive woman in lilac athleisure, floating behind the glass door of my marble shower. There was a large, ragged hole in her torso through which I could see the shower caddy behind.

Carody had died in her forties after becoming financially free through adopting an abundance mindset.

'Julie,' she said to me, 'I believed that I could do anything, and I did.'

Carody had always been an overachiever. She had worked at an executive level in a range of fields, including banking and insurance.

'My goalposts kept shifting,' she told me. 'Every time I achieved a dream, it rotted in my hand, so I reached for the next gleaming thing. I raced against myself to optimise my output, looking for a sense of satisfaction I was never able to find.'

Several years into her career, Carody began to experience burnout. She rectified this by engaging in self-care practices such as sitting cross-legged in the shower and sobbing inconsolably. She also bought a rainbow-coloured whip online and flogged herself regularly. With each lash she would shout, 'I am happy. I am manifesting abundance! I believe and I achieve.'

Eventually, she pulled herself together and decided on a new career goal: to become a full-time investor. She enrolled in an online course on using astrology to guide personal investment decisions, and consequently decided during a New Moon to invest her life savings in a US-based company that specialised in the development of lethal autonomous weapons. In its third year of operations, it became one of *Bortune*'s 600 Fastest-Growing Startups.

Carody built a supersized yurt on a parcel of land on the Sunshine Coast and conducted day-long philanthropic workshops there for underachieving women, teaching them how to become financially free through gratitude practices and investment in robotic warfare technology. She taught her students how to tap into the stream of abundance, asking them to ask themselves: 'What do you want to manifest this financial year?'

As an under-the-table gift for her support, the company offered to send Carody a domestic robot engineered to her specifications. Given that she lived alone and had always feared the possibility of choking on string cheese with no one around to help her, she asked for the robot to be equipped with a single skill – to be able to perform the Heimlich manoeuvre.

The robot was soon delivered. It was meant to blend in with furniture, so was disguised as a pouf.

One sunny morning in that high-ceilinged mid-century-Moroccan yurt with its famous south-facing aspect, Carody was standing by the window admiring the view when she began to chuckle, remembering her foolish period of burnout.

The pouf mistook this as choking. It barrelled towards her, expanding vertically into a tall cylindrical form.

'Carody,' it said. Two steel arms shot out from its body and enveloped her, its fists meeting above her navel. In its tight embrace, Carody felt an emotional tug, stemming from a sense of profound satisfaction that all was finally well with her life. Then the robot reached in and disembowelled her while reciting the Third Geneva Convention on the treatment of prisoners of war.

At Carody's funeral, her devotees spoke tearfully of how financially free she had been.

Carody regretted nothing, telling me to tell her mourners: 'God wanted me to be rich.'

CYNICAL CIEON

Over time I came to learn that one of the least understood principles of existence is that the Universe is an intelligent yet simple organism. Researchers at the University of Stoke-on-Trent recently found that 100 per cent of the time, the Universe is listening. If you think negative thoughts, you manifest negativity. If you think positive thoughts, you manifest abundance and freedom. It's as simple as that.

Take Cieon, for example. I met her on stage in a Sydney convention centre during the first stop of my very first tour, in front of a sell-out crowd. I had just started connecting with the energies in the space when Cieon stepped forward in spirit. She was a sweet eighteen-year-old with a radiant face, broken neck and bleeding on the brain.

Cieon had lost her parents due to war and had come to Sydney for a peaceful life. As she explored the streets of her new city, she saw happy children with their parents, and wondered why her life had turned out the way it had. She envied the innocence of those children, who had not yet seen the worst that humanity had to offer, and whose futures would be blessed with good things. She felt instantly bitter, and pessimistic about her own trajectory.

Cieon was a talented gymnast. She took up a gig doing stunts for a show in the very convention centre in which we were speaking. During the show's dress rehearsal, Cieon had been fitted with a safety harness and suspended above the audience, the plan being that she would descend slowly towards the stage. But the harness was not secured properly and she fell forward from a great height.

On the concrete floor, losing consciousness, Cieon knew that it was her own fault for having an underlying victim complex.

She had realised a fundamental truth of existence: that the Universe is merely a mirror of one's own perceived reality. Everything and everyone around Cieon had been a reflection of herself, and she had been co-creating her experiences with the Universe. Nothing could have been achieved with her lack mindset and this was why she had been unable to go towards the light.

People who are entrenched in their own victimhood are in denial about this universal principle.

'But Julie,' they say, 'what if my failures are just not my fault?' This is the victim mentality of killjoys. People who believe this should be taken into a field and shot.

A PETTY POLTERGEIST

What I recall in particular about those early days was that many beings tried to stand in the way of my success. Having failed to achieve their own dreams, they projected their issues onto me, even if that meant making false accusations that would, in all likelihood, ruin my lifestyle.

The worst instance of this occurred just as I was on the verge of ascending to fame on a massive scale. I realised later that it was a final test sent by Source, to see if I was fully ready to step into my power.

It all happened after meeting Cieon. I had escaped from the city for a luxury farm stay to unwind after my first appearance when Tague texted me in a panic from my penthouse. Strange things had been happening there, and they were escalating.

There had been shadowy figures moving between rooms, phantom footsteps on the balcony and loud crashing noises that had no perceptible origin. That morning, Tague had found the washing machine split clean in half as if struck by lightning.

I took the first flight back. Upon opening the front door, I saw my *Investor's Bible* on the hallstand spontaneously burst into flames. Tague came to greet me, clearly shaken up. As we moved through the penthouse, lights flickered on and off. The visitor intercom kept buzzing of its own accord. Sounds of hissing and heavy breathing emanated from the smart speakers in every room.

I directed Tague to retrace our steps and switch the devices off. Then I entered the kitchen. A bar stool at the kitchen island slid towards me at breakneck speed. I sprang out of the way. It slammed into the wall behind me. I rushed to the sink, which began filling with blood.

At that point, the poltergeist progressed from hissing and breathing to speech. It began communicating in my voice through the speaker on the countertop.

'I don't care,' my voice was saying. 'It won't work without a skydive re-enactment, so just get in the harness… Keep it on the down low, but my hot tip for the New Moon is investing in military robotics… Well, she clearly wanted my turf, so why not put her onto a startup run by muppets? What a waste *not* to give a charming eulogy and convert all her yurt ladies… So I was drunk. She brought the wrong order. Of course I went after her in the convertible… Katie. Don't give me that look. It's your own fault I'm stuffing these down your throat… So just arrange an accident when his boat gets to Capri!'

It was clearly a calculated concoction of sounds I had once uttered at home, derived from what my speakers had previously recorded. I had been spiritually hacked – my precious, darling voice deepfaked.

'Show yourselves!' I shrieked. 'I will not be framed!'

But the entities behind the poltergeist were too cowardly to materialise.

A foul odour filled the room. I looked down at the fruit bowl before me. In it was a disgusting new arrangement – a mouldy pile of string cheese topped with a single filthy bliss ball.

'What do you want?' I asked. 'Some sort of groundless apology? *I'm sorry you feel that way!*'

Tague appeared in the doorway to the kitchen. His eyes widened in terror as he looked in the direction of the balcony. I whirled around to see the glass bifold doors sliding closed. Painted in giant red capitals on the panes were the words 'Happy Leak Day'. With an almighty sound, the glass shattered, raining shards.

I was still standing by the sink, frozen. Around me, the kitchen drawers and cupboards began opening and closing. Plates hurtled down from the shelves above me. I crouched, covering my head with my hands. Tague leapt to shield me, trying to catch plate after plate as they came faster and faster, attempting to stack them into a pyramid.

'Enough!' I shouted. 'Enough!'

I shut my eyes tight and remembered my greatness. Then I stood up, elbowing Tague out of harm's way. I raised my hands and clapped twice, calling on the power of the Divine. Immediately, the smart skylight opened above our heads and a bright white bathed the kitchen. A golden bubble of sacred protection descended upon me.

I held my arms wide, and from the floor rose literally millions of glass and plate shards, along with a set of authentic Santokus from my knife block. They hung suspended in the air around me. I then began to direct their movements with masterful precision, creating a swirling vortex so powerful that the wayward spirits would not be able to resist its magnetic pull.

As I stood calm in the eye of this tornado of glass and blades and ceramics, I compelled it, and the spirits, upwards.

'Go towards the light!' I commanded.

The vortex of darkness lingered for a moment, then spun up and out of the penthouse.

The vibration of my home immediately shifted, as a feeling of calm permeated the air. The poltergeist was over. From inside my robe, I took a hip flask of activated holy water and scattered drops around. I called my lawyers, demanding that they plug the leak and ensure that no person's voice would ever be so criminally manipulated again.

Tague and I sat side by side on the kitchen island, surveying the aftermath of the bloody scene. He took my hand in his and we stared into each other's eyes. It was at that moment that I fell radically in love. He was the yin to my yang. I had no choice but to follow my intuition and marry him.

Tague became my fifth husband and thus the final piece of my dream life fell into place. A month later, while he was building a monument I had dreamed of to honour our indestructible love – a structure that also had the potential to break the Guinness World Record for the largest pyramid of washing machines – Tague was sadly flattened by a freefalling Somsang Bubblewish front-loader. In a state of enlightened bliss, he ascended to the afterlife.

I am now not only a healer but also the new owner of a multi-billion-dollar media empire, continuing the legacy built by Tague's father. Despite my wealth, I still insist on touring tirelessly in person, telling my side of the story while helping struggling failures the globe over.

I would not be the success I am today if I had bowed to those who sought to prevent me from fulfilling my destiny. Know that when you, too, step into your power and work to transform your reality for the better, you *will* attract haters. But what they do in the darkness will always come to light and you must have unshakeable faith that the Divine will prepare a sunflower-lined table for you in the presence of your oppressors.

Julie Koh is a globally renowned psychic shaman oracle medium visionary prophet saint and *Forbergs* World 1000 CEO. Enrol in her latest course on astrology for investors at thefictionaljuliekoh.com

Lawdenmarc Decamora

The Wrestling of Art

> *Spectatorship is not a passivity that must be turned into activity.*
>
> Jacques Rancière

In the interest of fairness, please submit to your opponent not by tapping
out, but by covering you (hee-haw mass esemplastic) one! two! three!
I tell you *not* to break the hold once & for all. The approximate length &
width of the ring can testify to the size of The Big Show puffing smoke
rings ('cause moths are oracular) from the steel cage that you (hee-haw
mass esemplastic) thought was an ancient gumbad of manuscripts &
cathode rays. In light of new brutalist art & peer reviews, please follow
the submission guidelines & observe the smooth delivery of debut
vignettes guided by an abstract of 300 to 500 words ('cause moths are
oracular). After your proposal is approved, you will be invited to cheer
on the hope of the other paper: to apply a submission hold on politics and
aesthetics. Unpublished words always turn into birds. You (hee-haw mass
esemplastic) remember that! Art, like wrestling, is about breaking kayfabe.
After the wrestling match, perhaps our doubt could launch a fighter
plane on a slew of heads disappearing before the WWE Thunderdome,
perhaps an attacker line booming, *How did they do that? That storyline
almost stank.* Every word is vital to the conclusion. I buy it, and there's a
revolution that power-slams the Daydream-*nasium* of the mind, *If vying
for the gold, the technique must be sexy, artsy, no, sexy.* And that win we saw is
full of kingdom. We're tired. We're tired of the caged horizon, the canned
emotion. But the spectacle of the crimson world is a real slobber-knocker
of a struggle. It is the flesh of the outside, the babyface-turned-heel
character that shoots on the sky of flaky *isms*. The new normal *machina*,
as we know, is ideologically the border-shunning pipe bomb.

Lawdenmarc Decamora is a Pushcart-nominated poet who has published
two full-length collections, *Love, Air* (Atmosphere Press, 2021) and *TUNNELS*
(Ukiyoto Publishing 2020). His chapbook *Dream Minerals One* was recently
published by Ghost City Press.

Living in kayfabe

Beyond masks and make-believe

Beau Windon

THE MOST CONSISTENT presence throughout my life has always been professional wrestling. The fake sport that calls itself *Sports Entertainment*. But I've never really understood why wrestling wants to be talked about as if it were sport. Isn't being a piece of melodramatic physical theatre enough? It was enough to make professional wrestling become my lifelong obsession – what autistic experts would refer to as my 'special interest'.

In Grade 3, in front of my entire class, I pretended my pencil was a microphone so I could address the room and *cut a promo*, giving an animated interview in character as '80s/'90s wrestling superstar 'Macho Man' Randy Savage during show 'n' tell (*Oh yeahhh, dig it!*). The class was in hysterics as I spoke in a tough-guy drawl, making my voice as gravelly as I could, curling my mouth so it forced my left eye into a squint, holding my hands up like I was speaking an alien sign language. After that day, other kids would often quote me quoting the Macho Man when I passed them around school ('I'm the tower of power – too sweet to be sour. I'm funky like a monkey – sky's the limit and space is the place!'), and I thought to myself: *I'm so cool.* From that day on, everyone knew me as the wrestling kid.

'Watch out, that's the wrestling kid.'

'I saw him talking to himself yesterday. Probably one of those wrestling speeches.'

'Don't talk to Beau unless you want to be talked at about wrestling for hours.'

I didn't have any friends, but I was at the peak of school popularity.

On free-dress days, I wore my sister's dance tights to school because they made me feel like I was a real wrestler. I would've worn my Speedos if my mum let me. Other kids stared at me and asked 'What are you wearing?' and I'd tell them that this was my wrestling gear. They'd smile and whisper to each other. I was ecstatic that so many people were talking about me because this meant I was an interesting person.

At lunchtime, I played wrestling alone on the school oval. I threw myself around on the grass, imagining that my invisible opponent was slamming me on the mat. Sometimes kids would watch and comment on what I was doing. My very own fans.

Eventually another kid from the special education unit saw me wrestling on my own and came to join in. One day I bought a fake blood capsule to school and we exploded it over my forehead while playing. When lunchbreak ended, I went to class wearing my *crimson mask* and everyone erupted in excitement. In wrestling lingo they were *marking out* – the crowd was going wild for me.

My teacher didn't *mark out*. She sent me to the principal's office. My classmates cheered as I left the room. I was glowing with how *over* I was with them. They saw me. They talked about me. I felt wanted.

HERE WE SEE an autistic child in his natural untamed state. Note how he misreads others' perceptions of him due to his single-mindedness. He is wrapped up in the world of professional wrestling and believes that everyone has the same interest as him. He can't comprehend that they don't. The taunts and the teasing are read as compliments rather than acts of aggression towards his differences.

Wrestling is the child's world. It is how you get through to him. It is his language. A bridge to his mind. And professional wrestling has a secret world all of its own: kayfabe. It's an illusionary world like kayfabe that the child must enter if he ever hopes to truly fit in.

Kayfabe is the mask wrestling wears that allows its participants and spectators to accept it as a real sport rather than as a television show about a sport. It's the code word that's been used for decades so that wrestlers can let other wrestlers know if they've been hurt in kayfabe rather than genuinely injured. It's how they relay to one another what's real and what isn't.

Wrestlers are like magicians – everything they do forms part of the act that integrates them into kayfabe.

The child must build his own mask to achieve the similar illusion of acceptance that kayfabe conjures. It will be a realm he can step inside to maintain his own illusion – the illusion of fitting in.

As the child grows older, we can see him slowly become aware that he isn't well liked by the other kids in his pack. It dawns on him that his all-consuming love of professional wrestling makes others look down on him and exclude him.

The child realises that if he ever wants to fit in, he must conceal this part of himself. And so, he finally creates a mask to hide his true self. But since wrestling is the tool he uses to understand and relate to the world, he becomes withdrawn and quiet. A background character in his own life. A nameless spectator during other people's wrestling matches. After all, kayfabe is an illusion that everyone is in on, spectators and performers alike – but the child's illusion is one that he must carry all on his own.

IN GRADE 10, I hated my life. I would go to school and disappear into nothingness. During class I would fall into a daydream where I hit a reverse 450 splash on my opponent to win a shot at the world championship – then I would fail my exam. Lunchbreaks were spent finding places to hide from others so I could write short stories about wrestling. Mostly other kids ignored me. They all felt alien to me, and yet somehow I knew that I was the real alien. I was the one character that my grade wouldn't accept into their kayfabe.

There was only one kid in my grade who ever talked to me – a boy named Tommy who would call me Silent Beau because I never spoke. After a year of this, I was informed by one of my cousins that this nickname was a reference to a fictional duo of stoners called Jay and Silent Bob. I was not a stoner and, to be totally honest, I didn't understand what a stoner was – I thought it had something to do with stones.

One day, a new girl started at our school and tried speaking to me.

'I like your hair. It reminds me of Jeff Hardy.'

I should've been thrilled – I had modelled my hairstyle on Jeff Hardy, a pro wrestler, and the fact that she recognised this meant two things: my hairstyle was doing its job, and here was someone else who liked wrestling. But her comment caught me off guard, and my agitated reaction to someone other than Tommy talking to me probably caught her off guard, too. As her words slowly settled into my brain, excitement rose through me, but before I could respond…

'Oh, don't mind Silent Beau,' Tommy said. 'He doesn't speak to anyone. Come hang with us.'

She didn't even think twice about it. My annoyance must've been obvious because when Tommy looked at me, his expression was disgusted.

'The fuck are you looking at, freak?

I'm not a violent person, but something in me broke when he said those words. I grabbed a nearby steel trash can – one of the things I was usually afraid to touch because of all the germs and the feeling of the dirty steel, which made my skin shriek – and then I tossed it at Tommy's head like I was Donkey Kong and he was a plumber harassing me for having a conversation with a princess.

All of his friends got between us, a couple holding Tommy back and a couple swearing at me. There were so many sounds, my ears couldn't keep up. I'd thrown the trash can so fast the action hadn't fully registered in my head, and when it did, my hands felt like I'd soaked them in sewer water, so I puked a little. The kids around me started laughing and I didn't know what to do. Why was I such a fuck-up?

I ran.

Eventually I changed schools, and one of my new classmates had a friend from my old school who told them that I'd hit a kid with a trash can. This made all the popular kids want to befriend me for being such a 'rebel'. I thought this could be the start of my *push* – in pro wrestling, this is when a character ascends through the rankings – but it was nothing like the fantasy I had built. They didn't like wrestling and I didn't like any of the things they liked. They made a lot of mean jokes that I didn't understand. I laughed anyway. And when they spoke about sports or drugs or hooking up or other things that didn't make sense to me, I nodded along and they never questioned me. Their personalities were laying the foundation for me to fit into my new school's kayfabe.

WHEN THE AUTISTIC child enters his rebellious teenage years, the desire not to be a target of his pack becomes stronger. He has learnt – albeit slower than most – that not everyone will think the same way he does. He keeps his obsession to himself. Single-minded devotion attracts taunting and taunting makes him feel alone.

Locking the gate on what he loves makes him appear more human. He is assimilating into the kayfabe that he must adhere to for survival.

In the kayfabe of professional wrestling, there are three categories of wrestlers:

Babyfaces: the heroes, the good guys. They do what they need to do to pop the crowd and get people rallying behind them. Everyone loves a good babyface, and they inspire others to reach for greatness.

Heels: the villains. They can be both bad and good because their morality isn't what makes them a villain – it's their reaction to how others treat them. If a babyface lashes out, justified or not, it often indicates their transformation into a heel character. This heel turn presents a new chapter in the wrestler's career and often leads to greater success, even though spectators and other wrestlers alike have now turned against them.

The last category is the rarest, the tweener. Tweeners jump seamlessly between babyface and heel, assuming the role they need to for the story to play out. Tweeners often have a cool, rough demeanour that can be tweaked ever so slightly to manipulate the crowd into either cheering or booing them. Tweeners often find themselves lost in major storylines.

The teen knows that being a babyface should be his goal. Babyfaces are adored by everyone. They're the happiest and the most successful. Yet, when he watches pro wrestling, he finds himself siding with the heel. Often, they're not inherently bad characters – they've just been pushed too far and are doing what they need to survive.

The teen doesn't understand how to be adored as a babyface and he lacks the confidence to be a heel. So as he enters a new chapter of life, he becomes a tweener. He wears his babyface mask for as long as he can, but it isn't a natural fit, so occasionally it slips and the heel mask shows through. Not a cool heel like a wolf, but a dud heel like a bull ant.

IN MY LATE twenties, I started working at a sort-of-popular-but-sort-of-really-not-popular tourist attraction in Melbourne. By now I'd crafted a whole heap of masks to ensure my survival. All of them came with rules:

Take at least five seconds to thoroughly understand what you're about to say before saying it.

Ask more questions than you give answers. Ever confused or worried about how to answer someone? Find a way to turn your response into a question. If someone says something and looks at you expecting a response that you aren't sure how to give, the safest bet is a release of breath followed by a neutral-sounding 'Awwwh'.

Avoid talking about yourself and your interests – especially if people ask about aspects of your out-of-work social life. Do not engage.

If you stim (an unusual repetitive movement used to mitigate strong emotions) or tic (similar to stimming but less controllable and often vocal), play it off like an allergy and find a way to take a bathroom break so you can work through it out of sight.

No matter my mask, adhering to these rules kept me safe.

Years and years of therapy had helped me figure out how to blend into life's kayfabe despite not truly understanding the rules of engagement. Personal experience had taught me that when people hear the terms 'autistic' or 'anxious' or 'depressed' or 'OCD', they instantly build a character for you, and that character represents a burden. So when people would start to see that I was different, I was very quick to claim that 'I'm just very eccentric'.

Then I took three months off work to study in some intensive improvisational theatre programs in the US. Theatre had always come naturally to me. Pretending not to be me was my most finely honed skill. But it was during these programs that my masks started to slip.

THE TEEN, NOW a full adult, has trained himself well.

Funny, then, that it is three months of dedication to playing other people that is the cause of his exhaustion. Like a world wrestling champion on the run of his life – setting attendance records, eclipsing merch sales and getting five-star-rated match after five-star-rated match – eventually the hard work takes its toll.

I WAS OUT drinking with some of the people in the theatre program after we finished our final showcase performance. Hanging out with them felt different. Perhaps it was because they felt temporary. When the program was over, I would go back to Australia and never see them again. So if I messed up, it wouldn't follow me home. I could relax a bit.

They all thought I was so *cool. Easy to talk to. Funny. Chill.* And I knew this because they told me so. They mentioned it again that night as I got drunk and accidentally let slip about how down and miserable I can get. How heavy the darkness can lean on me. How much I can hate on myself. And rather than judge me, they refused to let me talk shit about myself.

Then I broke.

We did shots.

My masks fell away.

We danced and when they touched me I said, 'Please don't', and they accepted it.

I forgot my rules.

They asked me about the weird thing I was doing with my hand.

I told them that it was the taunt of a wrestling world champion.

Then they asked me about wrestling – something they said they were fascinated by but didn't understand.

What I had held in for so long burst out. Finally, I began to speak...

The funny thing about adults is that they have a tendency to outgrow their childish ways of being. Honesty. Vulnerability. These qualities, while looked down on by children, are often admired by adults. People that wield them are referred to as brave.

I am not entirely sure who I am. I think that moment in the US constituted a gimmick change. I was going from Ringmaster to Stone Cold, from Cactus Jack to Dude Love, from Razor Ramon to Scott Hall – only my new gimmick was no gimmick. I was just me, whoever that was.

In 1996, four of my favourite pro wrestlers (real-life best friends known by insiders as the Kliq) partook in an infamous moment at Madison Square Garden known as the *curtain call*. Two of the four wrestlers were on their way out of one company and signing with another, ending their time on the road together. At the end of the show, they stood in an emotional huddle in the centre of the ring and acknowledged their friendship. This was controversial, as two of them were babyfaces and two of them were heels. Bad guys and good guys were not meant to mingle. More than that, they had all just fought each other in the ring and were hated enemies in storylines.

'Kayfabe is dead!' The news spread across wrestling newsletters and fan sites. Four of the top guys in the business had acknowledged kayfabe as a fake aspect of their world.

Wrestling changed that night. Kayfabe was no longer an unspoken industry secret, and wrestlers would even begin to allude to it in a way that blended fact with fiction to create deeper story arcs.

IN THAT MOMENT at the bar in the US, I felt so free and unchained. It was a revelation.

My peers accepted me for who I was. They liked me. It didn't matter if I was a babyface or a heel or a tweener. Kayfabe be damned – they thought my honesty was refreshing and likeable.

After spending so long constructing a character based on what I thought I needed to survive, I felt that it was only in losing those constructions that I could survive the happiest.

When I returned to Melbourne, I strived to remember this new mindset. I dropped my masks more often, living both in and out of kayfabe. Similar to wrestling storylines, life is most interesting when fact and fiction blend together. Showing my vulnerable side continued to have a positive effect on the people around me.

After nearly thirty years of feeling like a fake person, I finally felt alive.

And so I hold my $500 World Wrestling Championship replica belt up to my shoulder, I bring both of my hands to my face and kiss them before letting them rocket out to my sides, and in a deep gravelly voice I say, 'I'm the tower of power – too sweet to be sour. Oooooooh yeah, DIG IT!'

A previous contributor to *Griffith Review*, Beau Windon is a neurodivergent writer of Wiradjuri heritage based in Naarm (Melbourne). He was a 2021 Writeability fellow and currently has grant funding to develop a hybrid memoir on all of the ways to fail well and fail often.